P9-CFV-453

Marvel Holsinger
1972

MORMONISM AND AMERICAN CULTURE

INTERPRETATIONS OF AMERICAN HISTORY

★ ★ ★ JOHN HIGHAM AND BRADFORD PERKINS, EDITORS

MORMONISM AND AMERICAN CULTURE

EDITED BY

Marvin S. Hill and James B. Allen
Brigham Young University

HARPER & ROW, PUBLISHERS
NEW YORK, EVANSTON, SAN FRANCISCO, LONDON

MORMONISM AND AMERICAN CULTURE

Copyright © 1972 by Marvin S. Hill and James B. Allen
Printed in the United States of America. All rights reserved. No part of this book
may be used or reproduced in any manner whatsoever without written permission
except in the case of brief quotations embodied in critical articles and reviews. For
information address Harper & Row, Publishers, Inc., 10 East 53rd Street, New
York, N.Y. 10022.

Standard Book Number: 06-042819-8

Library of Congress Catalog Card Number: 72-82900

CONTENTS

The Mormon Community: Twentieth Century Challenges

EDITORS' INTRODUCTION

This volume—and companions in the series "Interpretations of American History"—makes a special effort to cope with one of the basic dilemmas confronting every student of history. On the one hand, historical knowledge shares a characteristic common to all appraisals of human affairs. It is partial and selective. It picks out some features and facts of a situation while ignoring others that may be equally pertinent. The more selective an interpretation is, the more memorable and widely applicable it can be. On the other hand, history has to provide what nothing else does: a total estimate, a multifaceted synthesis, of man's experience in particular times and places. To study history, therefore, is to strive simultaneously for a clear, selective focus and for an integrated, overall view.

In that spirit, each book of the series aims to resolve the varied literature on a major topic or event into a meaningful whole. One interpretation, we believe, does not deserve as much of a student's attention as another simply because they are in conflict. Instead of contriving a balance between opposing views, or choosing polemical material simply to create an appearance of controversy, Professors Hill and Allen have exercised their own judgment on the relative importance of different aspects or interpretations of a problem. We have asked them to select some of what they consider the best, most persuasive writings bearing on Mormonism and American culture, indicating in the introductory essay and headnotes their reasons for considering these accounts convincing or significant. When appropriate, they have also brought out the relation between older and more recent approaches to the subject. The editors' competence and experience in the field enable them to provide a sense of order and to indicate the evolution and complexity of interpretations. They are, then, like other editors in this series, informed participants rather than mere observers, students sharing with other students the results of their own investigations of the literature on a crucial phase of American development.

JOHN HIGHAM
BRADFORD PERKINS

MORMONISM AND AMERICAN CULTURE

INTRODUCTION

That the Church of Jesus Christ of Latter-day Saints, commonly called Mormon, with but three million adherents in 1970, should merit a volume in this series may puzzle the reader. From the standpoint of direct influence upon the development of American culture, the Mormons would hardly compare with such movements as the American Revolution or the advance of democracy, nor would they compare in influence with other religious groups such as the Puritans or the Roman Catholics. It could well be argued that the Methodists or the Presbyterians are, from the standpoint of numbers and general impact, far more significant. Why then the Mormons?

One answer is related to the amorphous quality of American culture itself. A diverse people—all of whom at one time or another came from other countries and other cultures, spread across a sprawling landscape where departure from traditional ways of doing and thinking seemed a virtual necessity, governed by representative leaders responsible to the caprice of a numerical majority—Americans have been preoccupied with Hector de Crevecoeur's trenchant and difficult question, "What then is the American, this new man?" Frequently they have resorted to affirming what they are not rather than what they are, contrasting themselves with Europeans, Catholics, communists—or Mormons.

During most of the nineteenth and the first generation of the twentieth century, the Mormons attracted attention in the popular press and also among many scholars as a useful counterimage, a glaring example of what America was not and should not be. They were considered so different in their fundamental institutions—theocratic government, plural marriage, and communitarianism—that joining them seemed to consititute an un-American activity. John Wesley Hill, a Methodist minister in Ogden, Utah, put

I

the matter succinctly in 1889. Mormonism, he said, "is an enemy to this government, a traitor to the flag, and the foe of American civilization."[1] But in the last forty years, perhaps because other images have seemed more ominous, an alternative perspective has prevailed. According to this view Mormons have been, in varying degrees, not a counterpart to the American culture but its epitome. Ralph Barton Perry suggested in 1949,

> Mormonism was a sort of Americanism in miniature; in its republicanism, its emphasis on compact in both church and polity, its association of piety with conquest and adventure, its sense of destiny, its resourcefulness and capacity for organization.[2]

And in recent years these two have been combined in a third approach, which holds that Mormonism has been both unique and typical. William Mulder argued in 1957 that nineteenth-century Mormonism:

> . . . in its New England origins, its utopian experiments and reforms, its westward drive, and its early expansion to Europe resulting in a great program of immigration and settlement . . . expressed prominent traits and tendencies that were already shaping American Society. It was not simply a colorful reflection of the times; it was a dynamic reworking of the diverse elements of American culture.[3]

In the same year, Thomas F. O'Dea took a similar view, maintaining that,

> . . . throughout its history, as in its very origin, Mormonism was to be both typical of the larger American setting in which it existed and at the same time peculiarly itself, with its own special idiosyncratic emphasis and interpretations. Even when most at odds with its fellow Americans, it was to be typically American, and it was always to feel and express this combination of typicality and peculiarity.[4]

Despite the differences between the perspective of a late nineteenth-century Protestant minister engaged in a sectarian struggle in Utah, and that of twentieth-century historians, we can perceive a certain agreement between them. Most writers characteristically focus upon the Mormon community and suggest that its nature has special significance for the

[1] John Wesley Hill, *Americanism or Mormonism, Which?* (Salt Lake City: Salt Lake Tribune Publishing Co., 1889), p. 21.

[2] Ralph Barton Perry, *Characteristically American* (New York: Knopf, 1949), pp. 97–98.

[3] William Mulder, "The Mormons in American History," *Utah Historical Quarterly,* XXVII (January 1959), p. 60.

[4] Thomas F. O'Dea, *The Mormons* (Chicago: University of Chicago Press, 1957), p. 21.

American people. Those who have been unusually concerned with the Mormon style of community include John W. Gunnison, Jules Remy, Richard Burton, Hubert H. Bancroft, William Alexander Linn, Nels Anderson, and Leonard J. Arrington. Not all agree on the degree of Americanism within the Mormon community. Some, like the French traveler Remy, have seen Mormonism as a by-product of American religious freedom. Others, like Linn, have seen the Mormons as divergent. The perspective has tended to fluctuate roughly according to the degree of consensus prevailing in America at the time. At the height of the Cold War, William Mulder characterized Mormonism as "as native to the United States as Indian corn and the buffalo nickel." More recently, as America has experienced new internal conflict, Robert Flanders revived something of the nineteenth-century point of view by interpreting early Mormonism as a "counter-culture." The Mormon way, he affirmed, "eventuated in an alternative view of American history and an alternative way for Americans."[5]

We agree, however, with the general position of writers such as Mulder and O'Dea, that the history of Mormonism is, indeed, representative of American history and at the same time a unique American experience. We believe that to write about Mormonism significantly is to say something about America, and the essays included in this volume demonstrate this. We maintain that the central theme of Mormon history has been the search for community, and that this has also been the ultimate American concern. The Mormons were faced with the dilemma of seeking a close-knit community free from corrosive outside influence, while at the same time striving to relate harmoniously with the broader American society—a society that they believed had a divine origin and destiny. In this regard they were similar to the Puritans who sought to build a New Jerusalem in the wilderness of America but also to avoid any direct confrontation with the English crown. Quakers, Roman Catholics, and other religious groups have tried in different ways and at different times to establish a separate identity within the larger community, as have many of the utopian and communal movements of both the nineteenth and twentieth centuries. What institutions would permit individual freedom and still create and preserve social cohesiveness and social order? This constituted a central question for Americans and Mormons in the nineteenth and twentieth centuries.

When so much of the American social and political experience has concentrated upon the building of a cohesive community—at Jamestown, Plymouth, and Massachusetts Bay, at Philadelphia in 1787, at Washing-

---

[5] Robert Flanders, "To Transform History: Early Mormon Culture and the Concept of Time and Space," *Church History*, XL (March 1971), p. 109.

ton and Montgomery in the early 1860s, and at Birmingham and Berkeley in our time—it is not surprising that observers should also find the Mormon effort noteworthy. Some examples will illustrate how general this interest has been. In 1852 Lieutenant John W. Gunnison, an army engineer, published a widely read book, *The Mormons, or Lattery-day Saints,* in which the Mormon political community was characterized as outwardly republican but infused with and dominated by religious influences. Gunnison termed the system "Theo-democratic" and remarked that its power could most effectively be broken by leaving it alone. Taking another perspective, Progressive economist Richard T. Ely wrote in 1903 that the Mormons had established a highly disciplined society.

> We find in Mormonism, to a larger degree than I have ever seen in any other body of people, an illustration of the individual who is willing to sacrifice himself for the whole, and it is a religious sanction which impels him to do so.[6]

"The Mormon creed," Ely contended, "recognizes no interest external to the Church." All work under the guidance of the church was seen as religious, and it was common to hear leaders in religious meetings discuss irrigation and bridge-building.

Another who studied aspects of Mormon cooperation in the early 1900s was Ray Stannard Baker, who noted that the church absorbed the entire time and talent of its members. "The church never lets go its people," he commented, "even in their leisure hours. . . . Pursuing the policy of answering all the demands of a rational life, [it] has even assisted in the establishment of opera houses and theatres."[7] Whether considering its external relations with the rest of the nation or its internal social life, knowledgeable observers found community the central Mormon concern.

Bernard De Voto was no exception in this regard. Scorning Mormon doctrine as "a body of belief almost incredibly absurd," he focused upon the corporate enterprises of the church, saying acridly that the "five Mormon talents" had bred many times over in sugar trusts, rails, and industrials. Where the Progressives had looked upon Mormonism as unique, De Voto, in the midst of a depression, saw it as typical in its complete fusion of piety and business.[8]

The view that the Mormons were representative of America gained

[6] Richard T. Ely, "Economic Aspects of Mormonism," *Harper's Monthly,* CVI (April 1903), pp. 667–668.

[7] Ray Stannard Baker, "The Vitality of Mormonism," *The Century Magazine,* LXVIII (June 1904), p. 176.

[8] Bernard A. De Voto, "The Centennial of Mormonism," *The American Mercury,* XIX (January 1930), pp. 3, 12.

additional support in the 1940s and 1950s. Perhaps the rise of American social and intellectual history as a distinctive discipline during years of almost continuous international tension increased the tendency during this time to see Mormonism as a microcosm of America. One of the first statements of this point of view was historian Ralph Henry Gabriel's classic *The Course of American Democratic Thought* (1940). Gabriel proposed that three dominant ideals had guided the American people since 1787— faith in the fundamental law, in the free individual, and in the mission of America. He saw the Mormon commitment to building Zion in the West as a manifestation of the American mission. "The power of early Mormonism," he wrote with unusual perception, "was the millennial hope, the vision of Zion soon to arise upon the earth."

Alice Felt Tyler, in her influential *Freedom's Ferment* (1944), a study of pre-Civil War social movements, also saw Mormonism "filled with millennialism and utopian prophecy." The new church, she said, was "born on American soil," among the restless and dissatisfied from New England. Tyler titled her chapter on the Mormons "The Stake in Zion," thus recognizing the importance of community, although she had some difficulty in fitting them into her general framework of utopian societies.

Whitney Cross's *The Burned-Over District,* a thoughtful analysis of the social forces in western New York that influenced the rise of Mormonism, was published in 1950. He stressed the degree to which these Yorkers had been subjected to rigorous campaigning for Christ by sectarian revivalists and missionaries for a generation following the War of 1812, and how as a result many new religious groups emerged in the region. The Mormons, he insisted, were not frontiersmen responding to Frederick Jackson Turner's democratic processes, but easterners, who joined the Mormon church in an area that was rapidly maturing economically and culturally. Cross affirmed that Mormonism was a religious movement, not a quest for power or material gain, and that it must be understood within the context of religious developments in western New York. He made a noteworthy contribution to our understanding of the beginnings of Mormonism, but had little to say about the shape of the movement as a whole.

It remained for another student of American cultural history, David Brion Davis, to make a bolder attempt to characterize early Mormonism, and his article begins our collection of essays. Davis argued that the movement had its roots in New England, and thus possessed community and other values that can be identified as Puritan. The arguments of Davis and Cross brought a response from Mario De Pillis,[9] who affirmed that

---

[9] Mario S. De Pillis, "Social Sources of Mormonism," *Church History,* XXXVII (1968), pp. 50–79.

many aspects of Mormon culture emerged not in New England but in the West, and that much of what became distinctively Mormon after 1830 was contrary to Puritanism. The Mormons, De Pillis insisted, had to discover a new basis for solidarity at a time when old values were waning. Throughout the 1950s and 1960s others trained in intellectual and cultural history demonstrated interest in the Mormon community. In *Homeward to Zion* (1957) William Mulder, trained in American Studies at Harvard University, offered one of the first analyses of the close proximity between Mormon and other American approaches to immigration. He suggested his basic point of view in an article on "Mormonism's Gathering: An American Doctrine with a Difference," which is included in this volume. But in another piece, "Image of Zion," Mulder showed that the Mormons were considered an unwelcome American influence in Scandinavia. Thomas F. O'Dea, also a student of American Studies at Harvard, wrote a Ph.D. dissertation entitled "Mormon Values: The Significance of a Religious Outlook for Social Action" (1953), that emphasized the strong Mormon commitment to community but noted some strains and stresses in the twentieth century. Most of these ideas were presented in O'Dea's *The Mormons* (1957).

One of the forces that tended to promote cohesiveness among the Mormons was persecution. David Brion Davis, in a 1960 article on the public image of Mormons, Masons, and Roman Catholics,[10] suggested that in opposing the allegedly un-American aspects of these movements nativists gave lip service to the ideal of individualism. They thus provided themselves with a sense of stability when American society was otherwise marked with fluidity and social conflict. Later, Keith Huntress, a professor of humanities at Iowa State University, argued in a study of Governor Thomas Ford and the Mormons in Illinois that the tensions between the Mormon and non-Mormon communities were sharpened by the inability of the bankrupt and decentralized government of agrarian Illinois to deal efficiently with specific incidents such as the Mormon destruction of a dissenting newspaper, the *Nauvoo Expositor*.

While specializing in American Studies at the University of Wisconsin, Robert Flanders concentrated on the Mormon kingdom in Illinois. His book, *Nauvoo: Kingdom on the Mississippi* (1965), described the social, economic, and political dimensions of the kingdom, seeing it essentially as a "kingdom of this world" in business, military, and governmental aspects. The social ideals of the kingdom were those of Joseph Smith, and it was

---

[10] David Brion Davis, "Some Themes of Counter-Subversion: An Analysis of Anti-Masonic, Anti-Catholic, and Anti-Mormon Literature," *The Mississippi Valley Historical Review*, XLVII (September 1960), pp. 205–224.

these ideals that the Mormons took with them to Utah. A year later a British student of American Studies, P. A. M. Taylor, in *Expectations Westward* (1966), focused on the experience of the British Mormons who emigrated to America in the nineteenth century. Taylor agreed with Flanders that the kingdom "was in no sense other worldly," but added that it was perfectionist in orientation, hoping to "serve as the headquarters of Christ's millennial rule." He saw the Mormons achieving community solidarity by stressing the moral obligation to serve, to settle in compact villages, and to subordinate individual property rights to collective need.

Klaus Hansen, who studied American intellectual history at Wayne State University, considered in *Quest for Empire* (1967) the role of the Council of Fifty in influencing Mormon history until the turn of the century. Hansen argued that this Council, the executive and legislative arm of government which presided over the Mormon Kingdom of God, was not an un-American institution, that it had some non-Mormons participating in its sessions, and that the kingdom as a whole was the fulfillment of the American political dream. Yet Hansen himself noted in an article that the Kingdom of God often stirred bitter hostility among non-Mormons who saw its collectivism as anti-American, thereby raising some doubts that the kingdom was truly typical.[11]

Once these students of intellectual and cultural history began giving the Mormons attention, increased interest was also shown by those with other specialties. In *Great Basin Kingdom* (1958), Leonard J. Arrington, an economic historian, detailed the Mormon attempt to establish a viable economy in arid Utah and demonstrated that the Mormons experimented frequently in their search for an orderly and prosperous society. And his article on the law of "Consecration and Stewardship" showed that this experimental approach to community had its roots in the earliest period of the church's history.[12]

Sociologist Kimball Young studied the most controversial Mormon social experiment in *Isn't One Wife Enough?* (1954) and affirmed that polygamy was "neither the horrible system pictured by the anti-Mormon reformers nor the marital bed of roses alleged by the Church officials." The motivations to enter polygamy included sexual, economic, and other considerations, but, as Young observed, this deviant form of marriage was implemented successfully by the Mormons because they believed it was a

[11] Klaus Hansen, "The Political Kingdom of God as a Cause of Mormon-Gentile Conflict," *Brigham Young University Studies,* II (Spring-Summer 1960), pp. 241–260.
[12] Leonard J. Arrington, "Early Mormon Communitarianism: The Law of Consecration and Stewardship," *Western Humanities Review,* VII (Autumn 1953), pp. 341–369.

religious principle. In some ways polygamy enhanced certain ideals which reforming Americans considered virtuous. Most polygamists were highly puritanical, and, according to Young, their society was more "moral" than the "tandem polygamy" of the modern multiple divorce and marriage system. The popular image of the father as the autocratic ruler of a harem was highly exaggerated, as was the view that women played a less significant role in Mormon society than elsewhere.

But polygamy may not have been the most important issue in the accommodation of Mormonism to the American culture. Gustive O. Larson, a student of western America, argued in *The Americanization of Utah for Statehood* (1971) that political authoritarianism was more pivotal. He explained that "Americanization" did not imply a quest for moral reformation of the Mormons but "was a demand for undivided loyalty to the United States government, for the acceptance of the country's democratic process under the Constitution, including the separation of church and state." In "Statehood for Utah: A Different Path," an article included in this collection, Howard R. Lamar showed that in seeking statehood from 1847 to the middle 1880s the Mormons could be very accommodating. Their effort to sell a more favorable image to the nation, thus countering congressional fears that Mormon ways of thinking were alien, constitutes a fascinating story of the group's pursuit of self-determination through concilation.

Despite the rapid increase in Mormon studies, relatively little has been written about the Mormons in the twentieth century; historians have been preoccupied with the formative period of the church's history and with the political and economic struggles of the nineteenth century. Those who have studied recent times, however, have continued to be concerned with the Mormon quest for community and its interaction with the broader American culture. In an article on the origin of the Mormon welfare program, Leonard J. Arrington and Wayne K. Hinton argued that this innovation was not, as many have supposed, a reaction against the federal relief programs of the 1930s, but an effort to cooperate with the government in meeting the problems of the Great Depression.[13] Still another commentary on recent Mormonism is that already mentioned by Thomas F. O'Dea, who in a postscript to his earlier work, published here for the first time, analyzes the dilemmas presented to the Mormon establishment by the rise of black Americans in social status.

Significantly, the only major books since O'Dea's to attempt to analyze modern Mormonism have been written by popular journalists not historical scholars. William J. Whalen, in *The Latter-day Saints in the Modern*

---

[13] Leonard J. Arrington and Wayne K. Hinton, "Origins of the Mormon Welfare Plan," *Brigham Young University Studies*, V (Winter 1964), pp. 67–85.

Day World (1964), attempted to present a balanced view and praised the accomplishments of the church in organization, welfare work, family unity, and education, but was mildly critical of health rules, the policy vis-à-vis blacks, and certain theological positions. In *The Mormon Establishment* (1966) Wallace Turner was highly critical of current Mormon financial policy as well as the church's involvement in politics, and emphasized the various divisive forces within the church, particularly the question of race. Robert Mullen, however, in *The Latter-day Saints: The Mormons Yesterday and Today* (1966), was laudatory of Mormon achievements, but failed to discuss many of the serious social and political problems confronting the modern church.

One phase of contemporary Mormon history remains conspicuously unreported in either scholarly or popular literature. In the last two decades the church has experienced phenomenal growth in other countries, particularly in Latin America and in Asia. The effect of this growth has yet to be critically analyzed. Whether Mormonism will effectively carry its American values into foreign countries, thus establishing outposts of American culture abroad, or whether it will be forced to modify some of its Americanism to become more internationl in orientation will be decided only in the years ahead. The story of its past accommodation to American culture suggests that this latter alternative is not impossible.

In the meantime, our selections are divided into three sections. The first traces the evolution of the early Mormon movement, its nature and significance. The second considers in depth the Mormon struggle for a common social denominator in Missouri, Illinois, and Utah and how this quest both reflected and conflicted with the broader search for consensus among the American people. The final section explores the perils and prospects for contemporary Mormonism confronted by modern secular life and national cultural crisis. In so considering Mormon history we hope to shed some significant light on the problems that have confronted American civilization and culture in general.

PART I

THE MORMON COMMUNITY: ORIGINS

As a young man, according to his own account, the Mormon prophet Joseph Smith was deeply affected by a religious revival which occurred in western New York about 1820. Unable to decide which of several competing churches he should join, Smith knelt in prayer. His supplication was answered when a heavenly messenger informed him that he should join no church at that time because "their creeds were an abomination in His sight." Three years later another messenger revealed that the fulness of the Christian faith was contained in a book of golden plates buried long before in a hill near his home. When, "by the gift and power of God," Smith translated these early records and then published them as the Book of Mormon, he initiated a new American religious faith. On April 6, 1830, he organized a church and called special missionaries to spread the restored gospel abroad.

The New England Origins of Mormonism

DAVID BRION DAVIS

When Mormonism emerged in the 1830s as a new religion based on new revelation and new scripture, it challenged the Protestant tenant of the sufficiency of the Bible. This precipitated rigorous opposition to the validity of its claims. Today, in what some students have called a "Post-Protestant Era," most non-Mormon scholars are no longer concerned with determining the ultimate truth or untruth of Mormon doctrine but with understanding the nature of the movement and its relationship to the broader American culture. David Brion Davis, now of Yale University, affirmed that in its theocratic church government, its affirmation of a close and personal God, its providential view of history, and its gospel of works, Mormonism advocated Puritan ideals. Historians nowadays are not so certain as they were a generation ago whether a movement so diverse as Puritanism can be precisely defined. Yet, in stressing that the essential thrust of Mormonism, like that of Puritanism, was to fuse sacred and secular within the confines of a close-knit, religiously permeated community, Davis provides us with an enduring insight that illuminates the continuity of American cultural history.

I

It is a curious fact that the vast literature on Mormonism tends to treat the subject as everything but a religion. Until the twentieth century the issue was so incendiary that non-Mormon publications were usually either polemics written or preached by Protestant ministers or sensational exposes by people who claimed to have penetrated Brigham Young's iron curtain.

David Brion Davis, "The New England Origins of Mormonism," *The New England Quarterly*, XXVI (June 1953), pp. 147–168. Reprinted by permission of the publisher and the author. Footnotes deleted by permission.

But if the Woodruff Manifesto made polygamy and thus Mormonism an academic matter for most Americans, succeeding historians were not to profit by the less emotional perspective. Scholars grew indignant over Brigham Young's dictatorship and the criminal docility of a people who could not see the proper line between church and state. Joseph Smith's pretentious visions seemed absurd to an enlightened people. There was a blossoming of analyses proving him an epileptic, a paranoiac, or an impostor. Scholars amassed data proving that the Book of Mormon could not have been written in any other place than northeastern United States between 1815 and 1835. But most of the energy went into asserting or refuting the Spaulding-Rigdon theory of the origin of the golden plates.

There were some, however, who saw implications beyond the disputes over authorship. Why should the gibberish of a crazy boy send thousands of people trekking off to establish a theocracy beyond the Rocky Mountains? Here, these scholars reasoned, was the perfect example of the inexorable magic of the frontier. Mormonism was a purely American and western product. "Western New York in the frontier days, interest in Indians, an attempt to give America an ancient heritage; Ohio, Illinois, a Zion in Missouri (mid-America!); religion for the common man, free air and expansive ideas, polygamy—like to do things in a big way. Conceived in a frontier, driven further west by an angry frontier, first settlement and colonization of the western desert—the saga of a westering people, an epic in social history, Manifest Destiny with religion as its rationalization!"

These enthusiasts never suspected that they might be following the old pattern of a new religion consuming another and using it to prove its own doctrines. For the West and the frontier with its free air and expansive confidence was a sort of religion for Americans, and if the Mormons could absorb Columbus and George Washington into the grand scheme of Nephites and Lamanites, the scholarly frontiersmen could take Joseph Smith and Brigham Young and hitch them to Manifest Destiny.

So Mormonism has come down as an interesting phase of American social history, an autochthonous expression of the frontier. If it had any relation to previous religious developments, it was only as a reaction against stern New England Calvinism. Mormonism was not primarily a religion but a social movement.

II

Jan Matthys had a personal revelation that he should lead a sally against the pagans. On April 5, 1534, he led the assault, but Jan apparently did not realize what Joseph Smith (a later Enoch) knew: Revelations can also come from the devil. When Jan fell, Johann Bockhold, whom posterity has known as John of Leyden, became ruler of the saints. On August 31 he was officially proclaimed king of the Chosen and ruler of the world. As head of the Muenster theocracy he instituted polygamy, after citing biblical precedent and saying there was a surplus of women anyway. He outlawed infant baptism and produced a divinely revealed constitution for Israel. Twelve elders assumed joint worldly and spiritual powers, proclaimed free will, and told the people that Christ's kingdom was earthly. In the earlier Articles of Muenster the Anabaptists had refused to obey any pagan authority and now the day for the destruction of the Godless was approaching. But that year drew to a close and 1535 was a hungry year. On April 4 the Diet met and hurled the imperial armies against the Muenster walls. There was no possibility of retreat to the land of the honey bee.

There had been radical outbreaks before, but Muenster was incorporated in the Protestant tradition as a symbol of evil and a slogan for persecution precisely because it was the expression of a tendency latent in Protestantism itself. The early confessions and creeds were important because they checked the centrifugal force inherent in any biblical or personal religion. One of the fundamental articles of the Westminster Confession, for instance, was number six of Chapter I, which decreed that nothing was ever to be added to Holy Scripture, "by new revelations of the Spirit or traditions of men." But all the scholarship, logic, and authority of the age could not hold the fires under control. The Reformation made man aware of his sin and responsibility, gave him the Bible to study, and filled his soul with an awareness of history. Then when Renaissance optimism simmered down to groups of farmers and soldiers, combining confident materialism with a biblical sense of mission, the reaction was bound to be severe. Especially in the English civil wars, the combination of these forces produced radical sects like the Quakers, the "Fifth Monarchy" men, and Gerrard Winstanley's Diggers. While differing in many respects, these movements were all perfectionist and most entertained eschatological hopes for fulfillment in history.

The New England Puritans were as properly horrified as anyone by the outbreak of these "gangrena" during the Cromwellian period. They had promptly and severely dealt with antinomianism and were not a little disturbed by the new tolerance of the Restoration. But despite their orthodoxy on personal revelation and perfection, they had brought with them certain Anabaptist ideas of polity. The nonseparatist Puritans had dropped the conception of a national church and substituted the idea of individual, autonomous churches composed of visible saints.

Perhaps the single most important fact of early religious history in

America is this tendency away from the concept of the national church. The Revolution prevented the possible establishment of the Anglican Church and after a belated enchantment with deism, successive waves of religious enthusiasm only served to split further the existing churches. In early American Puritanism, the inherent conflict of orthodoxy and Anabaptist polity had brought a specious compromise with the Half-Way Covenant, but this in turn contributed to the collapse of Puritan church polity in the eighteenth century. More and more emphasis was placed on inducing conversions en masse, while large segments of the community were excluded from church membership. Thus an increasingly large group of New Englanders, whose ancestors had taken membership for granted, found themselves displaced and uncertain.

By the early nineteenth century, a small group along the seaboard was adapting religion to conform with trade, business, and a free and genteel life, while the back country smouldered with evangelism and literal Bible-mindedness. During the first quarter of the century, religion was effectively separated from society and politics, and the general trend seemed to be away from orthodox formulations of dogma. Especially among liberals in the East, God was elevated to an inscrutable height. He became a vague but ambient force or power, indifferent and imperturbable. The religious debates revolved around the nature of man, which seemed freer after God's elevation; but whether Hopkinsians argued that man was impotent or their opponents held that he had a fighting chance, God still remained distant and unaffected.

After assuming this knowable God, the tendency was to stress a divine immanence for man. The prevailing mood emphasized the importance of the present and forgot history, which was considered mostly dark ages anyway. The church, then, was not only separate from the state but was in no way coincident with a community. Theology moved away from history, providence, and revelation, and strove to give man individual freedom and a means to an easy conscience.

But as the canals and turnpikes pierced the Appalachians, a good many farmers and small townsfolk found themselves in a dilemma. On the actual frontier, conditions favored friendly interdenominational relations, and religion was accepted as just religion. But upstate New York in the 1820s was not a frontier and it experienced a certain amount of denominational competition. Hill people left Litchfield and Berkshire counties and the western ridges of Vermont to farm the rolling Finger Lakes country. They had a deep religious heritage. They had the tradition of strong men like Solomon Stoddard, who had ruled Northampton as an autocrat and had dispensed with such trivia as the Half-Way Covenant. Then there had been the Great Awakening with its emotion and emphasis on conversion. Religion was a main topic of conversation and the literate thought and wrote in Biblical terms. Now, in York State these people were besieged by exhorters and circuit riders, Methodists, Freewill Baptists, and Presbyterians. These divines painted dismal pictures of hell and called for immediate conversion. But which was the right church, *the* church? The York State population was a mobile one and in every new community, it seemed, there was a new sect and a new divinity. The people read their Bibles and wondered.

Since no organized force existed to check centrifugal aberrations, it was not surprising that people clustered around self-proclaimed prophets. Little dust devils sucked in a few particles and skittered across western New England and York State, which was the trough of the low pressure area—minute signals of larger storms to come. An ex-British officer led a group in Vermont and Massachusetts in the 1790s. A little later, Middletown, Vermont, broke out with millennial expectations, direct revelations, and treasure hunting. These were common occurrences among a people who yearned for salvation, a people whose ancestors had bequeathed both a religious passion and an inevitable frustration in a splintered church which had no place for them.

Meanwhile New England money and missionaries crossed the Hudson and concentrated on the area of new economic development. Revivals flared up after the War of 1812, and the evangelists illogically but effectively combined the broken fragments of Edwardean theology, with emphasis on both disinterested benevolence and what approached free will. The Methodists, Universalists, and Campbellites wielded hammer blows against the sterile residue which remained from seventeenth-century Puritanism. With all the barriers, systems, and formulizations gone, an emotional continent lay bared for all to exploit. In the autumn of 1821 a young Oneida County lawyer named Charles G. Finney went into the woods where no one could see him and received an ecstatic baptism from the Holy Ghost.

III

. . . so great were the confusion and strife among the different denominations, that it was impossible for a person, young as I was, and so unacquainted with men and things, to come to any certain conclusion who was right and who was wrong.

Thus Joseph Smith remembered the religious tumult in the burnt-over district when he was fourteen.

The Presbyterians were most decided against the Baptists and Methodists, and used all the powers of either reason or sophistry to prove their errors. . . . On the other hand, the Baptists and Methodists, in their turn, were equally zealous in endeavoring to establish their own tenets and disprove all others. In the midst of this war of words, and tumult of opinion, I often said to myself, What is to be done? Who, of all these parties, are right? or, are they all wrong together? If any one of them be right, which is it? and how shall I know it?

So in the spring of 1820 Joe Smith retired into the woods in response to James 1:5, but the Holy Ghost who lived in the York State woods in those days was even more familiar with Joe than he was with young Mr. Finney the next year. The fourteen-year-old ragamuffin saw both God and Christ.

God, it appeared, could make no more out of the multitudes of sects than could Joseph Smith. He thought that the reign of apostasy had lasted long enough and it was time to reëstablish the true Church, with real apostolic succession. Young Smith learned to his amazement that he was to be the custodian of the keys.

The frontier historians say that Mormon theology is mostly absurd and meaningless but can be explained as a western revolt against Calvinism. The important thing was that free land to the west gave this "insane movement" a chance to expand and members were attracted by economic opportunity. The origins and meaning of Mormonism are not, unfortunately, quite that simple. Upstate New York after 1825 had a booming economy and a maturing culture. With schools, libraries, canals, and taverns, it was no longer a frontier. The influences which shaped Mormonism came largely from New England. Even after Zion moved westward, the bulk of new members were recruited in the East. There were tens of thousands of conversions in Britain. As for economic opportunity, the Mormons, like their ancestors, saw no cleavage between speculation and providence. The works of Max Weber and R. H. Tawney have cast some doubt on the naive assumption that religion is merely the hypocritical side of exploitation. Actually, the frontier was the place where Mormonism was nearly extinguished, while the final settlement came a thousand miles beyond the frontier.

That Mormonism was a revolt against something is quite evident. But orthodox Calvinism was hardly a thing to revolt against in 1830, when Unitarians were becoming a settled and conservative element in Boston, when Campbellites and Universalists roamed the Genesee Valley, and when the prevailing mood even in the Plan of Union churches was against intellectual formulations and strict dogma. Rather, it was this rising tide of liberalism and individualism that presented a challenge to dissenting minds. The forgotten fact about Mormonism is that the New England settlers in York State had a tradition which held that a church is something more than a social group, that theology has concerns other than the nature of man.

In the one hundred years before Joseph Smith, intellectuals and scholars had gradually lost control of the main currents of religion. The contemporary feuds in the New England theological schools did not affect Joseph Smith or the farmers and merchants along the expanding Erie Canal. But the ideas of earlier divines had seeped down to the level of mechanics and day laborers. While these doctrines had been distorted and simplified, a movement from the bottom was bound to reflect them. The descendants of farmers from isolated valleys in Vermont and Connecticut instinctively thought of one church, *the* church, with a definite logical creed and reassuring covenants. Like Joseph Smith's father, they thought of a church of saints, directly descended from "the ancient order, as established by our Lord and Savior Jesus Christ, and his Apostles." The church of New England tradition was a church at one with society, without any division of temporal and spiritual power.

Though he was an immigrant, Alexander Campbell represented a part of this tendency. He thought of one church, the original pure church of the apostles. For this reason many disciples were absorbed into Mormonism and this has led to perhaps undue emphasis on Campbell's influence. Campbell was also part of the liberating, free, catholic temper of the times. He was opposed to dogma, was for extreme toleration and separation of church and state, and he was bitterly anti-Mormon. Discussing the intolerant certainties and pretensions of the Latter-day Saints, Campbell wrote:

> He decides all of the great controversies—infant baptism, ordination, the trinity, regeneration, repentance, justification, the fall of man, the atonement . . . even the question of freemasonry, republican government, and the rights of man.

Campbell was too much immersed in the Baptist spirit of tolerance to see that deciding all of the great controversies was exactly that function of religion which Mormonism sought to reëstablish.

The Latter-day Saints were as much in revolt against Baptists as they were against Methodists, Presbyterians, Finney's revivals, and Andrew Jackson Davis' spiritualists. Parley Pratt, one of the formulators of Mormon theology, lashed out at the spiritualistic tendency in emotional religion, the tendency to divide the body into two realms and to evoke manifestations "which neither edify nor instruct." If the Mormons were opposed to the separation of man's spiritual nature from his body, they were also against the omnipresent, inscrutable, "Buddhistic" God of modern Arminian religions.

While Mormon missionaries drew many converts from revival areas, their approach to doctrine was always by argument rather than emotional oratory. Since the revolt originated in the lower strata, the antinomian tendencies of John of Leyden and Anne Hutchinson were apparent in the early years. It was soon realized, however, that the doctrine of continual revelation was explosive and could divide the movement before it was well under way. The extreme mysticism which was necessary for the founding of the church was the very force which nearly brought its downfall. When people like Sydney Roberts, James C. Brewster, Martin Harris, and even Sidney Rigdon began having separate revelations, Joseph warned his people that "the devil can speak in tongues." He insisted that all revelations come through him, while his own revelations of this period were an attempt to stabilize the centrifugal weaknesses of his religion.

The theology and polity of the Latter-day Saints was a crude attempt on the part of untrained but sincere men to establish a simple and authoritative church, the church they had lost and now yearned for. While they attacked the prevailing religions of the day, the converts of Mormonism were able to retain almost all of the fundamental beliefs they had accepted since childhood. The theology was not against scholarship or a learned ministry. Indeed, it embodied part of the awe and reverence which unschooled Americans have always had for Education. At Kirtland, Nauvoo, and Deseret the Mormons were quick to establish schools. Joseph Smith and others made at least a pretense to study Hebrew and German, while Orson Pratt wrote treatises on calculus, astronomy, and romantic philosophy.

Of course, Mormon education had to conform to the Mormon world view and eschatology, but this world view in turn gave education a paramount importance. Since the Bible clearly showed that God was a chemist, biologist, ship-builder, horticulturist, architect, and surveyor, Parley Pratt included these arts and sciences in his definition of theology, saying that "all arts and sciences . . . [are] but branches growing out of *this, the root.*" Joseph Smith, who was practically illiterate, said that man is saved no faster than he gains intelligence. This meant that a man's station in the eternal celestial hierarchy would depend on the degree of perfectibility he achieved in this life. The Mormons wanted to set up education on their own terms and like the non-Mormon elements in the same culture, they were suspicious of formal, eastern education. They were not, however, in the tradition of Gilbert Tennent and the later evangelists. Many of the Mormons felt inferior because of their lack of education and even the Book of Mormon apologizes for literary "weaknesses" and stumbling "because of the placing of our words." But Joseph Smith compensated for this inferiority by making a pretense to philological erudition:

We say from the Saxon *good;* the Dane *god;* the Goth *goda;* the German *gut;* the Dutch *goed;* the Latin *bonus;* the Greek *kalos;* the Hebrew *tob;* and the Egyptian *mo.* Hence, with the addition of more, or the contraction *mor,* we have the word Mormon, which means literally, *more good.*

IV

The doctrines and beliefs of the Church of Jesus Christ of Latter-day Saints can be viewed from a number of perspectives. Since Mormonism is a biblical religion, taking every word literally, its peculiarities can be interpreted as what happens when all classes of ignorant and superstitious people have freedom to draw their own conclusions from scripture. Luther had feared such consequences (Muenster was an example), and he strove to separate the Gospel from the Bible itself. In America the various formulations and creeds had been undermined and Mormonism can be seen as the extreme result of the evils of literal-mindedness.

Another factor was the absorption and synthesis of the contemporary cultural and theological debates such as pseudo-Masonic rituals, immersion, and millennialism. But most important, and this fact has been largely ignored, Mormonism was a link in the Puritan tradition, asserting a close and personal God, providential history, predestination, an ideal theocracy, the importance of a Christian calling, and a church of saints. In this same tradition it opposed deism, evangelism, and the Arminianism of Methodists and Unitarians. Finally, the Latter-day Saints represented an outburst of mysticism and superstition, the belief in continued revelation and the perfectibility of man, which was at least a latent facet of American Puritanism.

In nearly all these aspects, the Mormons ran against the mainstream of American thought, and the tolerant and free Americans of the frontier found it difficult to be tolerant of such a diabolical unity of evils. This anachronistic residue of seventeenth-century New England just did not understand the meaning of individualism. Mormons voted the way their elders and apostles told them to vote. As a block they manipulated real estate and formed wildcat banks, which were not unknown on the frontier in the 1830s, but the idea of doing these things collectively was revolting. The Mormons did not seem to know that religion was one thing and politics and economics another.

One of the chief aims of Mormon theology was to redefine the nature of God, to recover the anthropocentric God of their forefathers. The Athanasian Creed was rejected, but not for the liberal Unitarian reasons. The tendency among Boston liberals was to raise and disperse the Father image, until He became an immaterial Force, while the Son was seen as the ideal man, a very, very good man. The Mormons reacted against orthodox Trinitarianism because "it would be difficult to conceive of a greater number of inconsistencies and contradictions expressed in words as few."

The Bible said man was created in God's image and it talked of God as having physical attributes and passions. How could such a God be in more places than one at a single instant? The answer was that Protestant churches were not churches at all but stray sects which had lost sight of God and had substituted Eastern, mystical conceptions of "immaterial substance." Such a notion was clearly ambiguous and unscriptural. Ancient philosophers had confused states or conditions of the mind with the mind itself and had then defined mind as an immaterial substance. When this conception was transferred to God, it gave Him a mystical quality and brought magic into religion. But this is really saying

. . . that there is a God who does not exist, a God who is composed of nonentity, who is the negative of all existence, who occupies no space, who exists in no time, who is composed of no substance, known or unknown, and who has no powers or properties in common with any thing or being known to exist, or which can possibly be conceived of as existing either in the heavens or on the earth.

Thus Mormonism, with astounding temerity, charted "sectarian" Christianity with atheism.

Since the Mormons lowered God to a personal, supervising individual, with body, parts, and passions, He became subject to the eternal laws of truth. But this lowering of God to a substance did not exclude various degrees of substance. Spiritual substance is finer and purer than the substance we deal with on earth. While God's features resemble man's, this does not mean that He is restricted by the same lowly qualities. He is omnipotent, omniscient, and omnipresent, but even these superior qualities do not give Him a mystical cast. For God does not function as the Father alone. The Son and the Holy Ghost, while separate substances, work in harmony with the Father and in their identical purpose lies their unity. Thus they can truly be said to be One. The Holy Ghost is an ambient, spiritual *substance* which is diffused throughout the universe:

The purest, most refined and subtle of all . . . substances. . . . [but] like all others, is one of the elements of material or physical existence, and therefore subject to the necessary laws which govern all matter. . . . [It] is the grand moving cause of all intelligences and by which they act. . . . It is the controlling agent or executive, which organizes and puts in motion all worlds, and which, by the mandate of the Almighty, or any of His commissioned agents, performs all the mighty wonders, signs, and miracles ever manifested in the name of the Lord. . . .

God's ability to function so efficiently and to take care of so many things at once is thus reconciled with his specific personality. Miracles are not a break in the laws of nature, but are merely orderly workings of the Holy Ghost which man can not comprehend. Christ is not reduced to a man in this Trinity, but becomes God's prime minister and public relations man. "Man is subordinate to Jesus Christ, does nothing in and of himself, but does all things in the name of Christ. . . ." Since Christ holds this same relationship to His Father, man's obedience to the Son is in reality obedience to the Father.

This is an ingenious triumph on the part of York State farmers to reconcile the personal God of the Bible and their heritage with their smattering knowledge of nineteenth-century science. Through the material agency of the Holy Ghost and the unity in *purpose* of the Trinity, they could accept what little of contemporary science they knew and still believe in a God who could show his finger of flesh and blood, "as the finger of a man. . . ."

Equally absurd as an immaterial God, was the doctrine that the universe was created out of nothing. If we are going to have eternity in one direction, the Mormons said, we must have preexistence in the other. Out of a chaos of elements, God molded a temporary environment in which preexistent spirits, now clothed in fleshly "tabernacles" of a grosser substance, could work out their salvation. Parley Pratt's description of this creation reminds one of Washington Allston's *The Deluge:*

> . . . darkness fled, the veil was lifted, light pierced the gloom, and chaos was made visible. . . . No sound broke on the stillness, save the voice of the moaning winds and of dashing, foaming waters. Again, a voice comes booming over the abyss, and echoing amid the wastes, the mass of matter hears and trembles, and lo! the sea retires, the muddy, shapeless mass lifts its head above the waters. Molehills to mountains grow. Huge islands next appear, and continents at length expand to view, with hill and vale, in one wide, dreary waste, unmeasured and untrodden.

Into this specially created world eternal spirits are born anew. The destiny of these spirits is determined by the lives they lead in finite existence. Evil in the world gives natural man the chance to choose the good and just, and through faith, baptism, and reception of the Holy Ghost from the hands of those who possess Him, a man can assure himself of future godhood. If one lived and died in an age of darkness, his homeless spirit can only hope that some enlightened descendant will take pity and baptize him in proxy. Then the spirit can escape his lonely exile and take his place among the godly. For man is coeternal with God, and "as man is God once was: as God is man may become." This conception of the cosmic evolution of spiritual substance enabled later Mormons to claim that Joseph Smith anticipated Darwin.

Every man on earth is a candidate for celestial glory, a glory undiminished by any vague merging with an ethereal being. The saint who achieves the celestial, or highest degree, can contemplate eternal existence as an individual "clothed in the finest robes of linen, pure and white, adorned with precious stones and gold . . . promenading or sitting beneath the evergreen bowers and trees . . . inhaling the healthful breezes, perfumed with odor, wafted from the roses and pinks of paradise. . . ." And if the olfactory sense can function in the celestial sphere, so can the sexual. When thinking in terms of eternity, a man might get rather lonely with a single wife. Since all future relationships are formed in this life, it pays not only to have multiple wives but scores of children to keep one company in the vastness of celestial space. The Mormons had a sense of astronomy.

But if Mormonism contemplated such a luxurious eternity, life on earth was not to be conceived in such terms. Joseph Smith, Brigham Young, the Pratt brothers, and most of the other early leaders came out of a strict New England culture which thought of idleness as one of the most inexcusable of sins. Orson Pratt and Young never tired of condemning idlers and Pratt asserted that they will find themselves "cast out, and entitled to no place among the people of God." Men who had spent their boyhood plowing around stones in Berkshire fields attacked missionary work with a zeal seldom paralleled. Parley Pratt preached the word of Moroni from the Chilean Andes to England. His brother Orson even attempted the seemingly impossible task of converting Scotland to Mormonism. The York State farmer spent nine months in Edinburgh and every day climbed the steep and barren slopes of Arthur's Seat to pray to Zion's God to warm the stony hearts of the Scots. Moreover, he apparently succeeded in gathering over two hundred converts. The same monism which made mind and body a united substance made religion synonymous with life. The Mormons recaptured part of that Puritan fervor which compelled one to work unceasingly for God.

Many commentators have been confused by the apparent ambivalence in early Mormon theology toward predestination. Lehi's speech in the Book of Mormon about "God's eternal purposes" would seem to deny the emphasis on man's acting for himself and choosing good from evil. Here Mormonism absorbed some of the cultural currents of the times, in trying to give man a certain "natural ability" within God's total scheme. By 1834 the Presbyterian General Assembly was complaining that New School "errors in doctrine" had seeped from New England into New York State.

The Mormons appropriated this emphasis on man's ability to do what God requires of him, without going to the extreme free will of Methodism. In an attempt to reconcile predestination with the necessity for prayer, Orson Pratt wrote: "Because God knows the nature of music, that is no reason why he may not rejoice in hearing music."

The seeming liberalism of such doctrines as general atonement can only be interpreted in terms of the Mormon emphasis on oneness. The Latter-day Saints stood opposed to individualism of any kind, even to the rather dubious individualism of the eternally damned. They never denied that the wicked must undergo epochs of torment, but this must take place within the unified system. The Puritan ancestors of Mormons who were led to hell by false priests can still be saved if their descendants help them. Even in recent times Mormon agents have circulated in New England towns taking microfilm records of ancestors' births, so that they might be baptized in proxy and saved.

The Mormons allowed no partiality and in a sense were more hard-boiled than the sternest Calvinist. While retaining his particular substance, the individual was subordinate to a social and cosmic unity. All possible stress was placed on order, in an attempt to recover the order and certainty of a former era. The amazing success in fulfilling Joseph Smith's dream was due to the efficient channeling of all individual effort to do God's work. The early Mormon communism differed significantly from that of the Shakers, Rappites, and Fourier groups. The United Order of Enoch used communism as a means to an end, and the church did not collapse when it was necessary to modify communism.

It is a fantastic spectacle. In the era of Jackson, of liberalizing religions, of individualistic society and competitive economics, a movement which represents the antithesis rises, fights its way across a continent, and comes into full fruition. It was more than the appeal of superstition which would make a man say, "If Brother Brigham tells me to do a thing, it is the same as though the Lord told me to do it. This is the course for you and every other Saint to take. . . ." The future leader, Wilford Woodruff, could admit that whatever conclusions he might come to in the study of arts and sciences must be abandoned if the prophet of God rejected them.

The preoccupation of Mormonism with material expansion in this world led many interpreters into thinking of its theology as mere rationalization. They failed to see that a Mormon's calling was conceived only in terms of his salvation and historical role. While most nineteenth-century religions were minimizing man's guilt and the difficulties of salvation, Mormonism advanced the extreme and fanatical doctrine of blood atonement. It was an acute awareness of guilt which invoked the necessity of bloodshed for justification. Brotherly love compelled a man to "help" his neighbor atone for his sins. This again was the antinomian undercurrent which the older revelatory religions had feared.

Around 1842 the Mormons began introducing certain pseudo-Masonic rituals. The simple rites of washing and anointing were transformed into a ceremony where a man said, "Brother, having authority, I wash you that you may be clean from the blood and sins of this generation." Since Mormon naturalism held that every transgression will bring its proportionate punishment, a severe sin came to require more than simple washing. At later times, this doctrine may have meant legal murder. After the persecutions and mobbings given the Saints by the frontier, people began to realize that this blood atonement might have serious implications for the United States. The shadow of John of Leyden and Muenster fell eastward from the Rocky Mountains.

V

In an age of self-congratulation, optimism, and progress, it was the ghost of another era who could write:

Wickedness keeps pace with the hurried revolutions of the age. Gross immoralities, drunkenness, debaucheries, adulteries, whoredoms, self-pollutions, sodomy, beastliness, thieving, robbing, murdering, have engulfed the nations in a deathly ocean of filth, and have transformed our world into a sickly, disgusting, loathsome cesspool of corruption, fit for the habitation of devils and unclean spirits. In the midst of all this overwhelming crime, millions of long-faced, hypocritical, heaven-daring priests and clergy will roll up their sanctimonious eyes and insult the great Majesty of heaven, under pretense of thanking him that they live in such a glorious day of Gospel light. . . .

Yet this is the way Orson Pratt saw the latter days of the great apostasy. He was not surprised by the corruptions, because they were part of the providential plan. But they confirmed his belief in his own mission and enabled him to continue publishing such sentiments in his English *Millennial Star*.

The Mormon conception of history was quite different from other nineteenth-century theories. Since their personal God presided over the most minute happenings, the ordinary sequences of cause and effect were meaningful only in light of the overall system. In the late spring of 1847, when the Mormon emigrants were occupying both sides of the North Platte near the present Casper, Wyoming, God sent miraculous rains which swelled the river so that Gentile wagons jammed up before the crossing.

Obviously, God intended His children to profit by the miracle and ferry the Gentiles across for good money. It was all part of the plan.

Providential history was the dynamo which harnessed the separate energies of York State farmers into a smoothly-running organization, an organization which would build a holy empire west of the Wasatch. For fourteen hundred years the world had slumbered in darkness and illusion, further perpetuated by false priests and prophets. The obvious evidence of the death of the true church was the lack of immersion for remission of sins, the absence of laying on of hands for the gift of the Holy Ghost, and the total disappearance of miracles, gifts, and powers of the Holy Ghost. True apostolic succession must be restored by "the man or men last holding the keys of such power. . . ." As ministering angels they must return to the world and restore the keys to God's chosen. So God appeared to Moses after a time of apostasy. So Christ appeared to the Nephites. And when the early church councils perverted the Christian religion in Europe, the last holders of the keys were the gallant and cultured Nephites of America. Their destruction at Cumorah meant that Moroni, son of Mormon, must appear to the leader of the Latter-day Saints and convey the apostolic succession. Thus it was the Catholic and Anglican were usurping sects.

But fourteen hundred years of darkness did not mean that God had been ignoring the destiny of man. God let the United States come into being so that religious liberty would enable the Latter-day Saints to found the Kingdom of God on earth. The great discoveries and inventions were God's way of fertilizing the soil for the coming millennium. Rapid transportation and communication meant that regenerate men could be gathered at Zion before the destruction of the ungodly. So another people with a similar outlook, a similar desire for unity and purpose, had seen parliamentary government, the Reformation, and the New World discoveries as a well-planned sequence in preparation for the true church.

Like their forefathers, the Mormons thought of themselves in the role of warners rather than warriors. Just as the Puritans could support the Crown from a good distance and work out their model state within an established framework, so the Mormons paid verbal homage to the Constitution. After all, the stream of history was on their side.

Like the seventeenth-century Puritans, the Mormons saw their political and religious work as the culmination of history. Their model Zion would be the focal point of the globe and the fulfillment of history. Unity would come through example. Both groups worked tirelessly for the inevitable. Both groups built theocracies in the wilderness and hoped to unite the races which had been dispersed from the Tower of Babel. Both felt the necessity of a solid social and economic unity for this purpose.

It would, of course, be an oversimplification to think of the Mormons merely as nineteenth-century Puritans, revolting against the innovations of the age. The Mormons lacked the sense of propriety, the stability of their forefathers. They lacked the sound intellectual leadership and were constantly on the point of splintering, until Brigham Young became president. They went off on a dozen tangents and absorbed a crazy tangle of mysticism and charlatanry from a variety of sources. Leaders drew in ideas at random from local preachers, pseudoscientific books, and "philosophers" like Thomas Dick.

Yet the converts to Mormonism were usually the descendants of those cast off by the Half-Way Covenant. They were the churchgoers who did not belong, the Bible readers who did not understand. The relation between religion and culture had broken down and tradition failed to explain the new civilization. Methodist exhorters and jolly Universalists could not wash away the doubts of soul-searching New England farmers. If scripture were true, there must be another meaning to history, a more convincing way to escape sin. Since the theologians had failed to understand the problem and quarreled among themselves, since the business leaders were too intent on exploitation to lead, it was up to some farmers to make their own religion, and their own society.

There is something dramatic about the shift between the poles of two centuries. A small band of Englishmen creating a Christian community on the shores of a wilderness—for them, the triumph of the Reformation and the consummation of history. And a York State farmer whose ancestor had marched with Thomas Hooker from Newtowne and had been given land in Saybrook, this farmer climbing to the summit of Arthur's Seat to pray that the Scots and English be allowed to see the light and be saved.

It was, after all, a seventeenth- and not a nineteenth-century phenomenon for a group of mechanics and farmers to make their religion a part of everyday life, to interpret daily happenings in light of their providential mission, to cut a swath two-thirds of the way across a continent, and to colonize successfully an uninhabited desert, a thousand miles from alien civilization, where there were "no friends to wellcome them, nor inns to entertaine or refresh their weatherbeaten bodys, no houses or much less townes to repaire too, to seeke for succoure."

The Quest for Religious Authority and the Rise of Mormonism

MARIO S. DE PILLIS

Mario De Pillis, an assistant professor at Massachusetts University, admits that the Mormon prophet Joseph Smith inherited certain Puritan attitudes of mind—moralism, commitment to social order, and individual self-control—but insists that in initiating Mormonism Smith responded to specific social conflict and social change in the rural America of the 1830s. Through the means of new revelation, new scripture, and new priesthood and church government, the prophet provided some socially uprooted Americans with authoritarian foundations for their community that were lacking in religiously pluralistic America. In so arguing, De Pillis seems to tie the Mormons, to some extent at least, to those conservative groups in New England and New York that promoted social reform for purposes of social control. If Mormon means were radical their purpose was essentially conservative.

If historians were to take Mormonism as seriously as, say, the Separatism of Plymouth, what could they discern as the chief religious appeal of the new revelation? For an answer they must look not merely to the Book of Mormon and the Doctrine and Covenants, but also to the sincere concerns of the intensely religious people of western New York in the 1820s and 1830s. A good place to start is the explanation, never closely read by non-Mormons, of Joseph Smith himself.

The prophet's neglected explanation of the events leading to his first vision are among the most significant and revealing in all of early Mormon history. . . . His explanation, following the bare facts of birth, family, and education, comes first as the very source of his whole life and career:

Excerpt from Mario S. De Pillis, "The Quest for Religious Authority and the Rise of Mormonism," *Dialogue: A Journal of Mormon Thought*, I (Fall 1966), pp. 68–88. Edited and reprinted by permission of the publisher. Footnotes deleted by permission.

When about fourteen years of age, I began to reflect upon the importance of being prepared for a future state, and upon inquiring [about] the plan of salvation, I found that there was a great clash in religious sentiment; if I went to one society they referred me to one plan, and another to another; each one pointing to his own particular creed. . . . Considering that all could not be right, and that God could not be the author of so much confusion, I determined to investigate the subject more fully. . . .

Retiring to a grove, he began to call upon the Lord for wisdom and while so engaged was suddenly enwrapped in a heavenly vision, brighter than the noonday sun, in which two persons appeared:

They told me that all religious denominations were believing in incorrect doctrines, and that none of them was acknowledged of God as His Church and kingdom: and I was expressly commanded "to go not after them," at the same time receiving a promise that the fullness of the Gospel should at some future time be made known unto me.

. . . . The Prophet related his search to the particular religious conditions in the vicinity of Manchester:

[About 1820–1821] there was in the place where we lived an unusual excitement on the subject of religion. It commenced with the Methodists, but soon became general among all the sects of that region. Indeed, the whole district of country seemed affected by it, and great multitudes united themselves to the different religious parties, which created no small stir and division amongst the people, some crying, "Lo here!" and others, "Lo there!" Some were contending for the Methodist faith, some for the Presbyterian, and some for the Baptist.

The prophet's family succumbed to Presbyterianism . . . [but] Joseph, then fifteen years old, remained uneasy and undecided:

So great were the confusion and strife among the different denominations, that it was impossible for a person young as I was, and so unacquainted with men and things, to come to any certain conclusion who was right and who was wrong.

Who was right and who was wrong?—that was the issue at the very root of Mormon beginnings. By what *authority* did the contending preachers lay claim to the one true road to salvation?

The issue of authority will not seem unusual to faithful, informed, educated members of the church. But in the writing of history this criterion of salvation is rarely cited as an important explanation of the origins and immediate success of the early church. Non-Mormon historians and, indeed, most Mormons, habitually attribute the rise and progress of the church to personalities: Joseph Smith, Sidney Rigdon, Oliver Cowdery, Brigham Young, or others; to the appeal of the Book of Mormon; to the "age of reform"; to the environment of the Burned-over-District of western New York, with all its revivalism and religious emotionalism, its "far-out" reform movements; to the frontier environment.

These traditional explanations are relevant and necessary. But they do not make complete sense of the revivalism, the visions, the handful of Mormon baptisms that took place before the organization of the church in April 1830, nor of the Mormon insistence on the necessity of a High Priesthood . . . , of the new revelations collected in the Doctrine and Covenants . . . , restorationism . . . , [and] communitarianism. . . . All these may be explained by the thirst of Joseph Smith and his contemporaries for the religious authority of one true church, i.e., for divine authority.

When this thirst has been recognized by leading historians, most of whom have belonged to the liberal tradition, it has been dismissed as "authoritarian." The use of this pejorative denies to Mormonism any sincere concern with divine authority—and thus abjures any need to analyze Mormonism as seriously as one would analyze a more orthodox denomination. Thus, a standard work in American intellectual history deals with Mormonism in this way:

> The weakness of Protestantism in the Middle Period was its sectarianism. . . . Inevitably some anxious souls sought the reassurance of an authoritarian Church. Two such organizations played minor roles in the United States during the Middle Period. One, the Catholic Church, was old; the other, the Church of Jesus Christ of Latter-day Saints, was new. The latter was indigenous.

The "anxious souls" were many, not "some." They all refused to accept the three evangelical orthodoxies of Baptism, Methodism, and Presbyterianism. Some rebelled against any kind of formal doctrine of salvation and became Universalists, Unitarians, and "infidels." These sought authority and truth by relying in varying degrees on some concept of reason; others joined splinter groups like the Reformed Baptists, Reformed Methodists, Free Will Baptists, and others; some followed minor prophets like Joseph Dylks or Isaac Bullard; many joined various "Christian" groups and communitarian societies.

One "Christian" group, the Campbellites, and one communitarian movement, Shakerism, were very strong advocates of religious authority as the foundation of salvation. And it is significant that these were the two groups whose history impinged most closely on Mormonism.

Alexander Campbell's quest for primitive Christianity and divine authority led him, between 1808 and 1812, from Secession Presbyterianism to a kind of Baptist congregationalism. Authority was to be found in the ability of a congregation to find truth in scriptures. Campbell called the first such congregation assembled by him the "Christian Association." He found authority to ordain in the consent of his congregation—unlike the Mormons, who found this crucial exercise of authority in new revelations, especially the revelation on the High Priesthood. For the Campbellites, sectarianism was the chief evil—one reason why they called themselves "The Church of Christ" and "The Disciples of Christ"; for the names implied nonsectarianism or "unity."

A second group that competed with the Mormons in the Western Reserve of Ohio and elsewhere was the United Society of Believers in Christ's Second Appearing, commonly called Shakers. The Shakers were also ardent antisectarians. Richard McNemar, who before his conversion to Shakerism had been one of the leading figures of the Kentucky Revival, wrote a poem in about 1807 ridiculing the sectarians of the age; one stanza runs:

> Ten thousand Reformers like so many moles
> Have plowed all the Bible and cut it [in] holes
> And each has his church at the end of his trace
> Built up as he thinks of the subjects of grace.

Thirty years later he was preaching the same message. He made it clear that antisectarianism was a general feeling among the nonorthodox seekers of the early nineteenth century. He and others like him sought one true church with the mark of divine approbation. It had become meaningless to pick one of the major contending denominations as an instrument of salvation.

Antisectarianism could, of course, lead to infidelity or to rationalist simplifications of doctrine, but it usually meant, as it did with Joseph Smith, a fundamental rejection of the three dominant denominations of the frontier and rural areas of the time: Baptism, Methodism, and Presbyterianism. A seeker hardly wasted time with those denominations, and perhaps the spiritual history of the many anxious souls of the day may be symbolized by the brief story of the religious experience of young Michael Hull Barton of western Massachusetts, an area that gave so much to the religious life of western New York.

After traveling extensively throughout New England seeking the one true church, Barton found himself torn between the Mormons and the Shakers. Finally, in 1831 he started from western Massachusetts for Portsmouth, New Hampshire, to be baptized by a Mormon elder. On the way back to his home his "conscience seized him and his sins stared him in the face." Retiring to the woods to pray, he received the spiritual light which turned him toward the nearest Shaker community in the town of Harvard, Massachusetts. If he had lived in western Pennsylvania, he might have joined the Campbellites.

Fully to understand the importance of authority in early Mormonism, one must do more than take into account the religious milieu of the 1820s and the extraordinarily direct testimony of Joseph Smith. One must examine in detail . . . the subsequent development of Mormon polity and doctrine. Does it prove the sincerity of Joseph's quest for authority? Did his followers also seek it? Does the extraordinary elaboration of Mormon doctrine after 1830, and especially between 1838 and 1844, cast doubt upon his original quest?

Aside from the Book of Mormon (1830), the Mormon conception of authority rests chiefly on a special Priesthood and on the revelations received by Joseph Smith. Most of the development of the Priesthood and most of the revelations came after 1830.

For Mormons authority means the right of those holding the Priesthood to act for God. This right and the Priesthood that exercises it are given a historical rationale in the Book of Mormon and acquired specific forms and goals through subsequent revelations and practices. Mormon religion was authoritative (a slightly different concept from that of authority) because God attested to its truth by direct revelation. To demonstrate that Mormonism was a continuing quest for authoritative religion, it is not necessary for the historian to enter into the question of whether these revelations were authentic or to show how the Mormons proved their doctrines to be true in contrast to those of all their competitors.

Both Mormon apologetics and anti-Mormon propaganda have always dwelt, and understandably for their purposes, on the issue of the historical authenticity of the golden plates and on the divine authenticity of Joseph Smith's visions and revelations. This question of authenticity is basic for explaining the rise of the new religion, but is not enough. What must be shown is how much stronger the Mormon quest for authority was than that of the Campbellites, Shakers, and others who preached against sectarianism, how much more elaborate and theologically central was the Mormon concern for authoritative religion than, for example, Campbell's exaggerated reliance on the New Testament or the Shaker's faith in the postmillennial ministry of their foundress. Despite the intricate elaboration of their Priesthood, Mormons never watered down its function: the right and power to act authoritatively for God. Only the restored Priesthood could save a torn and divided Christianity.

· · ·

To oversimplify, it may be said that there are three modes of establishing a theological claim to being the one true teaching church: apostolic succession, miracles and "gifts" (as signs of divine approbation), and special revelations. With certain modifications the prophet used all three methods. Since apostolic succession was Roman and alien, he turned to a more familiar source of Protestant tradition, the Old Testament: he claimed a *prophetic* succession through a dual priesthood that allegedly existed among the Hebrews. Miracles and gifts he used discreetly and sparingly; ambitious miracles, such as his attempt to raise a dead infant, were likely to fail. As for special revelations, they were central to the establishment of authority and Joseph adopted them even before the church was organized (1830); his mother, with her antinomian predilections for special inspiration, encouraged him to see visions and revelations. Joseph believed that his additions to orthodox Christian-Jewish scripture—his revelations, the Book of Mormon, "lost books" like the Book of Enoch, and his revision of the King James Bible—constituted the "fulness of the Gospel." In short, while using some of its doctrines, Joseph rejected Protestantism as well as Calvinism: he claimed to bring an entirely "new dispensation." "Truth," he later said, "is Mormonism. God is the author of it." This special status of Mormonism as a fourth major religion is generally accepted in American society.

The idea of a religious authority established by means of prophetic succession and direct revelation originated not in the Book of Mormon but in the mind of Joseph Smith. The historical foundation, or authority, supplied by that book was of little practical use to the prophet in defining the polity and doctrine of the new religion. For the non-Mormon it is almost as though he had simply composed a Hebrew-and-Indian novel with no thought of making it the bible of a new religion. Even the uneducated agrarians who had read it with relish seemed to sense this, for they usually felt compelled to visit the prophet and hear what was concretely required of them for salvation. At first the prophet had little to offer them beyond baptism and his own impressive personality. Many heard him preach, but by January 1831, less than eighty persons in western New York had embraced the gospel—eleven years after Smith's first vision and six months after the publication of the Book of Mormon.

Converts soon discovered that Mormon polity and doctrine would consist of what God revealed through Joseph Smith, month by month, in direct revelations. It was Smith's revulsion against the sectarianism of the Burned-over District and his consequent quest for a new source of authority that made direct revelations necessary.

PART II

THE MORMON COMMUNITY: THE SEARCH IN THE NINETEENTH CENTURY

Early in the year 1831 Joseph Smith and most of the small body of New York Latter-day Saints migrated to northern Ohio. Thus began a series of movements which culminated in the settlement of the Great Basin, and, eventually, statehood for Utah in 1896. It is in this period, 1831 to 1896, that the search for community within the context of the larger American effort is especially clear in Mormon history. Mormons were alienated from their contemporary society by economic and social exclusiveness, political autonomy under the Kingdom of God, and polygamy. At the same time their search for community included such typical American activities as communitarianism, encouragement of immigration, westward migration, and a quest for political self-determination through statehood. The selections in this section explore the uneasy relationship between the Mormons and their physical and social environment as they sought to build a cohesive and relevant community in the nineteenth century.

Early Mormon Communitarianism

LEONARD J. ARRINGTON

At about the time Robert Owen established New Harmony, and the
Transcendentalists their Brook Farm, and literally scores of additional
experiments in communal living flourished as part of the general spirit
of reform, the Mormons too indulged in a significant effort to create a
self-sustaining communal order, based on the Puritan assumption that in
the use of the goods of the earth man possessed only a lease, or "stewardship," from God. Here Leonard J. Arrington describes this experimental
effort of the 1830s, noting the differences between the Mormon system and
communal societies elsewhere, and also suggesting how the Mormon
failure reflected certain inherent weaknesses in any such economic system.
After the Mormons moved to the Great Basin they tried other forms of
social organization, the most notable of which was an almost completely
socialistic community at Orderville, Utah. This effort had no more
success than the earlier one, and for many of the same reasons.

The Mormons have occupied little space in the studies of sectarian
communitarianism in early nineteenth-century America. The "law of consecration and stewardship," which was the first of many Mormon experiments in economic reform, should be of particular interest because of the
light it sheds on the problems of community-building in the Mississippi
Valley in the 1830s. An attempt was made by the Latter-day Saints to live
according to the provisions of this law in their various communities in
Ohio and Missouri from 1831 to 1834; a less exacting system was proclaimed in 1838; and the law was replaced by the "lesser law of tithing"
in 1841. The inauguration of this imaginative mixture of individualism
and collectivism, and the acceptance of the philosophy underlying it, go
far toward explaining the social union and cohesiveness of the Latter-day
Saints, which antedated the persecutions usually credited with generating

Leonard J. Arrington, "Early Mormon Communitarianism: The Law of Consecration and Stewardship," *Western Humanities Review,* VII (Autumn 1953),
pp. 341–369. Reprinted by permission of the publisher. Footnotes deleted by
permission.

this outstanding characteristic of Mormon group life. The decision to suspend the practical operation of this "divine" economic system illustrates the difficulties in the way of harmonizing institutional growth and individual equality. Indeed, its failure is symbolic of the fate of any static pattern of economic reform in a society committed to membership expansion. Nevertheless, the "celestial" law of consecration and stewardship has continued for more than a hundred years to embody Mormon economic idealism, and devotees of the Mormon faith still look forward to the day when it will be restored "in all its fulness."

I

The law of consecration and stewardship, variously known as the "First United Order," the "Order of Enoch," the "Law of Consecration," and the "Order of Stewardships," was first outlined in a revelation to Joseph Smith, dated February 9, 1831. Briefly, the law comprised four elements: economic equality, socialization of surplus incomes, freedom of enterprise, and group economic self-sufficiency. Upon the basic principle that the earth and everything on it belongs to the Lord, every person who was a member of the church at the time the system was introduced or became a member thereafter was asked to "consecrate" or deed all his property, both real and personal, to a church leader called the "Presiding Bishop of the Church." The Presiding Bishop would then grant an "inheritance," or "stewardship," to every family out of the properties so received, the amount depending on the wants and needs of the family, as determined jointly by the bishop and the prospective steward. The stewardship might be a farm, building lot, store, workshop, or mill. It was expected that in some cases the consecrations would considerably exceed the stewardships. Out of the surplus thus made possible the bishop would grant stewardships to the poorer and younger members of the church who had no property to consecrate. The words of the basic revelation were as follows:

. . . behold, thou shalt consecrate all thy properties, that which thou hast unto me, with a covenant and a deed which cannot be broken; and they shall be laid before the bishop of my church, and two of the elders, such as he shall appoint and set apart for that purpose . . . the bishop of my church, after that he has received the properties of my church, that it cannot be taken from the church, he shall appoint every man a steward over his own property, or that which he has received, inasmuch as shall be sufficient for himself and family. . . .

This redistribution of wealth was designed to place all family heads on an equal economic footing, considering their respective family obligations, circumstances, needs, and "just wants." The law of consecration and stewardship was thus a great leveler, designed to bring about a condition of relative temporal equality among the early converts to the church, for according to another 1831 doctrine, "it is not given that one man should possess that which is above another, wherefore the world lieth in sin." It was not "dead level" equality that the system aimed at, however, but a condition in which men were given responsibilities proportionate to their needs, circumstances, and capacities. The system was intended to dispose once and for all of the problem of charity by giving the poor a stewardship over sufficient property to provide for their own wants.

Once the Saints had been placed on an equitable economic footing, the equality was to be maintained by requiring family heads to consecrate annually all their surplus production to the storehouse provided by the bishop for this purpose. This surplus (or "residue," as it was called) was to be used primarily to distribute to those who for one reason or another, perhaps unseasonal arrival, illness, improvidence, or misfortune, failed to produce sufficiently to provide for the needs and just wants of their families. The surplus was also to be used to provide for special church expenditures, such as for publications, temples, education, and to finance the stewards who needed funds for improvement and expansion. The wording of the revelation was as follows:

> . . . the residue shall be kept to administer to him who has not, that every man may receive according as he stands in need; and the residue shall be kept in my storehouse, to administer to the poor and needy, as shall be appointed by the elders of the church and the bishop; and for the purpose of purchasing lands, and the building up of the New Jerusalem, which is hereafter to be revealed; that my covenant people may be gathered in one. . . .

This annual consecration of the social surplus to the church for redistribution to the poor was a device to ensure continued (relative) temporal equality; it was also a means by which the church would control investment and ensure that the social surplus was used for purposes which the church felt were necessary and desirable. It mitigated against luxurious living and against competitive expansion. If the surplus was adequate, it also ensured primacy to those investment projects in which the church was most interested.

While the collection, administration, and investment of the initial and annual consecrations were to be under the supervision of the Presiding Bishop and his advisers, there was to be freedom of enterprise in production and in the management of properties held as stewardships. That is, the properties placed at the disposal of each family head were to be used in producing whatever goods and services he desired, with whatever combinations of factors of production he selected, from among the limited opportunities open. Church leaders might give advice on these matters, but the law of consecration and stewardship did not provide for minute and intimate regulation of economic activity. Each member was free to work as he pleased within the limitations of his stewardship. The profit system, the forces of supply and demand, and the price system presumably would continue to allocate resources, guide production decisions, and distribute primary or earned income. Some of the institutions of capitalism were thus retained and a considerable amount of economic freedom was permitted. Above all, there was to be no communism of goods. While "God's chosen" were counseled to "live together in love," they were also admonished to "pay for that which thou shalt receive of thy brother."

Despite a considerable measure of freedom of enterprise, however, the system was distinctly communitarian in conception and in application. An 1831 revelation, which paralleled the law of consecration and steward-ship, commanded the members of the infant church to "be one." Common suffering, persecution, and group migration strengthened the forces making for unity. Social union, in turn, was indispensable to the establishment and operation of an exemplary Mormon community whose convert-citizens would have the disposition and means to prepare the earth for the return of the Savior and the institution of the Kingdom of God. John Corrill, an apostate Mormon bishop, in one of the first published histories of the Latter-day Saints, emphasized the role of the law of consecration and stewardship as follows:

> It is believed by them [the Latter-day Saints] that the Church ought to act in concert, and feel one general interest in building up the "great cause"; and that every man ought to consider his property as consecrated to the Lord for that purpose. . . .

Orson Pratt, also a participant in church affairs in the 1830s, drew a distinction between dividing property, which he characterized as a "Gentile" doctrine, and uniting property, which was "God's plan of making His Saints equal in property," "as joint heirs with Him, or as His stewards."

The Latter-day Saint community was to be established as the result of a "gathering" of "the faithful in heart," from "out of the bosom of Baby-lon" to a place designated as "Zion." Thus, the Saints would be organized "in close bodies." Once gathered, the Saints were then to devote them-selves assiduously to the task of building up Zion: "Thou shalt not be idle; for he that is idle shall not eat the bread, nor wear the garments of the laborer." Plainness in living and financial self-sufficiency were to characterize this New Jerusalem: ". . . let all thy garments be plain, and their beauty the beauty of the work of thine own hands; . . . contract no debts with the world. . . ." Thus, an industrious, frugal, independent society was to be established under the direction of the priesthood. Nevertheless, in contrast with many contemporary communitarian societies, each family was to live separately, possessed of its own stewardship, and communal living was eschewed.

One crucial point in regard to the system has never been made clear; namely, the relationship of the law of consecration and stewardship to the common-stock systems of the Shakers, Harmonists, Ephratists, and other contemporary communitarian societies. The Mormons disclaimed any resemblances between their law and the many types of communal orders prevalent in early nineteenth-century America, holding that the incorporation of the stewardship principle permitted a large area of individual initiative and enterprise. It seems evident, however, that Mormon leaders did not originally intend that the stewardship be held in fee simple, with all the legal privileges which that form of property right might accord to the "owner." Indeed, the title to all property would seem to have been vested in the Presiding Bishop. The original revelation read: "he that sinneth and repenteth not shall be cast out, and shall not receive again that which he has consecrated unto me. . . ." This seems to imply that a stewardship was a life-lease, subject to revocation by the bishop. The theory and practice of stewardship also would seem to have disallowed transferrals by the steward to his wife, children, heirs, and others with whom sales and exchanges might be contemplated.

II

There seem to have been three specific reasons, historically speaking, for the initial revelation establishing the law of consecration and stewardship. The first was the desire of Joseph Smith to establish a latter-day alternative to a communal society. One of the earliest converts to Mormonism was Sidney Rigdon, a leading Protestant minister in the Western Reserve. Rigdon had been a follower of the noted leader of the Disciples of Chirst, Alexander Campbell, but had broken away from Campbell, partly over a dispute as to the wisdom of attempting to duplicate the communism of the early Christians, as described in the Acts of the Apostles: "And all that believed were together, and had all things common; and sold their possessions and goods and parted them to all men, as every man had need." Rigdon, a person of considerable intellectual stature in his earlier years, was familiar with the experiments of Robert Owen, the Rappists, and the German Separatists at Zoar, Ohio. Rigdon's followers at Mentor and Kirtland, Ohio, two communities on Lake Erie, east of Cleveland, attempted to establish communal societies called "The

Family." Rigdon and most of his Kirtland congregation were converted to Mormonism late in 1830. So important was this group that Joseph Smith moved immediately, with some of his followers, from New York to Kirtland. When the twenty-six-year-old Smith arrived at the new headquarters on or about February 1, 1831, one of his first acts was to request "The Family" to abandon the common-stock principle in favor of what he called "the more perfect law of the Lord." Some positive explanation of the "law of the Lord" was necessarily forthcoming. A week later the law of consecration and stewardship was revealed, thus serving to replace common stock with stewardship, and "The Family" with a considerable measure of individualism.

The need to suggest something positive to replace the impractical common-stock principle was one purpose of the revelation. A second function of the law of consecration and stewardship was to provide a religious incentive whereby the Kirtland Mormons would agree to divide their farming lands, building lots, and other property with poor families who had gone, upon Joseph Smith's recommendation, from New York and elsewhere to Ohio (and later to Missouri). The law was also a device by which a surplus could be accumulated to purchase additional lands, care for the temporal needs of those called into church service, finance the publication of books and periodicals, make possible the construction of meetinghouses, and supply means for carrying out other worthwhile spiritual and temporal projects. Insofar as converts were convinced of its practical efficacy or divine origin, the law of consecration and stewardship would assure the use of the social surplus for charitable and religious purposes. It is quite possible that the law would have been announced for this immediate and compelling financial reason even if the Kirtland Family situation had not confronted Joseph Smith and his associates.

There was undoubtedly a third and more far-reaching objective in the revelations on consecration and stewardship. As the founder of "restored Christianity" it was necessary for Joseph Smith to establish the social and economic basis for a Christian society. The passage in the Acts of the Apostles previously quoted was doubtless a challenge to the youthful prophet, as it was to Bible-reading Christians generally. And in that period of social ferment, religious enthusiasm, and economic reform which saw the origin of Mormonism, scores of communistic and/or communitarian societies and experiments sprang into existence. In 1840 Emerson wrote to Carlyle: "We are all a little wild here with numberless projects of social reform. Not a reading man but has a draft of a New Community in his waistcoat pocket." Joseph Smith was not unfamiliar with these utopian concepts and experiments. Within a few miles of the Vermont community in which he was born were the Groveland Society of the Shakers, in which all property was held in trust by the community, and the organized followers of Jemima Wilkinson. Furthermore, Smith's associate, Sidney Rigdon, as mentioned before, was well acquainted with the systems of the Rappites and the Owenite socialists. Thus, it was logical, and perfectly within the order of events, that the new prophet should have announced the Latter-day Saint version of "the more perfect law of the Lord." Sprinkled through his revelations on the subject are phrases which indicate the lofty ideal to be held up before his followers: "be alike . . . and receive alike, that ye may be one"; "let every man esteem his brother as himself"; "my people [must be] united according to the union required by the law of the celestial kingdom"; and "thou shalt live together in love."

Thus, the law of consecration and stewardship originated as the result of practical need and utopian idealism. It is not surprising that the plan should have been intensely practical, in certain respects, and that it should have overestimated the possibilities of human altruism in other respects. It was equalitarian, a potentially good revenue-producer, and communitarian. It was also individualistic, though with strong elements of group control and influence.

III

During the first few months after the enunciation of the law of consecration and stewardship an attempt was made by some of the Latter-day Saints in Ohio to comply with its provisions. A group of Saints from Colesville, New York, established themselves at Thompson, near Kirtland, Ohio, in May 1831, and consecrations were importuned to apply on the purchase of their farming lands. Before this group was completely organized, however, one or two of the wealthier members backed out and successfully sued in the civil courts for the return of their consecrations. This introduced such confusion in their affairs that the Thompson Saints and others were called to settle Jackson County, Missouri (or "Zion" as it was called, the New Jerusalem whose building up was anticipated in the revelation of February 9, 1831), arriving there in July 1831. Nevertheless, the introduction of the system, even for that brief period, did facilitate the removal of the poor as well as the rich from New York to Ohio, and from Ohio to Missouri.

In Jackson County, Missouri, the second attempt was made to institute the law of consecration and stewardship. The form of the settlement was to be in accordance with the "Plat of the City of Zion." Every family was to receive a building lot in the city. In addition, the farmers were to receive an allotment of land outside the city. The mechanic was to receive the necessary tools and materials for his trade, and teachers, writers, and musicians were to have a home site and a license or appointment to serve the community according to their respective abilities. The town residents, of course, would participate in the produce of the farmers through regular commercial channels or through the redistribution of a central storehouse.

To purchase lands for the new community missionaries and agents were asked to canvass congregations throughout the East and Midwest for donations. The principal source of funds, however, was expected to be the consecrations of those going to Independence to live. The Presiding Bishop of the church was instructed to receive these consecrations, to allot inheritances to properly certified family heads, and to notify the church-at-large from time to time as to "the privileges of the land," so that the gathering would not take place faster than lands were purchased. The bishop was further directed to establish a storehouse for the reception and distribution of consecrations. This enterprise, operated under his management, was a going concern by the end of 1831. A printing concern was also established, the first such firm west of the Missouri River, to publish weekly and monthly periodicals.

By July 1832, roughly a year after the call to settle Jackson County, between three and four hundred converts had arrived at Independence, almost all of whom were located upon their inheritances. By the following July, almost 1,200 had gathered in Missouri, of whom 700 were "disciples." While the group was officially reported to be "in good health and spirits," and "doing well," the burden of migrating, of purchasing land, of establishing the printing office and store, and, above all, of transforming a "wilderness and desert," into a "garden of the Lord," was greater than most had anticipated. Evidently, the consecrations were insufficient to provide inheritances for all those who were entitled to them. From the frequent exhortations in *The Star* and in revelations of Joseph Smith, one would also gather that idleness was a problem. Perhaps some of the emigrants, filled with the millenarian spirit of the times, did not understand the necessity of laboring to build up Zion. Officials found it necessary to caution prospective emigrants not to give away their property before leaving for Zion! Despite these hindrances, however, some participants later wrote of the Jackson County experiment with pronounced nostalgia.

> There was a spirit of peace and union, and love and good will manifested in this little Church in the wilderness, the memory of which will be ever dear to my heart. . . . Peace and plenty crowned their labors, and the wilderness became a fruitful field, and the solitary place began to bud and blossom as the rose. . . . In short, there has seldom, if ever, been a happier people upon the earth than the Church of the Saints now were.

Idyllic or not, two problems arose in the administration of the system in

Jackson County. One had to do with the nature of the property rights to be granted to the stewards; the second was concerned with the size of the "inheritance" to be given to each steward. In regard to the first, the Presiding Bishop of the church, Edward Partridge, in the allotment of land purchased for the purpose, took the attitude that the inheritances ought to be tentative, entitling each settler to a right of use only, with a lease subject to cancellation on the order of the bishop. Considering the uncertainty in the number of converts for which he would have to provide land, the temporary nature of the allotments would make it possible for Partridge to make a reapportionment, if necessary, to provide for new arrivals. This plan would also discourage opportunists who might join the group to acquire an inheritance, and promptly withdraw. Finally, the no-title policy gave Partridge the power, under threat of the forfeiture of the entire stewardship, to enforce standards of workmanship, social behavior, and personal morality among those receiving inheritances. The wealth of the community would never be lost to apostates, "trouble-makers," or idlers.

A specimen of the type of instrument drawn up by Partridge is reproduced in Joseph Smith's documentary *History of the Church* and shows that one Titus Billings consecrated to the bishop the following:

Item	Value
Sundry articles of furniture	$ 55.27
Two beds, bedding, and extra clothing	73.25
Farming implements	41.00
One horse, 2 wagons, 2 cows, 2 calves	147.00
Total	$316.52

In return the bishop leased Billings twenty-seven and one-half acres of land, and "loaned" him all of the personal property which he had consecrated. Billings agreed to pay all taxes on the property, and also to pay the bishop "all that I shall make or accumulate more than is needful for the support and comfort of myself and family." The "lease and loan," as it was called—recalling a more modern program—was to be binding during the life of Billings "unless he transgresses, and is not deemed worthy by the authority of the church." In the event of transgression, Billings agreed to forfeit all claim to the real estate and to pay to the church the value of the personal property. The bishop, in turn, agreed to assist Billings and his family in the event of their inability to provide for themselves. In the event of Billings' death, his wife and/or children succeeded to all his rights, provided he died while in good standing in the church.

As might be expected, the church encountered legal difficulties as the result of the "lease and loan" policy. Judges on the frontier viewed properties held in trust with noticeable disfavor. Some apostates successfully sued in the courts for the return of their consecrated properties. Moreover, Mormonism was being associated, in the minds of many, with such religioeconomic movements as that of the Shakers—an association which Mormon leaders, for some reason, viewed with profound distaste. A leader of the church in Missouri finally wrote to Joseph Smith "on the subject of giving deeds, and receiving contributions from brethren." On April 21, 1833, Smith replied: "I have nothing further to say on the subject than to recommend that you make yourselves acquainted with the commandments of the Lord, and the laws of the state, and govern yourselves accordingly." Ten days later, in a special letter to Bishop Partridge, the Prophet wrote:

> . . . concerning inheritances, you are bound by the law of the Lord to give a deed, securing to him who receives inheritances, his inheritance for an everlasting inheritance, or in other words to be his individual property, his private stewardship, and if he is found a transgressor and should be cut off, out of the church, his inheritance is his still, and he is delivered over to the buffetings of Satan till the day of redemption. But the property which he consecrated to the poor, for their benefit and inheritance and stewardship [in other words, his "surplus"], he cannot obtain again by the law of the Lord. Thus you see the propriety of this law, that rich men cannot have power to disinherit the poor by obtaining again that which they have consecrated. . . .

Thus, it became clear that the official church position had become one of requiring that a deed with no strings attached be made out at the time each inheritance was given out. In commenting on this modification—or clarification—the editor of the church monthly later wrote:

> . . . they [the Latter-day Saints] have frequently been ridiculed in consequence of certain items contained in the one [revelation] setting forth their faith on the subject of bestowing temporal gifts for the benefit of the poor. . . .

> Some have said, and still say, that this Church, "has all things common." This asserting is meant, not only to falsify on the subject of property, but to blast the reputation and moral characters of the members of the same.

> The church at Jerusalem in the days of the apostles, had their earthly goods in common; the Nephites [a tribe of inhabitants of ancient America described in the Book of Mormon], after the appearance of Christ, held theirs in the same way; but each government was differently organized from ours; and could admit of such a course when ours cannot.

Because of the nature of prevailing state and national laws with respect to property, therefore, church authorities finally came to agree that a steward should hold legal rights to "the Lord's property" placed in his charge. In consequence of this decision, the leaders of the Missouri colony issued public statements in June 1833, declaring, among other things, that each family head had received, or was about to receive, "a warranty deed securing to himself and heirs, his inheritance in fee simple forever. . . ." However, it is doubtful that the new policy was completely carried out because of the developing friction between Mormons and non-Mormons in Missouri.

In regard to the second problem encountered in administering "the law" in Missouri—the amount of inheritance to be granted each steward—the revelation specified, in general terms, that each person was to have as much as was "sufficient for himself and family"; that every man should receive "according to his family, according to his circumstances . . . and his wants and needs. . . ." What were a family's wants and needs? Who was to determine them? Evidently, there was some difference of opinion on the matter, for Joseph Smith found it necessary to direct a letter to Bishop Partridge in June 1833, explaining the procedure that was to be followed:

> . . . every man must be his own judge how much he should receive and how much he should suffer to remain in the hands of the Bishop. I speak of those who consecrate more than they need for the support of themselves and their families.
>
> The matter of consecration must be done by the mutual consent of both parties; for to give the Bishop power to say how much every man shall have, and he be obliged to comply with the Bishop's judgment, is giving to the Bishop more power than a king has; and upon the other hand, to let every man say how much he needs, and the Bishop be obliged to comply with his judgment, is to throw Zion into confusion, and make a slave of the Bishop. The fact is, there must be a balance or equilibrium of power between the Bishop and the people, and thus harmony and good will may be preserved among you.
>
> Therefore, those persons consecrating property to the Bishop in Zion, and then receiving an inheritance back, must reasonably show to the Bishop that they need as much as they claim. But in case the two parties cannot come to a mutual agreement, the Bishop is to have nothing to do about receiving such consecrations; and the case must be laid before a council of twelve High Priests, the Bishop not being one of the council, but he is to lay the case before them.

These instructions, as with those pertaining to the granting of a deed, were too late to be applied in the Jackson County experiment.

Throughout the period of its operation, the active, on-the-job, management and supervision of the system was vested in the Presiding Bishop and his counselors. This imposed a heavy administrative task since these men were also spiritual leaders. In April 1832, the Central Council was created. This was a group of five men, three from Kirtland, two from Independence, later seven men, who were to serve as a board of directors for the supervision of business affairs in Kirtland and Zion. The Central Council, in turn, immediately created a "United Firm," or "United Order," which was a joint stewardship of the members of the Council with the responsibility of holding properties in trust, assisting the poor, and supervising the establishment of merchandising stores in Ohio and Missouri. The creation of this agency set the pattern for the assignment of responsibilities for the management of large companies and corporations: this was to be done by the method of joint stewardship.

While the creation of the Central Council removed overall temporal policy considerations from the province of the Presiding Bishop, a thousand miles, mostly wilderness, separated Kirtland from Independence, and it is probable that the control of the Central Council was not very effective.

IV

From a purely economic point of view, one fault of the law of consecration and stewardship was the transferral of consecrated properties from the relatively well-to-do to the poor, when the latter were incapable of wise management of property. Another fault in the system was the diminution of incentive which might be brought about by the requirement that stewards were to consecrate all their surplus income. This eventuality need not have resulted among a zealous and faithful people, but was a probability without that condition. We have Brigham Young's word for it that the system did not operate long enough, or successfully enough, to obtain much of a surplus:

> I was present at the time the revelation came for the brethren to give their surplus property into the hands of the Bishops for the building up of Zion, but I never knew a man yet who had a dollar of surplus property. No matter how much one might have he wanted all he had for himself, for his children, his grandchildren, and so forth.

Whether these difficulties could have been surmounted, as they were in many contemporary American idealistic communities, or whether church leaders would have modified the system sufficiently to take these two factors into account, can never be known for certain. About a year and a half after "Zion" had been founded, and before the system was completely organized and put into running operation, the Latter-day Saints in Missouri ran into the stiff opposition of their Gentile neighbors. Systematic persecution of the Mormons in Missouri commenced in April 1833. In July 1833, the Mormon printing establishment was wrecked and the Presiding Bishop and his companion were tarred and feathered. The printing establishment was about to issue 3,000 copies of the *Book of Commandments,* the first edition of the revelations received by Joseph Smith, and also a quantity of hymn books. All of these were destroyed, with the exception of a few sets of signatures of the uncompleted *Book of Commandments.* On July 23, 1833, what came to be known as the "Missouri Mob" reassembled, thoroughly armed and bearing a red flag, and required the Latter-day Saints to leave the county within a fixed time. In November 1833, armed mobs drove the Mormons from Jackson County.

The condition of the Saints during these and succeeding months was not such as to make the administration of the law of consecration and stewardship possible or effective. In December 1833, one of their number wrote Joseph Smith from Clay County, Missouri, describing their plight as follows:

> The condition of the scattered Saints is lamentable, and affords a gloomy prospect. No regular order can be enforced, nor any usual discipline kept up. . . . I should like to know what the honest in heart shall do? Our clothes are worn out; we want the necessaries of life, and shall we lease, buy, or otherwise obtain land where we are, to till, that we may raise enough to eat?

After exhausting all peaceful means of repossessing their land, church leaders in Ohio organized a group called "Zion's Camp" to march to Missouri to "redeem Zion." While this group was preparing to leave Kirtland, a revelation was announced separating the Jackson County and Kirtland orders. Instructions were given in relation to the establishment of "the Lord's law" in Kirtland. A treasury was created into which the cash receipts of the late Jackson County order were to be placed. This seems to have been particularly designed to receive the proceeds, or "avails," from the sale of lands in Jackson County, if any such sales were consummated. The Saints were to draw out of this treasury for their needs in getting established in Clay County, their new home. Thus, the treasury was a means of sharing the meager resources of the community among the needy.

These matters arranged for, Zion's Camp, with Joseph Smith as commander and some one hundred and thirty men, left for Missouri. They were destined not to reach their goal or to accomplish their purpose. An outbreak of cholera took a heavy toll of the little army and it was necessarily disbanded. Chastened and discouraged, the living heard Joseph

Smith announce a revelation on June 22, 1834, suspending the operation of the law of consecration and stewardship until such a day as Zion could be redeemed by purchase rather than by blood. This suspension apparently applied to the Mormon settlements in Ohio as well as to those in Missouri.

Zion—that is, Jackson County—was, of course, never "redeemed" by the Mormons, although some factions returned there after 1846; and the law of consecration and stewardship was never reinstated, in its pristine form, by church officials in Missouri or in any of the subsequent habitations of the Mormons in the Mississippi Valley. However, an "inferior" system which bore considerable resemblance to "the Lord's law" was officially introduced by Joseph Smith in 1838, at Far West, Caldwell County, Missouri. Far West, approximately fifty miles north of Independence, was the third Missouri gathering place of the Mormons—the first having been Jackson County, and the second having been Clay County, from which approximately 10,000 Mormons were called to settle Caldwell County late in 1837. There they bought up most of the land claims of value and established Far West as their new Zion. It was at this place, on July 8, 1838, that the following watered-down version of the law of consecration and stewardship was announced to the church:

> Verily, thus saith the Lord, I require all their surplus property to be put into the hands of the Bishop of my Church in Zion, for the building of mine house, and for the laying of the foundation of Zion [the purchase of lands?], and for the Priesthood, and for the debts of the Presidency of my Church.

> And this shall be the beginning of the Tithing of my people. And after that, those who have thus been tithed, shall pay one tenth of all their interest annually; and this shall be a standing law unto them forever. . . .

> . . . all those who gather unto the land of Zion shall be tithed of their surplus properties, and shall observe this law, or they shall not be found worthy to abide among you.

This admittedly "inferior" law, as it was called, was introduced because "the people had polluted their inheritances" while in Jackson County. In principle, however, it was not greatly different from the so-called "celestial" law of 1831. First of all, the revelation required the consecration of "surplus" property at the time the convert joined the community of Saints. In this respect, the law was precisely the same in effect as the 1831 law of consecration. The 1831 law required that the convert, at the time he joined the community of Saints, consecrate all his property and receive back a stewardship measured by his wants and needs. The 1838 law obviated the transfer and reverse transfer by requiring that he consecrate only his surplus and retain the remainder. The equalizing effect was identical. While the gesture of placing all his property on the altar was not required in the later law, the principle of stewardship was still retained, at least as a religious principle. Furthermore, whereas the original law of consecration and stewardship required that all the annual surplus income, or "residue," be placed in the storehouse for distribution to the poor and needy, the 1838 law required that a tithe, or a tenth, be universally paid on the annual increase. This might be regarded as a more precise definition of the "residue," or surplus income, and resulted in the same transferral of annual savings to the church for community-investment purposes that was to have been effected under the law of consecration and stewardship.

Because of the unsettled nature of the economic affairs of the Mormons at the time, it is difficult to determine to what extent the Latter-day Saints complied with the Far West revelation and consecrated their surplus property. Less than three weeks after the revelation was announced, Joseph Smith mentioned in his journal that church officials, including himself, met at Far West "to dispose of the public properties of the Bishop, many of the brethren having consecrated their surplus property according to the revelations." Brigham Young thought that the law "seemingly was not fully understood or practised." In a pulpit statement which reflects his gift for hyperbole as well as the problems raised by the revelation, Young explained:

When the revelation . . . was given in 1838, I was present, and recollect the feelings of the brethren. . . . The brethren wished me to go among the Churches, and find out what surplus property the people had, with which to forward the building of the Temple we were commencing at Far West. I accordingly went from place to place through the country. Before I started, I asked brother Joseph, "Who shall be the judge of what is surplus property?" Said he, "Let them be the judges themselves. . . ."

Then I replied, "I will go and ask them for their surplus property"; and I did so; I found the people said they were willing to do about as they were counselled, but, upon asking them about their surplus property, most of the men who owned land and cattle would say, "I have got so many hundred acres of land, and I have got so many boys, and I want each one of them to have eighty acres, therefore this is not surplus property." Again, "I have got so many girls, and I do not believe I shall be able to give them more than forty acres each." "Well, you have got two or three hundred acres left." "Yes, but I have a brother-in-law coming on, and he will depend on me for a living; my wife's nephew is also coming on, he is poor, and I shall have to furnish him a farm after he arrives here." I would [go] on to the next one, and he would have more land and cattle than he could make use of to advantage. It is a laughable idea, but is nevertheless true, men would tell me they were young and beginning in the world, and would say, "We have no children, but our prospects are good, and we think we shall have a family of children, and if we do, we want to give them eighty acres of land each; we have no surplus property." "How many cattle have you?" "So many." "How many horses, &c?" "So many, but I have made provisions for all these, and I have use for everything I have got."

Some were disposed to do right with their surplus property, and once in a while you would find a man who had a cow which he considered surplus, but generally she was of the class that would kick a person's hat off, or eyes out, or the wolves had eaten off her teats. You would once in a while find a man who had a horse that he considered surplus, but at the same time he had the ringbone, was broken-winded, spavined in both legs, and had the pole evil at one end of the neck and a fistula at the other, and both knees strung.

Whatever the status of the 1838 law of consecration in Far West, some Latter-day Saints took a further step at the time to consolidate their property by forming voluntary cooperative enterprises called "United Firms." Joseph Smith mentions in his journal having attended meetings on August 20, 21, 1838, at which groups of farmers organized the Western Agricultural Company, the Eastern Agricultural Company, and the Southern Agricultural Company. In the case of one of these companies, at least, a decision was reached to enclose a field of twelve sections, containing 7,680 acres of land, for the growing of grain. According to other accounts, plans were underway to organize, in addition to these agricultural companies, three other "corporations" uniting mechanics, shopkeepers, and laborers, respectively. Thus, the land, machinery, and skills of the church members would be utilized "for the common good." The four corporations, together with the modified law of consecration described above, were to implement the four goals of the law of consecration and stewardship; namely, economic equality, socialization of surplus incomes, freedom of enterprise, and group economic self-sufficiency. John Corrill, who observed these plans at Far West, wrote of them as follows:

Every man was to put in all his property by leasing it to the firm for a term of years; overseers or managers were to be chosen from time to time, by the members of the firm, to manage the concerns of the same, and the rest were to labor under their direction. . . . Many joined these firms, while many others were much dissatisfied with them, which caused considerable feeling and excitement in the Church. Smith [Joseph] said every man must act his own feelings, whether to join or not. . . .

Whether these plans, unofficial and voluntary as they seem to have been, would have materialized into a successful substitute for the law of consecration and stewardship, or whether they would have run aground on the rocks of human selfishness, can never be known. Late in 1838 the Mormons were once more driven from their homes and forced to leave Missouri and all their cooperative hopes behind. According to one report, more than $300,000 worth of property was forcefully abandoned.

The church took refuge in Illinois, with headquarters at Commerce (rechristened "Nauvoo"), on the banks of the Mississippi. And it has seemed strange to many students of Mormonism that in seven years of comparative freedom and isolation there—years marked by growth and worldly affluence—no attempt was made to restore "the Lord's plan." When some church members living in Iowa undertook, in 1840, to establish the law of consecration and stewardship, Joseph Smith advised, according to the historian, that

> The law of consecration could not be kept here and that it was the will of the Lord that we should desist from trying to keep it; and if persisted in, it would produce a perfect defeat of its object, and that he assumed the whole responsibility of not keeping it until proposed by himself.

The views of the prophet during his Nauvoo sojourn were perhaps expressed even more forcibly in a notation made in his journal on September 24, 1843: "I preached on the stand about one hour on the 2nd chapter of Acts, designing to show the folly of common stock. In Nauvoo every one is steward over his own."

One student of Mormon history has reminded the writer that the circumstances surrounding the settlement of Nauvoo were sufficiently different from those attending previous settlements to account for Joseph Smith's seeming neglect of the law of consecration and stewardship in that location. The church had to make far larger unit investments in land in Nauvoo than it had ever been called upon to do before, and its resources, financial and otherwise, were relatively fewer, partly because of forced property sales and partly because of the heavy expenses of frequent moving and establishing service enterprises. From the standpoint of economics, the law of consecration and stewardship was simply not feasible. Because of basic economic necessity, then, property institutions in Nauvoo were undiluted except by such restrictions as those imposed by conscience and the principle of stewardship.

In 1841 the Law of Tithing was officially adopted as a substitute more suited to financial necessity and the weaknesses of human nature. This law has been retained by the church to this day. The Law of Tithing contained no device for the reform of property institutions or for achieving a more equitable distribution of wealth and income. Henceforth, church members would participate in church programs by donating the equivalent of one-tenth of their possessions at the time of their conversion, and one-tenth of their annual increase (or more) thereafter. Those who had no property, and therefore no annual increase, were expected to labor one day in ten for the church.

The stewardship phase of "the Lord's law" lapsed into an informal, voluntary, less-than-universal arrangement in which the faithful were urged to regard their property rights, however legal, as something less than absolute, and as subject to a measure of control by the priesthood. Church revenues came to depend to a considerable extent upon sources other than consecrations, such as borrowings, capitalistic business enterprises, and profit-making sales of property. In an account of the history and doctrines of the Latter-day Saints prepared shortly before his death, Joseph Smith made no mention whatever of the law of consecration and stewardship.[1]

V

The failure of church leaders to reinstitute the law of consecration and stewardship in Nauvoo and elsewhere leads one to the conclusion that they regarded it as a practical failure, with little hope of succeeding even without Gentile opposition. Several factors militated against its success during the short period of its operation in Ohio and Missouri. (1) Most of the converts to the early church were poor and had nothing to consecrate. Yet inheritances had to be provided for them. (2) Most of the consecrations which were made were in kind, while most of the church's investments (in real estate and so on to provide stewardships for those who needed them) required liquid resources. Conversion of the former into the latter was difficult on the Missouri frontier. (3) Constant persecution made property accumulation almost impossible. (4) The opposition of the courts to the Mormons, and to cooperative (and communal) ventures generally, made it easy for apostates, who had made gifts to the church, to disrupt the financial affairs of the system by demanding and securing the return of all their consecrated properties. (5) The converts were not faithful in making their initial and annual consecrations.

Although all five of these factors have been recognized by Mormon apologists, church leaders have consistently emphasized the last-named factor: selfishness, unfaithfulness, unrighteousness. In the revelation which counseled the suspension of the law, mention was made of "the transgressions of my people," who "have not learned to be obedient." They

---

[1] Joseph Smith, "Latter Day Saints," in I. Daniel Rupp, ed., *An Original History of the Religious Denominations Existing in the United States* (Philadelphia, 1844), pp. 404–410.

"do not impart of their substance, as becometh saints. . . . ." Brigham Young, who was a member of the church during most of this early period, later explained that "Persons would conceal from Joseph that they had any money; and, after they had spent or lost it all, would come to him and say, 'O how I love you, Brother Joseph!' " On another occasion, many years after the system had been tried, George A. Smith said:

> The Lord endeavored to establish the order of Zion then, but while some considered it a privilege to consecrate their property to the Lord, others were covetous, and thought about looking after their own interests in preference to those of the Work of God.

Since the plan provided that each steward voluntarily consecrate his annual surplus, the faithful gave much, the unfaithful little. A premium was placed on liberality and honesty. In the distribution of charity out of the surplus, some demanded much, others little, and there was not always correspondence between need and participation in the consecrated surpluses.

As a means of enforcing the plan according to the revealed standard, the rich were constantly exhorted to participate in this equalitarian plan. Indeed, the rich who failed to participate would be damned:

> Wo unto you rich men, that will not give your substance to the poor, for your riches will canker your souls! and this shall be your lamentation in the day of visitation, and of judgment, and of indignation: The harvest is past, the summer is ended, and my soul is not saved!

> Therefore, if any man shall take of the abundance which I have made, and impart not his portion, according to the law of my gospel, unto the poor and the needy, he shall, with the wicked, lift up his eyes in hell, being in torment.

At the same time, the unworthy poor were also exhorted not to take advantage of the plan:

> Wo unto you poor men, whose hearts are not broken, whose spirits are not contrite, and whose bellies are not satisfied, and whose hands are not stayed from laying hold upon other men's goods, whose eyes are full of greediness, who will not labor with their own hands!

That the plan must have been operating very imperfectly during the 1831–1834 period is evident from a study of the revelations and correspondence of Joseph Smith during those years. J. Reuben Clark, Jr., who made such a study, concluded:

> All of these communications, these callings to repentance, these reproofs against covetousness, light mindedness and the various other ills which

were afflicting the brethren in Zion, indicate that Zion, as a whole, was not conducting itself in a way that the Lord could give unto them blessings. . . . It is perfectly clear from the kind of evils which it is indicated as having afflicted the brethren in Zion, that it would not be possible for such a group of Saints to live the law of consecration and the United Order as it had been laid down unto them.

The stress of church leaders on the failure of the people to "live up to" the system, and the acknowledgment of continued disregard of heavenly and prophetic exhortation, was, in reality, an admission that the system presupposed a level of altruism which was incompatible with a rapidly growing membership and extensive proselyting. While it was not without utopian overtones, the plan undoubtedly could have been made to operate as successfully as those of similar nineteenth-century sectarian societies by a systematic program of membership restriction. Certainly the Mormons were not less altruistic and self-forgetting than the Shakers, the Perfectionists, the Harmonists, the German Separatists, and the Amana Inspirationists.

It is quite possible that the plan may have been regarded from the outset as a temporary measure, designed particularly to replace the Kirtland Family and to share the wealth during the earliest months of the church when poor converts were being gathered and settled. Some method of raising funds was inevitable and in response to this immediate need "the Lord's law" was revealed. The initial problem of providing the means of a living for all the poor Saints, with only a small capital amongst them, was strategic. Once that hurdle was surmounted, and the membership of the church had grown sufficiently large, the strict, formalized "law of the Lord," in response, once more, to new conditions and circumstances, was abandoned in favor of a less drastic arrangement involving fewer administrative procedures and problems.

Whatever the initial intention, there can be no doubt that if a prolonged attempt had been made to make the plan succeed, which certainly could have been done by carefully screening converts and carefully devised procedures and policies, continued expansion in the size of the church would have been rendered more and more difficult, if not impossible. Communitarian societies were seldom successful except in small, homogeneous, well-contained groups. Heterogeneity produces internal friction, while a constantly growing group creates administrative problems of insurmountable magnitude. After reaching a certain condition of well-being, these societies usually have barred themselves off and refused to accept new members. Two thousand to three thousand members seems to have been a typical maximum. True, similar communities could be established in other locations, permitting the whole group to multiply, but the supervisory problem usually was such that each community became a relatively autonomous unit and was but poorly integrated with the others.

The instructions (believed to have been divinely inspired) to suspend the law of consecration and stewardship, at a time when the membership of the church was climbing well above 2,500 and the failure to restore its operation except in modified form after 1834, indicated that church leaders were impressed to rule that it was more important to drop the system and allow the church to grow than to try to make the system succeed and thus limit church membership to a few thousand stalwarts, or a few dozen communities. The suspension of the law of consecration and stewardship, with the retention of the concepts of consecration and stewardship in more flexible succeeding institutions, was one reason for the amazing growth of Mormonism while many comparable contemporary communitarian movements grew for a space, then withered, then died. In saving their community from the drastic restrictionism essential to the system's success, church leaders removed the conditions without which nationwide and worldwide proselyting would have been unsuccessful. The wholesale gathering of the "pure in heart" from out of "the world," and the building of a constantly expanding kingdom, seem to have been regarded as more important to the Saints of the latter-day than the attempt to perfect a particular social and economic program. Church leaders, whether "inspired" to do so or not, thus abandoned the attempt to fix a static pattern of social organization upon the infant church and demonstrated a preference for a provisional or instrumental concept of social reform and betterment. The Kingdom of God was not to be the endless repetition of a fixed pattern of social relationships, but a progressive and developing society characterized by a diligent reworking of institutions and a pluralistic experimentation with new policies and practices.

However, it would be misleading to make too much of the suspension of the law of consecration and stewardship in 1834. The system has remained to this day in the minds of the Latter-day Saints as the ideal economic order—the blueprint of a Christian economic society. Accepting it as a literal commandment of God which has been suspended for a season because of the wickedness of the people, they have sought to approach it in many ways. In their revenue collections they have measured their efforts against the consecration of all their surplus. In their property institutions, their leaders have kept constantly before them the ideal of the good steward. Group economic self-sufficiency was the hallmark of Mormon policy on the Great Basin frontier. Above all, cooperative economic endeavor, which played such an important role throughout the history of the church, was to a large extent an outgrowth of this ideal economic system, or of the same ethic which produced it. An outstanding example of an institution built upon the principles of consecration and stewardship was the Perpetual Emigrating Fund Company, which received the consecrations of Latter-day Saints and assisted more than 80,000 European and American converts to migrate to Utah from 1849 to 1887. It utilized the social surplus to further the purposes of "the gathering" much as the law of consecration and stewardship was expected to do in the early 1830s.

Mormon economic history demonstrates that religiously motivated communitarianism, when not merely an escapism, can have important practical consequences. Prolonged insistence on the law and its workability might well have defeated the very purpose for which it was instituted and the idealism which gave such vitality to subsequent Mormon endeavors. As an experimental forecast of a better future, the law of consecration and stewardship mollified the rigors of frontier existence and provided an incentive for the establishment of ameliorative social and economic institutions. Beyond its life as a program of action, early Mormon communitarianism has continued to exert an undeniable influence as a dream of perfection.

Some Themes of Counter-Subversion

DAVID BRION DAVIS

Where Arrington treats the experimental efforts to establish an integrated economic life within the Mormon community, David Brion Davis in this article on counter-subversion looks at the effect which such experimentation and integration had upon the nervous psyche of some other Americans. In a period of rapid social change with accompanying dislocation of values, as he indicates, early nineteenth-century Americans were hostile toward any group that seemed contemptuous of the traditional ways. In studying the social roots of the anti-Masonic, anti-Catholic, and anti-Mormon movements before the Civil War, Davis finds that the most prominent element within these societies to which the antis were opposed was their secrecy and seeming loyalty to an autonomous group. Americans in this period wrestled with the inner conflict between a desire for individual and group identity, and an identification with the larger society. Davis explains deftly how persecution of minorities gave nativists a sense of identity and of identification they otherwise lacked. Such means provided a community spirit for some at the expense of others who desperately sought the same thing.

During the second quarter of the nineteenth century, when danger of foreign invasion appeared increasingly remote, Americans were told by various respected leaders that Freemasons had infiltrated the government and had seized control of the courts, that Mormons were undermining political and economic freedom in the West, and that Roman Catholic priests, receiving instructions from Rome, had made frightening progress in a plot to subject the nation to popish despotism. This fear of internal subversion was channeled into a number of powerful counter movements which attracted wide public support. The literature produced by these movements evoked images of a great American enemy that closely resembled traditional European stereotypes of conspiracy and subversion. In

David Brion Davis, "Some Themes of Counter-Subversion: An Analysis of Anti-Masonic, Anti-Catholic, and Anti-Mormon Literature," *The Mississippi Valley Historical Review*, XLVII (September 1960), pp. 205–224. Reprinted by permission of the publisher. Footnotes deleted by permission.

Europe, however, the idea of subversion implied a threat to the established order—to the king, the church, or the ruling aristocracy—rather than to ideals or a way of life. If free Americans borrowed their images of subversion from frightened kings and uneasy aristocrats, these images had to be shaped and blended to fit American conditions. The movements would have to come from the people, and the themes of counter-subversion would be likely to reflect their fears, prejudices, hopes, and perhaps even unconscious desires.

There are obvious dangers in treating such reactions against imagined subversion as part of a single tendency or spirit of an age. Anti-Catholicism was nourished by ethnic conflict and uneasiness over immigration in the expanding cities of the Northeast; anti-Mormonism arose largely from a contest for economic and political power between western settlers and a group that voluntarily withdrew from society and claimed the undivided allegiance of its members. Anti-Masonry, on the other hand, was directed against a group thoroughly integrated in American society and did not reflect a clear division of economic, religious, or political interests. Moreover, anti-Masonry gained power in the late 1820s and soon spent its energies as it became absorbed in national politics; anti-Catholicism reached its maximum force in national politics a full generation later; anti-Mormonism, though increasing in intensity in the 1850s, became an important national issue only after the Civil War. These movements seem even more widely separated when we note that Freemasonry was traditionally associated with anti-Catholicism and that Mormonism itself absorbed considerable anti-Masonic and anti-Catholic sentiment.

Despite such obvious differences, there were certain similarities in these campaigns against subversion. All three gained widespread support in the northeastern states within the space of a generation; anti-Masonry and anti-Catholicism resulted in the sudden emergence of separate political parties; and in 1856 the new Republican party explicitly condemned the Mormons' most controversial institution. The movements of counter-subversion differed markedly in historical origin, but as the image of an un-American conspiracy took form in the nativist press, in sensational exposés, in the countless fantasies of treason and mysterious criminality, the lines separating Mason, Catholic, and Mormon became almost indistinguishable.

The similar pattern of Masonic, Catholic, and Mormon subversion was frequently noticed by alarmist writers. The *Anti-Masonic Review* informed its readers in 1829 that whether one looked at Jesuitism or Freemasonry, "the organization, the power, and the secret operation, are the same; except that Freemasonry is much the more secret and complicated of the two." William Hogan, an ex-priest and vitriolic anti-Catholic, compared the menace of Catholicism with that of Mormonism. And many later anti-Mormon writers agreed with Josiah Strong that Brigham Young "out-popes the Roman" and described the Mormon hierarchy as being similar to the Catholic. It was probably not accidental that Samuel F. B. Morse analyzed the Catholic conspiracy in essentially the same terms his father had used in exposing the Society of the Illuminati, supposedly a radical branch of Freemasonry, or that writers of sensational fiction in the 1840s and 1850s depicted an atheistic and unprincipled Catholic Church obviously modeled on Charles Brockden Brown's earlier fictional version of the Illuminati.

If Masons, Catholics, and Mormons bore little resemblance to one another in actuality, as imagined enemies they merged into a nearly common stereotype. Behind specious professions of philanthropy or religious sentiment, nativists discerned a group of unscrupulous leaders plotting to subvert the American social order. Though rank-and-file members were not individually evil, they were blinded and corrupted by a persuasive ideology that justified treason and gross immorality in the interest of the subversive group. Trapped in the meshes of a machine-like organization, deluded by a false sense of loyalty and moral obligation, these dupes followed orders like professional soldiers and labored unknowingly to abolish free society, to enslave their fellow men, and to overthrow divine principles of law and justice. Should an occasional member free himself from bondage to superstition and fraudulent authority, he could still be disciplined by the threat of death or dreadful tortures. There were no limits to the ambitious designs of leaders equipped with such organizations. According to nativist prophets, they chose to subvert American society because control of America meant control of the world's destiny.

Some of these beliefs were common in earlier and later European interpretations of conspiracy. American images of Masonic, Catholic, and Mormon subversion were no doubt a compound of traditional myths concerning Jacobite agents, scheming Jesuits, and fanatical heretics, and of dark legends involving the Holy Vehm and Rosicrucians. What distinguished the stereotypes of Mason, Catholic, and Mormon was the way in which they were seen to embody those traits that were precise antitheses of American ideals. The subversive group was essentially an inverted image of Jacksonian democracy and the cult of the common man; as such it not only challenged the dominant values but stimulated those suppressed needs and yearnings that are unfulfilled in a mobile, rootless, and individualistic society. It was therefore both frightening and fascinating.

It is well known that expansion and material progress in the Jacksonian era evoked a fervid optimism and that nationalists became intoxicated with visions of America's millennial glory. The simultaneous growth of prosperity and social democracy seemed to prove that Providence would bless a nation that allowed her citizens maximum liberty. When each individual was left free to pursue happiness in his own way, unhampered by the tyranny of custom or special privilege, justice and well-being would inevitably emerge. But if a doctrine of laissez-faire individualism seemed to promise material expansion and prosperity, it also raised disturbing problems. As one early anti-Mormon writer expressed it: What was to prevent liberty and popular sovereignty from sweeping away "the old landmarks of Christendom, and the glorious old common law of our fathers"? How was the individual to preserve a sense of continuity with the past, or identify himself with a given cause or tradition? What, indeed, was to ensure a common loyalty and a fundamental unity among the people?

Such questions acquired a special urgency as economic growth intensified mobility, destroyed old ways of life, and transformed traditional symbols of status and prestige. Though most Americans took pride in their material progress, they also expressed a yearning for reassurance and security, for unity in some cause transcending individual self-interest. This need for meaningful group activity was filled in part by religious revivals, reform movements, and a proliferation of fraternal orders and associations. In politics Americans tended to assume the posture of what Marvin Meyers has termed "venturesome conservatives," mitigating their acquisitive impulses by an appeal for unity against extraneous forces that allegedly threatened a noble heritage of republican ideals. Without abandoning a belief in progress through laissez-faire individualism, the Jacksonians achieved a sense of unity and righteousness by styling themselves as restorers of tradition. Perhaps no theme is so evident in the Jacksonian era as the strained attempt to provide America with a glorious heritage and a noble destiny. With only a loose and often ephemeral attachment to places and institutions, many Americans felt a compelling need to articulate their loyalties, to prove their faith, and to demonstrate their allegiance to certain ideals and institutions. By so doing they acquired a sense of self-identity and personal direction in an otherwise rootless and shifting environment.

But was abstract nationalism sufficient to reassure a nation strained by sectional conflict, divided by an increasing number of sects and associations, and perplexed by the unexpected consequences of rapid growth? One might desire to protect the Republic against her enemies, to preserve the glorious traditions of the Founders, and to help ensure continued expansion and prosperity, but first it was necessary to discover an enemy by distinguishing subversion from simple diversity. If Freemasons seemed to predominate in the economic and political life of a given area, was one's joining them shrewd business judgment or a betrayal of republican tradition? Should Maryland citizens heed the warnings of anti-Masonic itinerants, or conclude that anti-Masonry was itself a conspiracy hatched by scheming Yankees? Were Roman Catholics plotting to destroy public schools and a free press, the twin guardians of American democracy, or were they exercising democratic rights of self-expression and self-protection? Did equality of opportunity and equality before the law mean that Americans should accept the land claims of Mormons or tolerate as jurors men who "swear that they have wrought miracles and supernatural cures"? Or should one agree with the Reverend Finis Ewing that "the 'Mormons' are the common enemies of mankind and ought to be destroyed"?

Few men questioned traditional beliefs in freedom of conscience and the right of association. Yet what was to prevent "all the errors and worn out theories of the Old World, of schisms in the early Church, the monkish age and the rationalistic period," from flourishing in such salubrious air? Nativists often praised the work of benevolent societies, but they were disturbed by the thought that monstrous conspiracies might also "show kindness and patriotism, when it is necessary for their better concealment; and oftentimes do much good for the sole purpose of getting a better opportunity to do evil." When confronted by so many sects and associations, how was the patriot to distinguish the loyal from the disloyal? It was clear that mere disagreement over theology or economic policy was invalid as a test, since honest men disputed over the significance of baptism or the wisdom of protective tariffs. But neither could one rely on expressions of allegiance to common democratic principles, since subversives would cunningly profess to believe in freedom and toleration of dissent as long as they remained a powerless minority.

As nativists studied this troubling question, they discovered that most groups and denominations claimed only a partial loyalty from their members, freely subordinating themselves to the higher and more abstract demands of the Constitution, Christianity, and American public opinion. Moreover, they openly exposed their objects and activities to public scrutiny and exercised little discrimination in enlisting members. Some groups, however, dominated a larger portion of their members' lives, demanded unlimited allegiance as a condition of membership, and excluded certain activities from the gaze of a curious public.

Of all governments, said Richard Rush, ours was the one with most to fear from secret societies, since popular sovereignty by its very nature required perfect freedom of public inquiry and judgment. In a virtuous republic why should anyone fear publicity or desire to conceal activities, unless those activities were somehow contrary to the public interest? When no one could be quite sure what the public interest was, and when no one could take for granted a secure and well-defined place in the social order, it was most difficult to acknowledge legitimate spheres of privacy. Most Americans of the Jacksonian era appeared willing to tolerate diversity and even eccentricity, but when they saw themselves excluded and even barred from witnessing certain proceedings, they imagined a "mystic power" conspiring to enslave them.

Readers might be amused by the first exposures of Masonic ritual, since they learned that pompous and dignified citizens, who had once impressed non-Masons with allusions to high degrees and elaborate ceremonies, had in actuality been forced to stand blindfolded and clad in ridiculous garb, with a long rope noosed around their necks. But genuine anti-Masons were not content with simple ridicule. Since intelligent and distinguished men had been members of the fraternity, "it must have in its interior something more than the usual revelations of its mysteries declare." Surely leading citizens would not meet at night and undergo degrading and humiliating initiations just for the sake of novelty. The alleged murder of William Morgan raised an astonishing public furor because it supposedly revealed the inner secret of Freemasonry. Perverted by a false ideology, Masons had renounced all obligations to the general public, to the laws of the land, and even to the command of God. Hence they threatened not a particular party's program or a denomination's creed, but stood opposed to all justice, democracy, and religion.

The distinguishing mark of Masonic, Catholic, and Mormon conspiracies was a secrecy that cloaked the members' unconditional loyalty to an autonomous body. Since the organizations had corrupted the private moral judgment of their members, Americans could not rely on the ordinary forces of progress to spread truth and enlightenment among their ranks. Yet the affairs of such organizations were not outside the jurisdiction of democratic government, for no body politic could be asked to tolerate a power that was designed to destroy it. Once the true nature of subversive groups was thoroughly understood, the alternatives were as clear as life and death. How could democracy and Catholicism coexist when, as Edward Beecher warned, "The systems are diametrically opposed: one must and will exterminate the other"? Because Freemasons had so deeply penetrated state and national governments, only drastic remedies could restore the nation to its democratic purity. And later, Americans faced an "irrepressible conflict" with Mormonism, for it was said that either free institutions or Mormon despotism must ultimately annihilate the other.

We may well ask why nativists magnified the division between unpopular minorities and the American public, so that Masons, Catholics, and Mormons seemed so menacing that they could not be accorded the usual rights and privileges of a free society. Obviously the literature of counter-subversion reflected concrete rivalries and conflicts of interest between competing groups, but it is important to note that the subversive bore no racial or ethnic stigma and was not even accused of inherent depravity. Since group membership was a matter of intellectual and emotional loyalty, no *physical* barrier prevented a Mason, Catholic, or Mormon from apostatizing and joining the dominant in-group, providing always that he escaped assassination from his previous masters. This suggests that counter-subversion was more than a rationale for group rivalry and was related to the general problem of ideological unity and diversity in a free society. When a "system of delusion" insulated members of a group from the unifying and disciplining force of public opinion, there was no authority to command an allegiance to common principles. This was why oaths of loyalty assumed great importance for nativists. Though the ex-Catholic William Hogan stated repeatedly that Jesuit spies respected no oaths except those to the Church, he inconsistently told Masons and Odd Fellows that they could prevent infiltration by requiring new members to swear they were not Catholics. It was precisely the absence of distinguishing outward traits that made the enemy so dangerous, and true loyalty so difficult to prove.

When the images of different enemies conform to a similar pattern, it is highly probable that this pattern reflects important tensions within a given culture. The themes of nativist literature suggest that its authors simplified problems of personal insecurity and adjustment to bewildering social change by trying to unite Americans of diverse political, religious, and economic interests against a common enemy. Just as revivalists sought to stimulate Christian fellowship by awakening men to the horrors of sin, so nativists used apocalyptic images to ignite human passions, destroy selfish indifference, and join patriots in a cohesive brotherhood. Such themes were only faintly secularized. When God saw his "lov'd Columbia" imperiled by the hideous monster of Freemasonry, He realized that only a martyr's blood could rouse the hearts of the people and save them from bondage to the Prince of Darkness. By having God will Morgan's death, this anti-Mason showed he was more concerned with national virtue and unity than with Freemasonry, which was only a providential instrument for testing republican strength.

Similarly, for the anti-Catholic "this brilliant new world" was once "young and beautiful; it abounded in all the luxuries of nature; it promised all that was desirable to man." But the Roman Church, seeing "these irresistible temptations, thirsting with avarice and yearning for the reestablishment of her falling greatness, soon commenced pouring in among its unsuspecting people hordes of Jesuits and other friars." If Americans were to continue their narrow pursuit of self-interest, oblivious to the "Popish colleges, and nunneries, and monastic institutions," indifferent to manifold signs of corruption and decay, how could the nation expect "that the moral breezes of heaven should breathe upon her, and restore to her again that strong and healthy constitution, which her ancestors have left to her sons"? The theme of an Adamic fall from paradise was horrifying, but it was used to inspire determined action and thus unity. If Methodists were "criminally indifferent" to the Mormon question, and if "avaricious merchants, soulless corporations, and a subsidized press" ignored Mormon iniquities, there was all the more reason that the "*will of the people* must prevail."

Without explicitly rejecting the philosophy of laissez-faire individualism, with its toleration of dissent and innovation, nativist literature conveyed a sense of common dedication to a noble cause and sacred tradition. Though the nation had begun with the blessings of God and with the noblest institutions known to man, the people had somehow become selfish and complacent, divided by petty disputes, and insensitive to signs of danger. In his sermons attacking such self-interest, such indifference to public concerns, and such a lack of devotion to common ideals and sentiments, the nativist revealed the true source of his anguish. Indeed, he seemed at times to recognize an almost beneficent side to subversive organizations, since they joined the nation in a glorious crusade and thus kept it from moral and social disintegration.

The exposure of subversion was a means of promoting unity, but it also served to clarify national values and provide the individual ego with a sense of high moral sanction and imputed righteousness. Nativists identified themselves repeatedly with a strangely incoherent tradition in which images of Pilgrims, Minute Men, Founding Fathers, and true Christians appeared in a confusing montage. Opposed to this heritage of stability and perfect integrity, to this society founded on the highest principles of divine and natural law, were organizations formed by the grossest frauds and impostures, and based on the wickedest impulses of human nature. Bitterly refuting Masonic claims to ancient tradition and Christian sanction, anti-Masons charged that the Order was of recent origin, that it was shaped by Jews, Jesuits, and French atheists as an engine for spreading infidelity, and that it was employed by kings and aristocrats to undermine republican institutions. If the illustrious Franklin and Washington had been duped by Masonry, this only proved how treacherous was its appeal and how subtly persuasive were its pretensions. Though the Catholic Church had an undeniable claim to tradition, nativists argued that it had originated in stupendous frauds and forgeries "in comparison with which the forgeries of Mormonism are completely thrown into the shade." Yet anti-Mormons saw an even more sinister conspiracy based on the "shrewd cunning" of Joseph Smith, who convinced gullible souls that he conversed with angels and received direct revelations from the Lord.

By emphasizing the fraudulent character of their opponents' claims, nativists sought to establish the legitimacy and just authority of American institutions. Masonic rituals, Roman Catholic sacraments, and Mormon revelations were preposterous hoaxes used to delude naive or superstitious minds; but public schools, a free press, and jury trials were eternally valid prerequisites for a free and virtuous society.

Moreover, the finest values of an enlightened nation stood out in bold relief when contrasted with the corrupting tendencies of subversive groups. Perversion of the sexual instinct seemed inevitably to accompany religious error. Deprived of the tender affections of normal married love, shut off from the elevating sentiments of fatherhood, Catholic priests looked on women only as insensitive objects for the gratification of their frustrated desires. In similar fashion polygamy struck at the heart of a morality based on the inspiring influence of woman's affections: "It renders man coarse, tyrannical, brutal, and heartless. It deals death to all sentiments of true manhood. It enslaves and ruins woman. It crucifies every God-given feeling of her nature." Some anti-Mormons concluded that plural marriage could only have been established among foreigners who had never learned to respect women. But the more common explanation was that the false ideology of Mormonism had deadened the moral sense and liberated man's wild sexual impulse from the normal restraints of civilization. Such degradation of women and corruption of man served to highlight the importance of democratic marriage, a respect for women, and careful cultivation of the finer sensibilities.

But if nativist literature was a medium for articulating common values and exhorting individuals to transcend self-interest and join in a dedicated union against evil, it also performed a more subtle function. Why, we may ask, did nativist literature dwell so persistently on themes of brutal sadism and sexual immorality? Why did its authors describe sin in such minute details, endowing even the worst offenses of their enemies with a certain fascinating appeal?

Freemasons, it was said, could commit any crime and indulge any passion when "upon the square," and Catholics and Mormons were even less inhibited by internal moral restraints. Nativists expressed horror over this freedom from conscience and conventional morality, but they could not conceal a throbbing note of envy. What was it like to be a member of a cohesive brotherhood that casually abrogated the laws of God and man, enforcing unity and obedience with dark and mysterious powers? As nativists speculated on this question, they projected their own fears and desires into a fantasy of licentious orgies and fearful punishments.

Such a projection of forbidden desires can be seen in the exaggeration of the stereotyped enemy's powers, which made him appear at times as a virtual superman. Catholic and Mormon leaders, never hindered by conscience or respect for traditional morality, were curiously superior to ordinary Americans in cunning, in exercising power over others, and especially in captivating gullible women. It was an ancient theme of anti-Catholic literature that friars and priests were somehow more potent and sexually attractive than married laymen, and were thus astonishingly successful at seducing supposedly virtuous wives. Americans were cautioned repeatedly that no priest recognized Protestant marriages as valid, and might consider any wife legitimate prey. Furthermore, priests had access to the pornographic teachings of Dens and Liguori, sinister names that aroused the curiosity of anti-Catholics, and hence learned subtle techniques of seduction perfected over the centuries. Speaking with the authority of an ex-priest, William Hogan described the shocking result: "I have seen husbands unsuspiciously and hospitably entertaining the very priest who seduced their wives in the confessional, and was the parent of some of the children who sat at the same table with them, each of the wives unconscious of the other's guilt, and the husbands of both, not even suspecting them." Such blatant immorality was horrifying, but everyone was apparently happy in this domestic scene, and we may suspect that the image was not entirely repugnant to husbands who, despite their respect for the Lord's Commandments, occasionally coveted their neighbors' wives.

The literature of counter-subversion could also embody the somewhat different projective fantasies of women. Ann Eliza Young dramatized her seduction by the Prophet Brigham, whose almost superhuman powers enchanted her and paralyzed her will. Though she submitted finally only because her parents were in danger of being ruined by the church, she clearly indicated that it was an exciting privilege to be pursued by a Great Man. When Anti-Mormons claimed that Joseph Smith and other prominent Saints knew the mysteries of Animal Magnetism, or were endowed with the highest degree of "amativeness" in their phrenological makeup, this did not detract from their covert appeal. In a ridiculous fantasy written by Maria Ward, such alluring qualities were extended even to Mormon women. Many bold-hearted girls could doubtless identify themselves with Anna Bradish, a fearless Amazon of a creature, who rode like a man, killed without compunction, and had no pity for weak women who failed to look out for themselves. Tall, elegant, and "intellectual," Anna was attractive enough to arouse the insatiable desires of Brigham Young, though she ultimately rejected him and renounced Mormonism.

While nativists affirmed their faith in Protestant monogamy, they obviously took pleasure in imagining the variety of sexual experience supposedly available to their enemies. By picturing themselves exposed to similar temptations, they assumed they could know how priests and Mormons actually sinned. Imagine, said innumerable anti-Catholic writers, a beautiful young woman kneeling before an ardent young priest in a deserted room. As she confesses, he leans over, looking into her eyes, until their heads are nearly touching. Day after day she reveals to him her innermost secrets, secrets she would not think of unveiling to her parents, her dearest friends, or even her suitor. By skillful questioning the priest fills her mind with immodest and even sensual ideas, "until this wretch has worked up her passions to a tension almost snapping, and then becomes his easy prey." How could any man resist such provocative temptations, and how could any girl's virtue withstand such a test?

We should recall that this literature was written in a period of increasing anxiety and uncertainty over sexual values and the proper role of woman. As ministers and journalists pointed with alarm at the spread of prostitution, the incidence of divorce, and the lax and hypocritical morality of the growing cities, a discussion of licentious subversives offered a convenient means for the projection of guilt as well as desire. The sins of individuals, or of the nation as a whole, could be pushed off upon the shoulders of the enemy and there punished in righteous anger.

Specific instances of such projection are not difficult to find. John C. Bennett, whom the Mormons expelled from the Church as a result of his flagrant sexual immorality, invented the fantasy of "The Mormon Seraglio" which persisted in later anti-Mormon writings. According to Bennett, the Mormons maintained secret orders of beautiful prostitutes who were mostly reserved for various officials of the church. He claimed, moreover, that any wife refusing to accept polygamy might be forced to join the lowest order and thus become available to any Mormon who desired her.

Another example of projection can be seen in the letters of a young lieutenant who stopped in Utah in 1854 on his way to California. Convinced that Mormon women could be easily seduced, the lieutenant wrote frankly of his amorous adventures with a married woman. "Everybody has got one," he wrote with obvious pride, "except the Colonel and Major. The Doctor has got three—mother and two daughters. The mother cooks for him and the daughters sleep with him." But though he described Utah as "a great country," the lieutenant waxed indignant over polygamy, which he condemned as self-righteously as any anti-Mormon minister: "To see one man openly parading half a dozen or more women to church . . . is the devil according to my ideas of morality, virtue, and decency."

If the consciences of many Americans were troubled by the growth of red-light districts in major cities, they could divert their attention to the "legalized brothels" called nunneries, for which no one was responsible but lecherous Catholic priests. If others were disturbed by the moral implications of divorce, they could point in horror at the Mormon elder who took his quota of wives all at once. The literature of counter-subversion could thus serve the double purpose of vicariously fulfilling repressed desires, and of releasing the tension and guilt arising from rapid social change and conflicting values.

Though the enemy's sexual freedom might at first seem enticing, it was always made repugnant in the end by associations with perversion or brutal cruelty. Both Catholics and Mormons were accused of practicing nearly every form of incest. The persistent emphasis on this theme might indicate deep-rooted feelings of fear and guilt, but it also helped demonstrate, on a more objective level, the loathsome consequences of unrestrained lust. Sheer brutality and a delight in human suffering were supposed to be the even more horrible results of sexual depravity. Masons disemboweled or slit the throats of their victims; Catholics cut unborn infants from their mothers' wombs and threw them to the dogs before their parents' eyes; Mormons raped and lashed recalcitrant women, or seared their mouths with red-hot irons. This obsession with details of sadism, which reached pathological proportions in much of the literature, showed a furious determination to purge the enemy of every admirable quality. The imagined enemy might serve at first as an outlet for forbidden desires, but nativist authors escaped from guilt by finally making him an agent of unmitigated aggression. In such a role the subversive seemed to deserve both righteous anger and the most terrible punishments.

The nativist escape from guilt was more clearly revealed in the themes of confession and conversion. For most American Protestants the crucial step in anyone's life was a profession of true faith resulting from a genuine religious experience. Only when a man became conscious of his inner guilt, when he struggled against the temptations of Satan, could he prepare his soul for the infusion of the regenerative spirit. Those most deeply involved in sin often made the most dramatic conversions. It is not surprising that conversion to nativism followed the same pattern, since nativists sought unity and moral certainty in the regenerative spirit of nationalism. Men who had been associated in some way with un-American conspiracies were not only capable of spectacular confessions of guilt, but were best equipped to expose the insidious work of supposedly harmless organizations. Even those who lacked such an exciting history of corruption usually made some confession of guilt, though it might involve only a previous indifference to subversive groups. Like ardent Christians, nativists searched in their own experiences for the meanings of sin, delusion, awakening to truth, and liberation from spiritual bondage. These personal confessions proved that one had recognized and conquered evil, and also served as ritual cleansings preparatory to full acceptance in a group of dedicated patriots.

Anti-Masons were perhaps the ones most given to confessions of guilt and most alert to subtle distinctions of loyalty and disloyalty. Many leaders of this movement, expressing guilt over their own "shameful experience and knowledge" of Masonry, felt a compelling obligation to exhort their former associates to "come out, and be separate from masonic abominations." Even when an anti-Mason could say with John Quincy Adams that "I am not, never was, and never shall be a Freemason," he would often admit that he had once admired the Order, or had even considered applying for admission.

Since a willingness to sacrifice oneself was an unmistakable sign of loyalty and virtue, ex-Masons gloried in exaggerating the dangers they faced and the harm that their revelations supposedly inflicted on the enemy. In contrast to hardened Freemasons, who refused to answer questions in court concerning their fraternal associations, the seceders claimed to reveal the inmost secrets of the Order, and by so doing to risk property, reputation, and life. Once the ex-Mason had dared to speak the truth, his character would surely be maligned, his motives impugned, and his life threatened. But, he declared, even if he shared the fate of the illustrious Morgan, he would die knowing that he had done his duty.

Such self-dramatization reached extravagant heights in the ranting confessions of many apostate Catholics and Mormons. Maria Monk and her various imitators told of shocking encounters with sin in its most sensational forms, of bondage to vice and superstition, and of melodramatic escapes from popish despotism. A host of "ex-Mormon wives" described their gradual recognition of Mormon frauds and iniquities, the anguish and misery of plural marriage, and their breathtaking flights over deserts or mountains. The female apostate was especially vulnerable to vengeful retaliation, since she could easily be kidnapped by crafty priests and nuns, or dreadfully punished by Brigham Young's Destroying Angels. At the very least, her reputation could be smirched by foul lies and insinuations. But her willingness to risk honor and life for the sake of her country and for the dignity of all womankind was eloquent proof of her redemption. What man could be assured of so noble a role?

The apostate's pose sometimes assumed paranoid dimensions. William Hogan warned that only the former priest could properly gauge the Catholic threat to American liberties and saw himself as providentially appointed to save his Protestant countrymen. "For twenty years," he wrote, "I have warned them of approaching danger, but their politicians were deaf, and their Protestant theologians remained religiously coiled up in fancied security, overrating their own powers and undervaluing that of Papists."

Pursued by vengeful Jesuits, denounced and calumniated for alleged crimes, Hogan pictured himself single-handedly defending American freedom: "No one, before me, dared to encounter their scurrilous abuse. I resolved to silence them; and I have done so. The very mention of my name is a terror to them now." After surviving the worst of Catholic persecution, Hogan claimed to have at last aroused his countrymen and to have reduced the hierarchy to abject terror.

As the nativist searched for participation in a noble cause, for unity in a group sanctioned by tradition and authority, he professed a belief in democracy and equal rights. Yet in his very zeal for freedom he curiously assumed many of the characteristics of the imagined enemy. By condemning the subversive's fanatical allegiance to an ideology; he affirmed a similarly uncritical acceptance of a different ideology; by attacking the subversive's intolerance of dissent, he worked to eliminate dissent and diversity of opinion; by censuring the subversive for alleged licentiousness, he engaged in sensual fantasies; by criticizing the subversive's loyalty to an organization, he sought to prove his unconditional loyalty to the established order. The nativist moved even farther in the direction of his enemies when he formed tightly knit societies and parties which were often secret and which subordinated the individual to the single purpose of the group. Though the nativists generally agreed that the worst evil of subversives was their subordination of means to ends, they themselves recommended the most radical means to purge the nation of troublesome groups and to enforce unquestioned loyalty to the state.

In his image of an evil group conspiring against the nation's welfare, and in his vision of a glorious millennium that was to dawn after the enemy's defeat, the nativist found satisfaction for many desires. His own interests became legitimate and dignified by fusion with the national interest, and various opponents became loosely associated with the un-American conspiracy. Thus Freemasonry in New York State was linked in the nativist mind with economic and political interests that were thought to discriminate against certain groups and regions; southerners imagined a union of abolitionists and Catholics to promote unrest and rebellion among slaves; Gentile businessmen in Utah merged anti-Mormonism with plans for exploiting mines and lands.

Then too the nativist could style himself as a restorer of the past, as a defender of a stable order against disturbing changes, and at the same time proclaim his faith in future progress. By focusing his attention on the imaginary threat of a secret conspiracy, he found an outlet for many irrational impulses, yet professed his loyalty to the ideals of equal rights and government by law. He paid lip service to the doctrine of laissez-faire individualism, but preached selfless dedication to a transcendent cause. The imposing threat of subversion justified a group loyalty and subordination of the individual that would otherwise have been unacceptable. In a rootless environment shaken by bewildering social change the nativist found unity and meaning by conspiring against imaginary conspiracies.

The Murder of Joseph Smith

KEITH HUNTRESS

If, as David Brion Davis suggests, Mormon persecution of the 1830s was an example of the paranoid style of politics, Keith Huntress views the murder of Joseph Smith in 1844 as resulting from similar tendencies. The Mormons were viewed as interlopers in Hancock County, Illinois, and Huntress examines the sources of the paranoia that led to the Carthage tragedy. Against the background of misunderstanding and violence Huntress considers the dilemma imposed upon Governor Thomas Ford in trying to prevent civil war and still preserve the lives of Joseph and Hyrum Smith for whose protection he assumed responsibility. In viewing the murders at Carthage in this context, Huntress creates a new understanding of the complexity of political problems facing a western democratic society in an age of limited government.

I

Thomas Ford, Governor of Illinois from 1842 to 1846, saved the credit of the state, fought bravely against financial and civil chaos, wrote "one of the two or three remarkable books written in the state during the formative period," worked through his last illness in a courageous endeavor to leave some kind of estate to his children—and is remembered only as one of the villains in a drama far greater than his own. Ford was a perceptive and intelligent man; dying, he foresaw what his ultimate reputation would be. Toward the end of his *History of Illinois* he wrote,

> . . . the author of this history feels degraded by the reflection, that the humble governor of an obscure state, who would otherwise be forgotten in a few years, stands a fair chance, like Pilate and Herod, by their official connection with the true religion, of being dragged down to

Keith Huntress, "Governor Thomas Ford and the Murderers of Joseph Smith," *Dialogue: A Journal of Mormon Thought,* IV (Summer 1969), pp. 41–52. Reprinted by permission of the publisher. Footnotes deleted by permission.

posterity with an immortal name, hitched on to the memory of a miserable impostor.

Many judgments of Ford's conduct during the struggle in Hancock County in 1844–1845 have been moderately or severely critical. Fawn Brodie condemns Ford as "weak." John Hay said that he was "plagued by the foul fiend Flibbertigibbet." Though Joseph Smith himself relied upon Governor Ford for protection, and seemed not unfriendly to a man who, he wrote, "treats us honorably," and "continues his courtesies," the opinion of the Mormons after the Smith murders was strongly condemnatory. The governor was accused of ignoring warnings of the evil intentions of the militia—an accusation certainly correct—and of being party to the murder plot.

It is easy to condemn Governor Ford for his conduct at the time of the murders. He was the chief executive of the state, he was on the scene, and yet the murders took place. But few people realize or realized the difficulties under which he labored. Any full study of the murders of the Smiths must consider the society which demanded and condoned those murders, and the conditions, so different from our own, within which that society operated. In that June of 1844 Governor Thomas Ford faced really insuperable difficulties.

II

In 1842 the state of Illinois was still frontier territory, facing all the troubles of a changing and expanding society with few settled traditions, financial or social, from which to operate. A series of sanguine speculations and an almost unbelievably rickety financial structure had resulted in a state government that was bankrupt in everything but hope and name. When Ford was elected governor in 1842,

> . . . the state was in debt about $14,000,000 for moneys wasted upon internal improvements and in banking; the domestic treasury of the state was in arrears $313,000 for the ordinary expenses of government; auditors' warrants were freely selling at a discount of fifty percent; the people were unable to pay even moderate taxes to replenish the treasury, in which not one cent was contained even to pay postage to and from the public offices; . . . the banks, upon which the people had relied for a currency, had become insolvent, their paper had fallen so low as to cease to circulate as money, and yet no other money had taken its place, leaving the people wholly destitute of a circulating medium, and universally in debt. . . .

This lack of a circulating medium of exchange is made more vivid by

Ford's testimony that the half-million or so people of Illinois in 1842 possessed only two or three hundred thousand dollars in good money, about fifty cents apiece on the average, "which occasioned a general inability to pay taxes." The Mormons in Nauvoo were continually recording difficulties in collecting a couple of dollars, or even fifty cents, in good money, and Robert Flanders has noted that bonds for deeds and other evidences of land ownership were commonly used as currency in Nauvoo. This simple lack of an acceptable currency made difficult business transactions of ordinary life, encouraged counterfeiting, and made possible all kinds of chicanery.

Another major problem of the state was transportation. The Mississippi was a great highroad, but the interior of the state was a wilderness of trails and rutted lanes. In 1841, on a day when the price of wheat was one dollar a bushel in Chicago, the price in Peoria was forty cents. Springfield is but one hundred miles from Nauvoo, yet the *Sangamo Journal* for July 4, 1844, a week after the murders of the Smiths, reported only rumors of troubles in Hancock County. The railroads and the telegraph were only a few years away, but in 1844 the tired horseman and the mired wagon could have stood for symbols of the state.

The cow-town Westerns of the movies and television have almost obscured the fact that violence was a major factor on the American frontier long before Dodge City and Tombstone. Illinois' history was typical enough. The almost legendary bandits of Cave-in-Rock were eliminated early in the century, and in 1816 and 1817 regulators had whipped and run out of the state rogues who, according to Ford, had included sheriffs, justices of the peace, and even judges. But as late as 1831 a gang almost controlled Pope and Massac counties, and even built a fort which had to be taken by storm by a small army of regulators. In 1837 occurred the better-known riots at Alton. A mob threw into the river the press of the *Alton Observer,* an Abolition newspaper published by Elijah Lovejoy. Lovejoy and a member of the mob were killed in a subsequent clash, and a second press destroyed. At about the same time Ogle, Winnebago, Lee, and De Kalb counties all suffered from "organized bands of rogues, engaged in murders, robberies, horse-stealing, and in making and passing counterfeit money."

In 1841 in Ogle County a family of criminals named Driscoll shot down a Captain Campbell, of the respectables of the county, before the eyes of his family. Driscoll and one of his sons were convicted of the murder by a kangaroo court. "They were placed in a kneeling position, with bandages over their eyes, and were fired upon by the whole company present, that there might be none who could be legal witnesses of the bloody deed. About one hundred of these men were afterwards tried for the murder and acquitted. These terrible measures put an end to the ascendancy of the rogues in Ogle County."

One would think that the violence at Carthage Jail in 1844 would have sickened the people of the state, but the conflicts that followed in Hancock County were by no means the only disturbances to trouble Governor Ford. Another small civil war took place in Pope and Massac counties in 1846. The militia of Union County, called in to keep the peace, refused to protect the suspected bandits and left the counties to the government of regulators, who, as always, began by terrorizing known criminals, moved to threatening the suspected, and ended hated and feared by honest and peaceful men.

A party of about twenty regulators went to the house of an old man named Mathis. . . . He and his wife resisted the arrest. The old woman being unusually strong and active, knocked down one or two of the party with her fists. A gun was then presented to her breast accompanied by a threat of blowing her heart out if she continued her resistance. She caught the gun and shoved it downwards, when it went off and shot her through the thigh. . . . The party captured old man Mathis, and carried him away with them, since which time he has not been heard of, but is supposed to have been murdered.

Of Hancock County itself Ford wrote: "I had a good opportunity to know the early settlers of Hancock county. I had attended the circuit courts there as States-attorney, from 1830, when the county was first organized, up to the year 1834; and to my certain knowledge the early settlers, with some honorable exceptions, were, in popular language, hard cases."

All of these citations, and they could be multiplied, show clearly that the murders at Carthage Jail fitted a fairly common pattern. The people of Hancock County, of a good many places in Illinois in 1844, were not horrified at the idea of taking the law into their own hands. That had been done before by neighbors and friends, and would be done again. Thomas Ford was trying to govern a state without money, without effective transportation, and with no effective way of rallying public support in areas of the state not directly involved in the Mormon troubles. In a society where violence becomes commonplace, domestic peace must largely depend upon speed of communication and transportation. Local feuds, riots, even revolts, are best handled by forces not themselves directly involved and therefore relatively objective in their actions. In 1844, in Hancock County, the non-Mormons were bitter partisans, and *they* were judges, jury—and executioners.

We have enough violence, of course, in our own time, with wars declared and undeclared, and with demonstrations, riots, and assassinations.

But there are differences. Our acts of violence tend to be the result of pitting group against government of some kind, or individuals against individuals. In Illinois in the 1840s the conflicts were between groups, or between groups on one side and individuals on the other. Today there is a tacit understanding that the government, using the National Guard or the Army, can always repress group violence if it becomes too threatening; in the mid-nineteenth century the central government left these problems to the states, and the state governments were frequently almost powerless or were strongly partisan on one side or the other of each conflict.

III

If we search for causes of these resorts to violence in Illinois, there is no lack of possibilities. Criminals are always with us, quick to take advantage of weakness in government, of unstable currency, of flimsy jails, of poor communications. And common crime is not only harmful in itself; it begets crime through success—and through retribution.

Another cause for violence may well have been simple boredom, with its concomitant yearning for any kind of action. Anyone who reads the letters and records of the mid-nineteenth century is struck by how often a writer dropped whatever he had in hand and set off on some vaguely motivated journey, and by how easy it always was to attract a crowd.

William Daniels, who wrote an eyewitness account of the Smith murders, began his story:

> I resided in Augusta, Hancock county, Ill., eighteen miles from Carthage. On the 16th of June I left my home with the intention of going to St. Louis. . . .

> The next morning a company of men were going from . . . [Warsaw] to Carthage, for the purpose, as they said, of assisting the militia to drive the Mormons out of the country. Out of curiosity, as I had no particular way to spend my time. . . .

Daniels, setting out from his home on the sixteenth of June, was a witness of the murders eleven days later, and apparently never did arrive in St. Louis.

Sheriff J. B. Backenstos supplied a list of those whom he supposed to have been active in the "massacre at Carthage." Backenstos was not present at the murders and was using hearsay in these accusations, which could not have been proved in court. He listed about sixty men as active participants. Of these sixty, six are listed as having "no business," two as "land sharks," one as "loafer," and one Major W. B. Warren as "a damned villain"—apparently his full-time occupation. Out of about sixty men, ten apparently had no occupation known to the sheriff, and ten others were farmers at a season of the year when farming might have been expected to take all of a man's time.

The best pictures of the boredom, the deep inner need for excitement, for some kind of action, are in the writings of Mark Twain. Twain grew up in Hannibal, Missouri, a river town close to Warsaw and Nauvoo. One of the most famous passages of American writing, and one of the best, could have been a description of Warsaw, though it was Hannibal that Mark Twain wrote of:

> After all these years I can picture that old time to myself now, just as it was then: the white town drowsing in the sunshine of a summer's morning; the streets empty, or pretty nearly so; one or two clerks sitting in front of the Water Street stores, with their splint-bottomed chairs tilted back against the walls, chins on breasts, hats slouched over their faces, asleep—with shingle shavings enough around to show what broke them down; a sow and a litter of pigs loafing along the sidewalk, doing a good business in watermelon rinds and seeds; two or three lonely little freight piles scattered about the "levee"; a pile of "skids" on the slope of the stone-paved wharf, and the fragrant town drunkard asleep in the shadow of them. . . . Presently a film of dark smoke appears . . . instantly a Negro drayman, famous for his quick eye and prodigious voice, lifts up the cry, "S-t-e-a-mboat a-comin' " and the scene changes! The town drunkard stirs, the clerks wake up, a furious clatter of drays follows, every house and store pours out a human contribution, and all in a twinkling the dead town is alive and moving. . . . Ten minutes later the steamer is under way again, with no flag on the jack-staff and no black smoke issuing from the chimneys. After ten more minutes the town is dead again and the town drunkard asleep by the skids once more.

In *Huckleberry Finn* Mark Twain shows us a town in Arkansas, but the description, and particularly the bored cruelty at the conclusion, fit into the picture of possibilities for violence in any Mississippi river town:

> There were empty drygoods boxes under the awnings and loafers roosting on them all day long, whittling them with their Barlow knives and chawing tobacco and gaping and yawning and stretching—a mighty ornery lot. . . . You'd see a muddy sow and a litter of pigs . . . and pretty soon you'd hear a loafer sing out, "Hi! *so* boy! sick him, Tige!" and away the sow would go, squealing most horrible, with a dog or two swinging to each ear and three or four dozen more a-coming, and then you would see all the loafers get up and watch the thing out of sight and laugh at the fun and look grateful for the noise. Then they'd settle back again till there was a dog-fight. There couldn't anything wake them up

all over and make them happy all over, like a dog-fight—unless it might be putting turpentine on a stray dog and setting fire to him, or tying a tin pan to his tail and see him run himself to death.

From September 1845 until well into the spring of 1846 a substantial part of the population of Hancock County seems to have done little except to harass the Mormons. If only the loafers and poor farmers had been bitter against the people of Nauvoo, the Mormons could perhaps have lived on in Hancock County without very great problems, but the respectables of Warsaw and Carthage made common cause with the "butcher boys." The new religion was feared and condemned, of course, since any new religion is necessarily built upon a belief in the inadequacy of established tenets, but Nauvoo was also a threat to Warsaw's trade and to Carthage's position as county seat. When it became obvious that Nauvoo's voters were a bloc to be directed as he chose by Joseph Smith, and when the prophet declared himself a candidate for the Presidency, the old settlers united against the new. The Mormons, strangers and isolates, had to face a county, a population, accustomed to the idea of violence, contemptuous of government, filled with hate, and armed.

IV

It was deeply ironical that the beginning of the end came with the destruction of the press of the *Nauvoo Expositor*. In Alton, a few years before, the mob had twice destroyed presses belonging to the Abolitionist Lovejoy. They rioted against the freedom of the press. In Nauvoo the Mormons did the destroying, and the mob rioted for the freedom of the press. In truth, of course, the mob cared nothing for the abstract freedom of the Bill of Rights; it hated Abolitionists and Mormons, and did them both to death.

Governor Ford first became closely involved with the Mormon troubles on June 17, 1844, when a committee of men from Carthage waited on him in Springfield and asked that the militia of the state be called out to keep the peace in Hancock County. There was reason for their fear. The Mormons had destroyed the press of the *Expositor* on June 10; the very next day a mass meeting at Carthage adopted the following resolutions:

> *Resolved* . . . that we hold ourselves at all times in readiness to co-operate with our fellow citizens in this state, Missouri, and Iowa, to *exterminate*—UTTERLY EXTERMINATE, the wicked and abominable Mormon leaders, the authors of our troubles.
>
> . . .
>
> *Resolved* . . . that the time, in our opinion, has arrived when the

adherents of Smith as a body, shall be driven from the surrounding settlements into Nauvoo; that the Prophet and his miscreant adherents should then be demanded at their hands, and if not surrendered, A WAR OF EXTERMINATION SHOULD BE WAGED, to the entire destruction if necessary for our protection, of his adherents.

Ford, listening to the delegation from Carthage, made the first of three fateful decisions; he would go to Carthage and see himself what the situation was. This was a perfectly sensible thing to do, but it made possible the murders of the Smiths. If the governor had stayed in Springfield the Smiths would not have surrendered; only Ford's personal guarantee of protection persuaded Joseph Smith to ride to Carthage and give himself into custody.

Ford had to find out what the situation was, but Joseph Smith was under no illusions as to the attitude and plans of the mob. When Ford, after hearing the Mormon side of the *Expositor* affair, demanded that the Smiths surrender to the magistrate at Carthage, Joseph Smith stated the situation very accurately, and appealingly, in a letter dated June 22, 1844:

. . . we would not hesitate to stand another trial according to your Excellency's wish, were it not that we are confident our lives would be in danger. We dare not come. Writs, we are assured, are issued against us in various parts of the country. For what? To drag us from place to place, from court to court, across the creeks and prairies, till some bloodthirsty villain could find his opportunity to shoot us down. We dare not come, though your Excellency promises protection. Yet, at the same time, you have expressed fears that you could not control the mob, in which case we are left to the mercy of the merciless. Sir, we dare not come, for our lives would be in danger, and we are guilty of no crime.

You say, "It will be against orders to be accompanied by others if we come to trial." This we have been obliged to act upon in Missouri; and when our witnesses were sent for by the court (as your honor promises to do) they were thrust into prison, and we left without witnesses. Sir, you must not blame us, for "a burnt child dreads the fire." And although your Excellency might be well-disposed in the matter, the appearance of the mob forbids our coming. We dare not do it.

Joseph Smith's plan to leave for the far West, his crossing the river to Montrose, and his final decision to return and give himself up to the law were crucial for his life but were unknown to Governor Ford, who would probably have been best pleased had that plan been followed.

The Smiths arrived in Carthage at about midnight, June 24–25. They were exhibited to the militia the next day, were charged with riot—the *Expositor* case—and were released on bail. Joseph and Hyrum Smith were immediately rearrested on a trumped-up charge of treason, and were *not* released on bail; they were committed to the county jail "for greater security."

At this point Ford made his second crucial decision: he did not interfere in the jailing of the Smiths. In his *History* Ford gives a detailed explanation which is persuasive as to the technical legality of the charges and of his position, but which has little to do with the facts of the matter and the murderous intention of the mob. The magistrate in Carthage refused to accept bail on the charge of treason, and, without the kind of hearing required by law, committed the Smiths to jail in the midst of their enemies. A different kind of governor might have overborne the magistrate and freed the Smiths, but Ford had been a lawyer and a judge. He felt that, as governor, he was only another citizen of the state, with peculiar responsibilities, of course, but with those responsibilities sharply delimited. "In all this matter," wrote Ford,

> the justice of the peace and constable, though humble in office, were acting in a high and independent capacity, far beyond any legal power in me to control. I considered that the executive power could only be called in to assist, and not to dictate or control their action; that in the humble sphere of their duties they were as independent, and clothed with as high authority by the law, as the executive department; and that my province was simply to aid them with the force of the State.

A more forceful and less legalistic chief executive could almost certainly have freed the Smiths; indeed, Ford wrote of the planned trip to Nauvoo on June 27. "I had determined to prevail on the justice to bring out his prisoners and take them along." If he could have persuaded the magistrate to release the prisoners on the twenty-seventh, he could have done the same thing on the twenty-fifth. But this begs the question. A more forceful and less legalistic chief executive would have been likely, in those times, to have been more violently anti-Mormon than was Ford. Governor Boggs of Missouri would probably not have hesitated to override a magistrate, but neither would he have hesitated to authorize the killing of the Smiths.

Once the prisoners were in Carthage Jail, events moved rapidly to the tragic ending. Visitors came and went; a pair of pistols was left with the prisoners; there was something of the feeling of a state of siege. Ford told Joseph Smith that he could not interfere with the slow—and in this case partial—process of the law. Ford had planned to take the Smiths to Nauvoo if he went there on the twenty-seventh, but on that morning the governor changed his mind—and this was his third crucial decision. He wrote, "I had determined to prevail on the justice to bring out his prisoners, and take them along. A council of officers, however, determined that this would be highly inexpedient and dangerous, and offered such substantial reasons for their opinions as induced me to change my resolution." It is interesting and significant that in his *History* Ford passed over this decision as rapidly as possible, did not give the "substantial reasons" of the officers, and moved immediately to the story of the expedition. Had the Smiths been taken to Nauvoo they might have been shot on the road, or they might have been killed in a trumped-up attack in Nauvoo if the original plan to take the whole militia to that city had been followed. That would have meant war. If the Smiths had been taken along with the small company that finally made the journey, they might very well have been kidnapped by the Nauvoo Legion. It is hard to believe that had the Smiths once returned to Nauvoo they would have been willing to come back to Carthage and the jail; they had seen and heard the mob and knew what justice to expect from everyone but the governor.

The rest of the story is familiar to anyone who has studied Mormon history. The governor, having decided to leave the Smiths in jail, ordered almost all the militia to be disbanded. He left with a small force for Nauvoo, where he made a hurried speech to the assembled citizens and exacted a pledge against violence. In the meantime the militia from Warsaw had marched north toward Golden's Point and had been met "at the shanties" with the governor's order to disband, and the news that the governor had left Carthage for Nauvoo and that the Smiths were still in Carthage Jail. John Hay's retelling of the story is probably accurate; his father was with the troops and knew all the men, and the story must have been told and retold in Warsaw:

> Colonel Williams read the Governor's order . . . Captain Grover soon found himself without a company. Captain Aldrich essayed a speech calling for volunteers for Carthage. "He did not make a fair start," says the chronicle [it would be interesting to know what *chronicle* Hay referred to] "and Sharp came up and took it off his hands. Sharp, being a spirited and impressive talker, soon had a respectable squad about him. . . ." The speeches of Grover and Sharp were rather vague; the purpose of murder does not seem to have been hinted. They protested against "being made the tools and puppets of Tommy Ford." They were going to Carthage to see the boys and talk things over. . . .

> While they were waiting at the shanties, a courier came in from the Carthage Grays. It is impossible at this day to declare exactly the purport of his message. It is usually reported and believed that he brought an assurance from the officer of this company that they would be found on guard at the jail where the Smiths were confined; that they would make no real resistance—merely enough to save appearances.

And so the men from Warsaw, led by Sharp, Grover, and Davis, and welcomed by the Carthage Grays under Frank Worrell, rushed the jail, disarmed the guard, and murdered Joseph and Hyrum Smith. Governor Ford heard the news when he met messengers two miles outside of Nauvoo; for safety's sake he took the two messengers with him back to Carthage, so that the knowledge of the murders would be kept from the people of Nauvoo as long as possible.

Everyone expected a war. The anti-Mormons had been violent enough, and the Mormons had been accused by their enemies so often of being bloodthirsty outlaws that the accusers had come to believe their own lies. In this case, the Mormons quite typically followed the advice of John Taylor, and kept the peace. But Ford, expecting the worst, felt that he could trust neither the Mormons nor the murdering Gentiles, and retreated to Quincy in a panic. His feelings about the murders he put into a letter to Nauvoo, of July 22, 1844:

> The naked truth then is, that most well-informed persons condemn in the most unqualified manner the mode in which the Smiths were put to death, but nine out of every ten of such accompany the expression of their disapprobation by a manifestation of their pleasure that they are dead.

> The disapproval is most unusually cold and without feeling . . . called for by decency, by a respect for the laws and a horror of mobs, but does not flow warm from the heart.

> The unfortunate victims . . . were generally and thoroughly hated throughout the country, and it is not reasonable to suppose that their deaths has produced any reaction in the public mind resulting in active sympathy; if you think so, you are mistaken.

Ford obviously foresaw the continuing persecution which resulted in the Mormon War of 1845 and the evacuation of Nauvoo.

V

How far, then, can Governor Ford be held responsible for the murders of Joseph and Hyrum Smith?

Ford arrived at Carthage on the morning of June 21. He discovered that Hancock County was already at the point of civil war, with approximately 1,700 men of the combined militia threatening to attack Nauvoo, which was defended by the Nauvoo Legion, 2,000 strong. His first act was to place the men of the militia under their regular officers and to get pledges of support from those officers. He then demanded the surrender of the Smiths for their part in the *Expositor* affair, which was the immediate cause of the threatened struggle. He then asked for and received the state arms from the Nauvoo Legion. After the Smiths were committed to jail, Ford met with the officers of the militia to consult on the next steps to be taken. He disbanded the militia, rode to Nauvoo with a small party, and pleaded with the Mormons to keep the peace. Then he was faced with the fact of the murders.

It seems obvious that Ford's primary concern was not to save the Smiths but to avoid civil war. He felt that he had to push for the surrender of the Smiths partly because of the legal requirement, but also because their immunity from punishment after the *Expositor* affair made furious the old settlers of Hancock County. He first put the militia under their regular officers in an attempt to enforce discipline, and then, finding the officers as bad as the men, discharged almost the whole militia, feeling that they would be less dangerous as individuals and that many would return to their homes. He took the state arms from the Nauvoo Legion in order to relieve the fears of the old settlers, and then discovered that those fears were mainly pretended and that the old settlers themselves were the real danger. Ford felt a responsibility for the Smiths—he had guaranteed their safety—but when he had to choose between leaving the Smiths and making another effort for peace he chose to meet what he thought was his first responsibility.

No one can tell what *might* have happened, but there seems every reason to believe that if Ford had stayed in Springfield and the Smiths had remained at Nauvoo, civil war would have occurred; that if Ford had arranged for the Smiths to escape to Nauvoo, civil war would have occurred; that if Ford had taken the Smiths with him to Nauvoo, civil war would have occurred. He did none of these things, and civil war occurred. The old settlers of Hancock County did not want peace and would not have peace. Hay reports of the Warsaw militia on the last grim march to Carthage, "These trudged . . . towards the town where the cause of all the trouble and confusion of the last few years awaited them. . . . The farther they walked the more the idea impressed itself upon them that now was the time to finish the matter totally. The avowed design of the leaders communicated itself magnetically to the men, until the whole company became fused into one mass of bloodthirsty energy."

Those writers who have called Ford weak, and who have pointed out, quite correctly, that he changed his mind during those last days of Carthage, have never suggested just what Ford should have done to save the Smiths and prevent the war. The governor tried almost everything in his endeavor to keep the peace; it was not his fault that nothing worked.

The mob wanted Joseph Smith dead and the Mormons out of Illinois.

Even after the Smiths were killed and the Mormons leaderless, civil war broke out the next year and the Mormons were finally expelled. The lesson that Thomas Ford learned is given in his *History:*

> In framing our governments, it seemed to be the great object of our ancestors to secure the public liberty by depriving government of power. Attacks upon liberty were not anticipated from any considerable portion of the people themselves. It was not expected that one portion of the people would attempt to play the tryant over another. And if such a thing had been thought of, the only mode of putting it down was to call out the militia, who are, nine times out of ten, partisans on one side or the other in the contest. The militia may be relied upon to do battle in a popular service, but if mobs are raised to drive out horse thieves, to put down claim-jumpers, to destroy an abolition press, or to expel an odious sect, the militia cannot be brought to act against them efficiently. *The people cannot be used to put down the people.*

Ford failed to save the lives of the Smiths, and he failed to prevent civil war. It is doubtful whether anyone, given that time, that place, those people, could have succeeded.

The Mormon Gathering

WILLIAM MULDER

The flooding of Mormons into Hancock County, as Huntress has observed, precipitated the crisis that culminated at Carthage. But such clustering into communities did not begin in Illinois. As William Mulder explains below, the doctrine of "the gathering," Mormonism's "oldest and most influential doctrine," profoundly affected Mormon history from 1830 into the 1890s. He examines its intellectual sources and its impact on Mormon eschatology, westward migration, and settlement in Utah.

In accentuating the gathering, the Mormon prophet struck upon a central aspect of the American experience. The Mormons were only typical of what Daniel Boorstin, in *The Americans: The National Experience,* has called "a new *homo Americanus* more easily identified by his mobility than by his habitat." The American transients, he affirmed, were a new phenomenon.

> Where before had so many people been continually in motion over a continental landscape? . . . Where had so many people of their own accord taken a one-way passage? Where had so many men moved to unknown, remote places, not to conquer or convert or fortify nor even to trade, but to find and make communities for themselves and their children?

Among the Mormons the one-way passage was taken not only by native Americans, but also by thousands of European immigrants who took seriously the doctrine that America was the land of Zion. Typical of such immigrants was William Clayton, an Englishman, for whom the attraction of Zion was so strong that after the trials of a hazardous voyage to America in 1840 he recorded in his diary on arriving in Nauvoo, "we were pleased to find ourselves once more at home."

America in 1830 could have taken Joseph Smith's Book of Mormon as portent and symbol. Itself the narrative of an ancient religious migration,

William Mulder, "Mormonism's 'Gathering': An American Doctrine with a Difference," *Church History,* XXIII (September 1954), pp. 248–264. Reprinted by permission of the publisher and the author. Footnotes deleted by permission.

the book begot a greater wandering, an epic in-gathering of believers from Europe and the States seeking New Jerusalem on the American frontier. Every Mormon proselyte knew by heart and in his own tongue the words of Father Lehi, refugee from Babylon, American immigrant circa B.C. 600: "We have obtained a land of promise, a land which is choice above all other lands. . . . Yea, the Lord hath covenanted this land unto me, and to my children forever, and also all those who should be led out of other countries by the hand of the Lord." That was the book's portent, big with history and promise. America, it said, had always been promises.

A nation seized with a conviction of manifest destiny should have rejoiced in the book as symbol. It was so very national. It was, in fact, aboriginal. It gave the young country the immemorial past its poets yearned for. With its central theme of the continent as a favored land providentially preserved for the gathering of a righteous people, it improved the American dream with scripture and endowed it with sacred legend. More faithfully than the prophet's neighbors in New England and upstate New York ever realized, his revelation reflected their most cherished myth. Descendants of Puritans and patriots should have recognized the doctrine.

Having given America its primeval migration story, Mormonism proceeded to make migration history—in two directions, both stemming from the same impulse to establish Zion: pioneering in the West and proselyting in Europe. In secular terms, call it building America. The Mormons called it building the Kingdom. Pioneering and proselyting, the frontier and immigration, forces which have so largely determined the national character, gave Mormonism the shape of the American tradition, with a difference. How traditional and how different may be seen in the origin and development of Mormonism's most distinctive doctrine, considerably less well known than the colorful history and institutions which were its consequences.

I

In 1884 in one of Mormonism's darkest hours—its back nearly broken by federal prosecution, many of its leaders in hiding, and hundreds of its members in prison—John Taylor, successor to Brigham Young, addressed an assembly of the Saints in Salt Lake City on their most cherished principle: "They form all kinds of opinions with regard to our gathering," he said: It was an emigration scheme to make money; missionaries were sent out to deceive the weak and ignorant, to make merchandise of them; it was for licentious purposes. Such were the accusations. But there was only one interpretation: "The Lord has gathered us together in these valleys of the mountains, that He might have a people who would be prepared to receive the eternal truths of heaven, and be governed by them."

"The gathering," not polygamy, was Mormonism's oldest and most influential doctrine. It was the signature of the "new and everlasting covenant" which the Lord had made with his elect in this last of all gospel dispensations. The doctrine and the threefold program of evangelism, emigration, and colonization which it had called into being had survived the calamities of over half a century: a prophet's martyrdom, a people's flight into the wilderness, a war with the United States, a running battle with Gentile carpetbaggers and crusaders, persecutions and prosecutions abroad, and now antipolygamy raids by deputy marshals, attended with disfranchisement and the threat of disincorporation as a church. Such tribulation was a sign the Latter-day Saints were still God's people, being tried and not found wanting. Trial was the gathering's great selective principle, winnowing the chaff from the wheat among the faithful. It united them, and they were constantly reminded that "Except ye are one, ye are not mine." "Trials and afflictions," said Apostle Lorenzo Snow just before his imprisonment for unlawful cohabitation in 1886, "will cause our hearts to turn towards our Father who has so marvelously wrought out our redemption and deliverance from Babylon." With his people shut up safely in the "chambers of his mountains," God's wrath and indignation would soon sweep the nations "as with a besom of destruction."

The words of John Taylor and Lorenzo Snow, spoken to congregations largely immigrant, touched a living experience. They reflected a tradition of golden dreams and fierce desires reaching back to the promises made to Israel and forward to the Second Coming. The gathering was as new as the latest proselyte, as old as prophecy. It was a still small voice and a mounting whirlwind, at once the product of a thousand personal decisions and of the Divine Will unfolding itself in history. A little girl in Sweden plays a game, rocking back and forth in the family rocker: she calls it "Going to America." A Danish shoemaker toasts his friends on New Year's Eve: "May next year find us together in Zion." A Norwegian, released from his labors as a missionary, rejoices in his return to Zion: "My absence has been to me an exile." It was all one and the same manifestation: it was the spirit of gathering. The phrase abounds in the literature, personal and official, the theme of countless songs and sermons and endless exposition. It describes a universal yearning among the proselytes, an experience private yet common to which they loved to bear witness after their arrival in Zion, spellbinding the young with tales of the Lord's wonder-working providences on their behalf. After baptism by immersion, they said, and the laying on of hands at confirmation, came the baptism of desire, a strange and irresistible longing which ravished them and filled them with a nostalgia for Zion, their common home.

> Oh Zion when I think of thee
> I long for pinions like the dove
> And mourn to think that I should be
> So distant from the land I love.

In some it leaped up like a flame and led them to leave kin and country in one fine careless rapture; in others it produced a steady glow, warming friends and family by its light and accomplishing through patient labor the final long journey to the sanctuary. "Gathering" came to be regarded the sign of one's faithfulness, and the convert who did not feel the pull was considered a queer fish in the gospel net.

The gathering was Mormonism's way of channeling what the nineteenth century called the religious affections; it disciplined into action the fervor that in revival faiths was dissipated in an aimless love affair with Christ. Though Mormonism, like other adventist faiths, was a millennial proclamation, a warning that the days were at hand when "kingdoms, governments and thrones are falling; . . . plague, pestilence, and famine are walking abroad; and whirlwind, fire, and earthquake proclaiming the truth of prophecy, . . ." it was also a program designed to deal with these eventualities: "Let the Saints be faithful and diligent in every duty and especially in striving to stand in chosen places, that they may watch the coming of the Holy One of Israel." The invitation and the promise were as magnetic as the warning and involved more than a trip to the sinner's bench. "To stand in chosen places" meant getting out of Babylon and uniting with God's people to build up the Kingdom and await greater spiritual endowments. The gathering was to be a roll call of Saints without halos, in whom divinity had yet to breed wings—of a people not already saved and sanctified but, one in faith and fellowship, eager to create conditions under which sainthood might be achieved. Building the Kingdom meant providing an environment that would regenerate the adult and rear the young so that they would never know themselves otherwise than Saints. Salvation was an ongoing process: "As man is, God once was; as God is, man may be." To become like God required an eternity, an endless unfolding of regenerated powers by study, faith, experience, and the intelligence which was the glory of God. George Q. Cannon, visiting Scandinavia in 1862, expressed this developmental aspect of the doctrine when he promised that

> Transplanting the Saints to Zion will benefit them in every way if they will do right. With all the rest, their physical beauty will be increased.

They are already strong and robust, but handsome forms and faces will
. . . become common. The heavenly influence of the Spirit of the Lord,
with more favorable circumstances and a more generous diet, will effect
this.

Inspiration for the gathering sprang from a literal interpretation of
scripture, from a providential reading of history, and from the circumstances of free-land society in early nineteenth-century America. Joseph
Smith, a "restorer among restorationists," saw the idea of the Kingdom of
God as the unifying theme of scripture, and he made the assembling of
the Saints which would have to precede that Kingdom—to him no mere
parable—the great unifying theme of Mormonism. Fired by a biblical
imagination which fused history and myth, Old Testament and New, into
one consuming vision, he reflected the highwrought excitement of the
millenarians all around him expecting an imminent divine event in
America, a state comparable to the confident expectation of the Reformers
in Milton's England before the disappointment of the Commonwealth.
The prophet would reenact an old drama, rehearsed in every gospel dispensation when the righteous sought to separate themselves from the wicked
in special gatherings: Enoch's holy city, Noah's seaworthy ark, Abraham's
intrepid family, the great migration of the tribes under Moses, the flights
of Book of Mormon peoples under Lehi, Mulek, and the brother of Jared,
the establishment of the Primitive Church—momentous gatherings
followed all too often by heartbreaking captivities and dispersions or dis-
solutions. But now, in the fulness of times, after the long night of Christian apostasy, Israel by blood and by adoption was being called home.
Rachel would weep no more for her children, Ezekiel's dry bones were
being quickened, the clay of Jeremiah's potter reworked, Isaiah's remnant
ransomed. It was Daniel's stone ready to roll forth, and St. John's heavenly
city about to come to earth. The proof texts were abundant and the signs
of the times unmistakable. This was to be the summing up. This was the
last dispensation, and the prophet had received the keys. The date is
exactly recorded.

On April 3, 1836, in Kirtland, Ohio, at the dedication of the Saints'
first temple—no bigger than a New England meeting-house but already
hallowed by their labor and sacrifice—Joseph Smith and his schoolteacher
companion Oliver Cowdery declared that they saw the heavens opened and
Moses appear, committing to them "the keys of the gathering of Israel from
the four parts of the earth, and the leading of the ten tribes from the land
of the north"; and Elijah, who came, he said, "to turn the hearts of the
fathers to the children, and the children to the fathers, lest the whole
earth be smitten with a curse." The young New Englanders were charged
with a great responsibility: "The keys of this dispensation are committed

into your hands; and by this ye may know that the great and dreadful day of the Lord is near, even at the doors." It was a double commission: to inaugurate the resettlement of Israel and to build temples to perform gospel ordinances on behalf of the unredeemed dead. Throughout Mormon experience this visitation related and motivated proselyting, emigration, and colonizing—which meant communities of temple-building Saints, for they held the Old Testament conviction that all that Jehovah could do and all that he could be for his people depended upon the existence of his temple. Only there could the Saints be washed clean from the blood and sins of their generation. In the minds of the converts, emigration and temple-building would be inseparable: the injunctions of Moses and Elijah would be reflected in mission ledgers where savings funds for the journey to Zion and for the temple there would be entered side by side.

If Moses and Elijah lifted the curtain on what was to be the last act in the centuries-old drama of Israel's dispersion and promised restoration, America was to be the stage. While other millenarians set a time, the Mormons appointed a place. Joseph Smith split the Hebrew metaphor of Zion and Jerusalem: he saw Judah returning to Jerusalem, Israel to Zion. And America was the land of Zion. To accommodate this stupendous homecoming would, in fact, require both continents, North and South. For this, all history had been mere prologue. The discovery of America by Columbus, the Reformation, the coming of the Pilgrim Fathers, the founding of the Republic, and the raising of "that glorious standard," the Constitution, were all preliminary to this design, while "the happiness of America," as Washington himself believed, was in turn to be but "the first link in a series of universal victories." The Mormons made this common Protestant view of providence controlling America's destiny peculiarly their own.

Joseph Smith's vision of Zion, a holy commonwealth, was nothing new in his America, freckled with communitarian societies, secular and religious, protesting a wicked and competitive world. What was different was the prophet's continental imagination, the magnitude of his dream, and its nativism. The Book of Mormon and the Doctrine and Covenants naturalized biblical prophecies and events to the American scene. America was the promised land, and Missouri, heart of the continent, was to be the site of the New Jerusalem. It had been, in fact, the site of old Eden; not Mesopotamia, but the great valley of the Mississippi had been the cradle of mankind, and the prophet pointed to the very spot where Adam, Ancient of Days, had once built an altar and where he would come again to preside over his righteous progeny. America as the promised land was the grand refrain of the Book of Mormon, which chronicles several migrations. Centuries before the Pilgrim Fathers, America had sheltered refugee bands from the Old World: the Jaredites from the Tower of Babel, the Mulekites and the followers of Lehi from Jerusalem in the days of Zedekiah. Their survivors were the Lamanites, Columbus' Indians, who were to be won back to a knowledge of their forefathers and become a "white and delightsome people." How many other migrations had peopled the Americas the ruins of ancient cities and forgotten mounds could only begin to tell. The Book of Mormon was just one record, but its message was unmistakable: only by serving the God of the land—Jesus Christ, who himself had trod American soil just before his ascension—had any civilization flourished. America on these terms, taught the prophet, had been held in special remembrance for the righteous in ages past, was even now fulfilling its characteristic role as a sanctuary, and for the redeemed would provide an inheritance in eternity.

The doctrine of inheritances went hand in glove with the doctrine of the gathering, domesticating and eternizing for the American freeholder the promises made to Abraham. Joseph Smith's four-square plat of the City of Zion, an idealized New England village with adjacent farm lands —pattern for the communities with which he hoped to fill up the earth— could have been conceived only in a freeland society. A simon-pure agrarian concept, the doctrine of inheritances taught that the meek would inherit the earth. Orson Pratt, early Mormonism's brilliant materialist, demonstrated by simple arithmetic how many acres the arable globe could afford the righteous who had lived since creation: 150 acres, or, if the New Earth contained only the same proportion of land as the old, about forty acres for every redeemed soul. When the earth, purified by fire in a baptism of the spirit as it had been baptized by water in the days of Noah, received its celestial glory and became the abode of the blessed, they could claim their inheritance. It was their stake in the Kingdom, and, since life here and hereafter was a continuum, the living Saints could make a headstart: the communities they founded through their gathering were the prelude to the Kingdom, in which they were first settlers. What for other millenarian faiths marked the end, for the Saints was just the beginning. Their expectation of the Second Coming was momentary, but they planned for mansions on earth rather than in the sky. The Advent itself would bring no more than a change in administration, so to speak—the beneficent monarchy of the King of Kings. The Kingdom, already established, would go right on, and its yeomanry would keep their inheritances, tilling their fields and tending their shops as they had done the day before. The materialism of this vision filled the Saints with security and made them eager to plant their vines and fig trees.

II

The earliest revelations and removals were the image and shadow of the gathering as it was to develop, giving Mormonism a history and largely determining its institutions. The Kirtland visitations actually culminated a series of pronouncements and looked to a worldwide expansion of what had been a statewide movement. At Fayette, New York, in September 1830, the prophet first specified a gathering of the elect "in unto one place upon the face of this land," and, though "no man knoweth where the city of Zion shall be built," it was to be "on the borders of the Lamanites," or Indian country. The church was already looking west. Kirtland, where Mormonism's strongest congregation flourished—the result of successful proselyting among Sidney Rigdon's Campbellites— became an early center and the jumping-off place for "the regions westward," into which a revelation in February 1831, directed elders to proceed, to raise up churches "until the time shall come when it shall be revealed unto you from on high, when the city of the New Jerusalem shall be prepared, that ye may be gathered in one, that ye may be my people, and I will be your God." The Saints were being called a "covenant people" and told to look to the day when the temple would be built. In March they were instructed to "gather out from the eastern lands . . .; go ye forth into the western countries. . . . And with one heart and with one mind, gather up your riches that ye may purchase an inheritance which shall hereafter be appointed unto you." This was to be the New Jerusalem, "a land of peace, a city of refuge, a place of safety. . . ." In June the prophet and over twenty leading elders left Kirtland, traveling west two by two by different routes to build up branches, agreeing to meet in conference in western Missouri, where the land in inheritance would be made known. At length, in July, at the frontier village of Independence, Jackson County, a thousand miles west of Kirtland, the prophet proclaimed Missouri the land consecrated for the gathering. He selected a temple site and, in the published revelation, urged the Saints to buy "every tract bordering by the prairies" and "every tract lying westward, even unto the line running directly between Jew and Gentile . . . inasmuch as my disciples are enabled to buy lands. Behold, this is wisdom, that they may obtain it for an everlasting inheritance." He appointed a land agent to make purchases for the Saints and a bishop to allot inheritances as they arrived.

Some converts from New York were already on the ground. Mormonism's oldest congregation, the Colesville Branch, keeping time with Joseph Smith's westering revelations, had made its way in the spring and summer of 1831 the 1,250 miles from Broome County, New York, to Independence: to Buffalo, by lake sloop to Fairport, Ohio, settling briefly at the neighboring town of Thompson, then taking passage to St. Louis, arriving on June 25 by the river boat *Chieftain* at Independence, actually ahead of the prophet. "I found it required all the wisdom I possessed," recorded Newell Knight, "to lead the company through so long a journey in the midst of their enemies." But the blessings were great: quite overcome at finding themselves at last "upon the western frontiers" and enraptured by the "pleasant aspect" of the country—its rich forest, beautiful streams, and widespread prairies, deep and rolling, "inviting the hand of industry to establish for itself homes upon its broad bosom"—they spoke the spirit of the gathering: "Our hearts went forth unto the Lord desiring fulfillment, that we might know where to bestow our labors profitably."

In August the prophet assisted the New Yorkers to lay the first log for a house as the foundation of Zion in Kaw Township, west of Big Blue a few miles from Independence. At the same time, Sidney Rigdon dedicated the land of Zion for the gathering. The next day the temple site was dedicated, a short distance west of Independence; and on the day following, the Saints held their first conference in Jackson County. With a mercantile house, a printing office, and a periodical—*The Evening and the Morning Star*—soon to follow, it was a hopeful beginning for the central stake of Zion's tent, which would "lengthen her cords and strengthen her stakes" as the arriving Saints filled up the countryside, establishing title to the Kingdom in good legal tender at the federal government's going rate of $1.25 an acre. The Saints had to purchase their inheritances; they were no handout. In 1833 the *Star* had to admonish mistaken zealots in realistic terms that would characterize all future immigration and settlement and be echoed in the instructions in coming mission periodicals, reflecting a sober and practical economics that once more distinguished the Saints from the adventists of the time: the "disciples of Christ" should not come without means to purchase their inheritances and the necessities of life; the Lord would not open the windows of heaven and rain down "angel's food" when their whole journey lay through "fertile country, stored with the blessings of life from his own hand for them to subsist upon." It was vain for them to build air castles. ". . . notwithstanding the fulness of the earth is for the saints, they can never expect it unless they use the means put into their hands to obtain the same in the manner provided by our Lord."

But in 1833 the drivings began. Less imaginative frontier neighbors, mistaking thrift and industry for high-and-mightiness, had little sympathy with the pretensions of New Jerusalem, and the Saints, temporarily abandoning the lands of their inheritance in successive withdrawals across

Missouri counties—Jackson, Clay, Caldwell, and Davis—at length in 1839 redeemed a swamp at a bend of the Mississippi River in Illinois and renamed the squalid hamlet of Commerce, Nauvoo the Beautiful. In a few years it was teeming with thousands from New England, the East, and the Ohio country, and from the British Isles. For in 1837, spurred by the Kirtland revelations of 1836, Mormon evangelists—persuasive and powerful figures like Wilford Woodruff, John Taylor, and Heber C. Kimball, and shortly Brigham Young—went to Great Britain, the first step in making the gathering as wide as Europe itself. By 1840 converts were arriving in Nauvoo from England—over three thousand before the fateful city's evacuation in 1846. With the migration from the states, Nauvoo became the regional capital of communities of Saints who were colonizing all round it in Illinois and across the river in Iowa. The Kingdom seemed here to stay, and the prophet, pleased beyond his expectations in the flow from abroad, told his apostles in 1843 that he planned to go with them to England and from there throughout the world conducting a great revival. "I will yet take these brethren through the United States and through the world, and will make just as big a wake as God Almighty will let me; we must send kings and governors to Nauvoo, and we will do it."

But, despite such optimism, Nauvoo also had to be abandoned, torn by hostilities as much from within as from without, and it became a silent and deserted city providing not even the hospitality of a way station on the road west. In January 1847, from the Camp of Israel's Winter Quarters among the Omahas, on the west bank of the Missouri River, Brigham Young rallied the Saints and hinted the new gathering place: in the Rocky Mountains, beyond the malice of the states, they would seek refuge. "Zion shall be redeemed in my own due time . . . I am he who led the children of Israel out of the land of Egypt; and my arm is stretched out in the last days to save my people Israel." Let the Saints only covenant to keep all the commandments, and the promises would yet be fulfilled. Let them be organized into companies of hundreds, fifties, and tens with their captains, and let each company choose a number of "able-bodied and expert men, to take teams, seeds, and farming utensils" to go as pioneers for putting in spring crops. Let each company look to the poor, the widows, the fatherless, and the families of those who had gone into the army headed for Mexico; and let the companies prepare houses and fields for those remaining behind that season. Let all use their "influence and property to remove this people." Let them keep their mutual pledges, ceasing to contend with one another, ceasing drunkenness. Let them return what was borrowed, restore what they found that another had lost. Let them be wise stewards. And if they felt merry, let them "praise the Lord with singing, with music, with dancing, and with a prayer of praise and thanksgiving." If sorrowful, let them "call on the Lord . . . with supplication, that your souls may be joyful." Let the ignorant learn wisdom by humbling themselves. The nation had rejected the testimony of the Saints; now would come the day of its calamity unless it speedily repent. The blood of the prophet cried out against it. As he sealed his testimony with his death, so let the Saints seal theirs with their diligence. The "Word and Will of the Lord" to Brigham Young was the Deuteronomy of the Saints' last journey into the wilderness. A renewal of their covenants and a strengthening of their hopes in the face of defeat, it was their Mayflower Compact, the civil and religious order of a people uprooted but saved by the ideology of the gathering from disintegration.

"We have created in the wilderness of the western world a commonwealth for Christ, a spiritual New Jerusalem," wrote the divines of New England. "We have established the political Promised Land, and have set up the Lamp of Liberty for a beacon light to all nations," wrote the fathers of the American Revolution. In the eyes of an astonished country, the New Canaan in the Valley of the Great Salt Lake seemed no less the work of zealots and rebels: Deseret would prosper, coming so clearly within the American tradition.

Though some wept at its desolation, to Brigham Young this was the destined place, and the Mormons, turning readily to scripture that spoke of deserts blossoming as the rose and of the mountain of the Lord's house being established in the tops of the mountains, found ample proof that the choice was prophetic. It was a land of promise and possibility, a region requiring only to be wrested from the dual menace of drouth and the squalid aboriginals who clung precariously to its hills. Communities could be founded by faith and nourished by irrigation, and the Indians could be fed, fought if necessary, and converted. If one believed, the land lay, almost, in the lap of God, who sent the sea gulls to save the grain from marauding crickets and covered the hills with sego lilies whose roots sustained the hungry settlers through the second hard winter.

The beginnings had been severe. "It has been hard times for bread," wrote Parley P. Pratt on July 9, 1849, to his brother Orson in England; but he could report that harvest had commenced and he had cut some fine wheat. Rye, oats, barley, corn, and vegetables were all doing well, and, in his opinion, "the best foundation for a living in this country would be a herd of young heifers, driven from the States, or a drove of sheep." To the scores, the hundreds, of travelers arriving in the valley daily on their way to the goldfields of California,

this spot suddenly bursts upon their astonished vision like a paradise in the midst of the desert. So great is the effect, that many of them burst forth in an ecstasy of admiration on emerging from the kanyon, and gaining a first view of our town and its fields and gardens. Some shed tears, some shout, some dance and skip for joy; and all doubtless feel the spirit of the place resting upon them, with its joyous and heavenly influence bearing witness that here live the industrious, the free, the intelligent, and the good.

By the fall of 1849 the First Presidency of the church, in a general epistle addressed to "the Saints scattered throughout the earth," could review an encouraging year. A provisional government for the new state of Deseret had been formed, with a constitution and elected officers, and Congress was being petitioned for admission into the Union. A good carriage road ran a hundred miles from the Weber River on the north to Provo River on the south, with "fine cultivated fields and civilized dwellings more or less from one extreme to the other." Good frame bridges crossed many of the streams, and ferries had been established on the Upper Platte during high water and at each crossing of Green River—important for next spring's immigration. Some fifteen to twenty thousand immigrants from the states bound for the coast had passed through the city, "filling the valley with goods" as in their haste they exchanged three heavy wagons for one light one and disposed of clothing, goods, and equipment at one quarter their New York or St. Louis wholesale value. The immigration of the Saints involved some five to six hundred wagons during the season, "besides many who come in search of gold, hear the gospel for the first time and will go no farther, having believed and been baptized . . . many of whom are among the most respectable and wealthy." New valleys were being explored and sites selected for settlement. Timber was abundant; three grist mills were operating. In Salt Lake City itself a spacious bowery for public worship had been built on the temple block; a council house was nearly completed; a foundation had been laid for an extensive storehouse and granary. A fund for helping poor Saints to immigrate had been created, since it had been covenanted that "we would never cease our exertions, by all the means and influence within our reach, till all the Saints who were obliged to leave Nauvoo should be located at some gathering place." The need now in all Zion was for laborers and multiplied means of farming and building: "We want men. Brethren, come from the States, from the nations, come! and help us to build and grow, until we can say, enough, the valleys of Ephraim are full."

III

With the prospect so fair for the future of Zion, it was time to turn once more to the wider obligations which the gospel of the gathering imposed: the warning, the invitation, and the promise must go to the oppressed continent of Europe:

> Ye Saints who dwell on Europe's shore,
> Prepare yourselves with many more
> To leave behind your native land,
> For sure God's judgments are at hand.

At a general conference of the church in October the appointments indicated that Mormonism was going to "the nations" in earnest: Apostle John Taylor to France and Germany, Apostle Lorenzo Snow to Italy and Switzerland, Apostle Erastus Snow and Elder Peter Hansen to Denmark, Elder John Foregren to Sweden.

They were a small company for so great an undertaking. But they went as the Lord's husbandmen, confident the harvest was waiting for them to thrust in the sickle before the great field of the world should be burned as stubble. That confidence was to die with them and their convert generation. They themselves could never imagine that the millennial hope would burn out, the program of the gathering come to a halt, and the doctrine itself, though its language remained the same, suffer a sea change. Only the fact that Utah's turbulence gave each new generation of Saints its own provocations with the enemy, making it as militant as the first with its own memories to pass on to the children, kept the ideology incandescent so long. The intoxicant biblical images, the apocalyptic rhetoric disappeared as the expectations subsided and as, with the renunciation of polygamy in 1890, the whiplash of persecution ceased to sting. Legislation aimed at drying up Mormon immigration hastened what changing social and economic conditions were already accomplishing.

Zion meant "the pure in heart," a people and a condition, and it meant the place where the pure in heart dwell. For the first generation it was Zion as a place that was preached with so much passion and commitment and that found expression in the practical program of immigration and settlement. But as outside influences broke in upon the harmony of one faith, one Lord, and one people, Zion became less provincial; the idea and the ideal expanded to mean any place where the pure in heart dwell. It meant permanent churches and at last even temples in Europe, once abhorred as Babylon. The great events which had seemed so imminent retreated into a future comfortably remote, and Mormonism settled down to an indefinite postponement of prophecy.

It was an accommodation to changing times. Abroad as at home, the newer generation, less literal in their reading of scripture—if they knew the Bible at all—were apathetic to issues that spelled the end of the world, and the beginning of another, to the earlier age. Europe, moreover, was finding itself by the end of the century less oppressed, and domestic programs which provided economic opportunities for more people and an outlet for social pressures weakened the old longing for distant utopias. Besides, the sky was no longer the limit in Zion. Once the encyclicals had urged, "Let all who can procure a loaf of bread, and one garment on their back, be assured there is water plenty and pure by the way, and doubt no longer, but come next year to the place of gathering, even in flocks, as doves fly to their windows before a storm." But in 1891, forty years later, they played a different tune: "Respecting the gathering, the elders should explain the principle when occasion requires; but acting upon it should be left entirely to the individual." To talk of emigration only "when occasion requires" reveals a startling transition from the days when the clarion call was to redeem the faithful and bring them singing to Zion. It was a day of pruning—the Saints were welcome, but at their own risk. The doctrine was at last most characteristically American.

Notes on Mormon Polygamy

STANLEY S. IVINS

If the gathering was Mormonism's most influential doctrine, it did not seem so to most Americans in the latter half of the nineteenth century. "Time was when, in the popular mind," Stanley Ivins reflects, "Mormonism meant only polygamy." But, as Ivins says, the practice of polygamy had only a short duration of about sixty-five years. Here he explores with insight what effect this institution had upon family life and indicates that it was not nearly so great as Mormons hoped and non-Mormons feared.

Time was when, in the popular mind, Mormonism meant only polygamy. It was assumed that every Mormon man was a practical or theoretical polygamist. This was a misconception, like the widespread belief that Mormons grew horns, for there were always many of these Latter-day Saints who refused to go along with the doctrine of "plurality of wives." It was accepted by only a few of the more than fifty churches or factions which grew out of the revelations of the prophet Joseph Smith. Principal advocate of the doctrine was the Utah church, which far outnumbered all other branches of Mormonism. And strongest opposition from within Mormondom came from the second largest group, the Reorganized Church of Jesus Christ of Latter-day Saints, with headquarters at Independence, Missouri.

This strange experiment in family relations extended over a period of approximately sixty-five years. It was professedly inaugurated on April 5, 1841, in a cornfield outside the city of Nauvoo, Illinois, with the sealing of Louisa Beeman to Joseph Smith. And it was brought to an official end by a resolution adopted at the seventy-fourth Annual Conference of the Utah church, on April 4, 1904. Since that time, those who have persisted in carrying on with it have been excommunicated. But the project was

Stanley S. Ivins, "Notes on Mormon Polygamy," *Western Humanities Review*, X (Summer 1956), pp. 229–239. Reprinted by permission of the publisher. Footnotes deleted by permission.

openly and energetically prosecuted during only about forty years. For the first ten years the new doctrine was kept pretty well under wraps, and it was not until the fall of 1852 that it was openly avowed and the Saints were told that only those who embraced it could hope for the highest exaltation in the resurrection. And during the fifteen years prior to 1904, there were only a few privately solemnized plural marriages. So it might be said that the experiment was ten years in embryo, enjoyed a vigorous life of forty years, and took fifteen years to die.

The extent to which polygamy was practiced in Utah will probably never be known. Plural marriages were not publicly recorded, and there is little chance that any private records which might have been kept will ever be revealed.

Curious visitors to Utah in the days when polygamy was flourishing were usually told that about one-tenth of the people actually practiced it. Since the abandonment of the principle this estimate has been revised downward. A recent official published statement by the Mormon church said: "The practice of plural marriage has never been general in the Church and at no time have more than 3 percent of families in the Church been polygamous." This estimate was apparently based upon testimony given during the investigation into the right of Reed Smoot to retain his seat in the United States Senate. A high church official, testifying there, referred to the 1882 report of the Utah Commission, which said that application of the antipolygamy laws had disfranchised approximately 12,000 persons in Utah. The witness declared that, since at least two-thirds of these must have been women, there remained no more than 4,000 polygamists, which he believed constituted less than 2 percent of the church population. The error of setting heads of families against total church membership is obvious. Using the same report, Senator Dubois concluded that 23 percent of Utah Mormons over eighteen years of age were involved in polygamy. Later on in the Smoot hearing the same church official testified that a careful census, taken in 1890, revealed that there were 2,451 plural families in the United States. This suggests that, at that time, 10 percent or more of the Utah Mormons might have been involved in polygamy.

Of more than 6,000 Mormon families, sketches of which are found in a huge volume published in 1913, between 15 and 20 percent appear to have been polygamous. And a history of Sanpete and Emery counties contains biographical sketches of 722 men, of whom 12.6 percent married more than one woman.

From information obtainable from all available sources, it appears that there may have been a time when 15, or possibly 20, percent of the Mormon families of Utah were polygamous. This leaves the great majority of the Saints delinquent in their obligation to the principle of plurality of wives.

While the small proportion of Mormons who went into polygamy may not necessarily be a true measure of its popularity, there is other evidence that they were not anxious to rush into it, although they were constantly reminded of its importance to their salvation.

A tabulation, by years, of about 2,500 polygamous marriages, covering the whole period of this experiment, reveals some interesting facts. It indicates that, until the death of the prophet Joseph Smith in the summer of 1844, the privilege of taking extra wives was pretty well monopolized by him and a few of his trusted disciples. Following his death and the assumption of leadership by the Twelve Apostles under Brigham Young, there was a noticeable increase in plural marriages. This may be accounted for by the fact that, during the winter of 1845–1846, the Nauvoo Temple was finished to a point where it could be used for the performance of sacred rites and ordinances. For a few weeks before their departure in search of a refuge in the Rocky Mountains, the Saints worked feverishly at their sealings and endowments. As part of this religious activity, the rate of polygamous marrying rose to a point it was not again to reach for ten years. It then fell off sharply and remained low until the stimulation given by the public announcement, in the fall of 1852, that polygamy was an essential tenet of the church. This spurt was followed by a sharp decline over the next few years.

Beginning in the fall of 1856 and during a good part of the following year, the Utah Mormons were engaged in the greatest religious revival of their history. To the fiery and sometimes intemperate exhortations of their leaders, they responded with fanatical enthusiasm, which at times led to acts of violence against those who were slow to repent. There was a general confession of sins and renewal of covenants through baptism, people hastened to return articles "borrowed" from their neighbors, and men who had not before given a thought to the matter began looking for new wives. And, as one of the fruits of the Reformation, plural marriages skyrocketed to a height not before approached and never again to be reached. If our tabulation is a true index, there were 65 percent more of such marriages during 1856 and 1857 than in any other two years of this experiment.

With the waning of the spirit of reformation, the rate of polygamous marrying dropped in 1858 to less than a third and in 1859 to less than a fifth of what it was in 1857. This decline continued until 1862, when Congress, responding to the clamor of alarmists, enacted a law prohibiting bigamy in Utah and other territories. The answer of the Mormons to this

rebuke was a revival of plural marrying to a point not previously reached
except during the gala years of the Reformation.

The next noticeable acceleration in the marriage rate came in 1868 and
1869 and coincided with the inauguration of a boycott against the Gentile
merchants and the organization of an anti-Mormon political party. But
this increased activity was short-lived and was followed by a slump lasting
for a dozen years. By 1881 polygamous marrying had fallen to almost its
lowest ebb since the public avowal of the doctrine of plurality.

With the passage of the Edmunds Act of 1882, which greatly strengthened the antipolygamy laws, the government began its first serious effort
to suppress the practice of polygamy. The Mormons responded with their
last major revival of polygamous activity, which reached its height in 1884
and 1885. But, with hundreds of polygamists imprisoned and most of the
church leaders driven into exile to avoid arrest, resistance weakened and
there was a sudden decline in marriages, which culminated in formal
capitulation in the fall of 1890. This was the end, except for a few under-
cover marriages during the ensuing fifteen years, while the experiment
was in its death throes.

II

If there is any significance in this chronicle of polygamous marrying,
it is in the lack of evidence that the steady growth of the Utah church was
accompanied by a corresponding increase in the number of such marriages.
The story is rather one of sporadic outbursts of enthusiasm, followed by
relapses, with the proportion of the Saints living in polygamy steadily
falling. And it appears to be more than chance that each outbreak of
fervor coincided with some revivalist activity within the church or with
some menace from without. It is evident that, far from looking upon
plural marriage as a privilege to be made the most of, the rank and file
Mormons accepted it as one of the onerous obligations of church membership. Left alone, they were prone to neglect it, and it always took some
form of pressure to stir them to renewed zeal.

The number of wives married by the men who practiced polygamy offers
further evidence of lack of enthusiasm for the principle. A common mis-
taken notion was that most polygamists maintained large harems, an idea
which can be attributed to the publicity given the few men who went in
for marrying on a grand scale. Joseph Smith was probably the most
married of these men. The number of his wives can only be guessed at,
but it might have gone as high as sixty or more. Brigham Young is usually
credited with only twenty-seven wives, but he was sealed to more than

twice that many living women, and to at least 150 more who had died. Heber C. Kimball had forty-five living wives, a number of them elderly ladies who never lived with him. No one else came close to these three men in the point of marrying. John D. Lee gave the names of his nineteen wives, but modestly explained that, "as I was married to old Mrs. Woolsey for her soul's sake, and she was near sixty years old when I married her, I never considered her really as a wife. . . . That is the reason that I claim only eighteen true wives." And by taking fourteen wives, Jens Hansen earned special mention in the *Latter-day Saint Biographical Encyclopedia,* which said: "Of all the Scandinavian brethren who figured prominently in the Church Bro. Hansen distinguished himself by marrying more wives than any other of his countrymen in modern times." Orson Pratt, who was chosen to deliver the first public discourse on the subject of plural marriage and became its most able defender, had only ten living wives, but on two days, a week apart, he was sealed for eternity to more than two hundred dead women.

But these men with many wives were the few exceptions to the rule. Of 1,784 polygamists, 66.3 percent married only one extra wife. Another 21.2 percent were three-wife men, and 6.7 percent went as far as to take four wives. This left a small group of less than 6 percent who married five or more women. The typical polygamist, far from being the insatiable male of popular fable, was a dispassionate fellow, content to call a halt after marrying the one extra wife required to assure him of his chance at salvation.

Another false conception was that polygamists were bearded patriarchs who continued marrying young girls as long as they were able to hobble about. It is true that Brigham Young took a young wife when he was sixty-seven years old and a few others followed his example, but such marriages were not much more common with the Mormons than among other groups. Of 1,229 polygamists, more than 10 percent married their last wives while still in their twenties, and more than one half of them before arriving at the still lusty age of forty years. Not one in five took a wife after reaching his fiftieth year. The average age at which the group ceased marrying was forty years.

There appears to be more basis in fact for the reports that polygamists were likely to choose their wives from among the young girls who might bear them many children. Of 1,348 women selected as plural wives, 38 percent were in their teens, 67 percent were under twenty-five and only 30 percent over thirty years of age. A few had passed forty and about one in a hundred had, like John D. Lee's old Mrs. Woolsey, seen her fiftieth birthday.

There were a few notable instances of high-speed marrying among the polygamists. Whatever the number of Joseph Smith's wives, he must have married them all over a period of thirty-nine months. And Brigham Young took eight wives in a single month, four of them on the same day. But only a few enthusiasts indulged in such rapid marrying. As a rule it proceeded at a much less hurried pace. Not one plural marriage in ten followed a previous mariage by less than a year. The composite polygamist was first married at the age of twenty-three to a girl of twenty. Thirteen years later he took a plural wife, choosing a twenty-two-year-old girl. The chances were two to one that, having demonstrated his acceptance of the principle of plurality, he was finished with marrying. If, however, he took a third wife, he waited four years, then selected another girl of twenty-two. The odds were now three to one against his taking a fourth wife, but if he did so, he waited another four years, and once more chose a twenty-two-year-old girl, although he had now reached the ripe age of forty-four. In case he decided to add a fifth wife, he waited only two years, and this time the lady of his choice was twenty-one years old. This was the end of his marrying, unless he belonged· to a 3 percent minority.

Available records offer no corroboration of the accusation that many polygamous marriages were incestuous. They do, however, suggest the source of such reports, in the surprisingly common practice of marrying sisters. The custom was initiated by Joseph Smith, among whose wives were at least three pairs of sisters. His example was followed by Heber C. Kimball, whose forty-five wives included Clarissa and Emily Cutler, Amanda and Anna Gheen, Harriet and Ellen Sanders, Hannah and Dorothy Moon, and Laura and Abigail Pitkin. Brigham Young honored the precedent by marrying the Decker sisters, Lucy and Clara, and the Bigelow girls, Mary and Lucy. And John D. Lee told how he married the three Woolsey sisters, Agatha Ann, Rachel, and Andora and rounded out the family circle by having their mother sealed to him for her soul's sake. Among his other wives were the Young sisters, Polly and Lovina, sealed to him on the same evening. The popularity of this custom is indicated by the fact that of 1,642 polygamists, 10 percent married one or more pairs of sisters.

While marrying sisters could have been a simple matter of propinquity, there probably was some method in it. Many a man went into polygamy reluctantly, fully aware of its hazards. Knowing that his double family must live in one small home, and realizing that the peace of his household would hinge upon the congeniality between its two mistresses, he might well hope that if they were sisters the chances for domestic tranquility would be more even. And a wife, consenting to share her husband with another, could not be blamed for asking that he choose her sister, instead of bringing home a strange woman.

III

The fruits of this experiment in polygamy are not easy to appraise. In defense of their marriage system, the Mormons talked much about the benefits it would bring. By depriving husbands of an excuse for seeking extramarital pleasure, and by making it possible for every woman to marry, it was to solve the problem of the "social evil" by eliminating professional prostitution and other adulterous activities. It was to furnish healthy tabernacles for the countless spirits, waiting anxiously to assume their earthly bodies. It was to build up a "righteous generation" of physically and intellectually superior individuals. It was to enhance the glory of the polygamist through a posterity so numerous that, in the course of eternity, he might become the god of a world peopled by his descendants. And there was another blessing in store for men who lived this principle. Heber C. Kimball, Brigham Young's chief lieutenant, explained it this way:

> I would not be afraid to promise a man who is sixty years of age, if he will take the counsel of brother Brigham and his brethren, that he will renew his age. I have noticed that a man who has but one wife, and is inclined to that doctrine, soon begins to wither and dry up, while a man who goes into plurality looks fresh, young and sprightly. Why is this? Because God loves that man, and because he honors His work and word. Some of you may not believe this; but I not only believe it—I also know it. For a man of God to be confined to one woman is small business; for it is as much as we can do now to keep up under the burdens we have to carry; and I do not know what we should do if we had only one wife apiece.

It does appear that Mormon communities of the polygamous era were comparatively free from the evils of professional prostitution. But this can hardly be attributed to the fact that a few men, supposedly selected for their moral superiority, were permitted to marry more than one wife. It might better be credited to the common teaching that adultery was a sin so monstrous that there was no atonement for it short of the spilling of the blood of the offender. It would be strange indeed if such a fearful warning failed to exert a restraining influence upon the potential adulterer.

There is, of course, nothing unsound in the theory that a community of superior people might be propagated by selecting the highest ranking males and having them reproduce themselves in large numbers. The difficulty here would be to find a scientific basis for the selection of the favored males. And there is no information from which an opinion can be arrived at as to the results which were obtained in this respect.

When it came to fathering large families and supplying bodies for waiting spirits, the polygamists did fairly well, but fell far short of some of their dreams. Heber C. Kimball once said of himself and Brigham Young: "In twenty-five or thirty years we will have a larger number in our two families than there now is in this whole Territory, which numbers more than seventy-five thousand. If twenty-five years will produce this amount of people, how much will be the increase in one hundred years?" And the *Millennial Star* reckoned that a hypothetical Mr. Fruitful, with forty wives, might, at the age of seventy-eight, number among his seed 3,508,441 souls, while his monogamous counterpart could boast of only 152.

With such reminders of their potentialities before them, the most married of the polygamists must have been far from satisfied with the results they could show. There is no conclusive evidence that any of Joseph Smith's many plural wives bore children by him. Heber C. Kimball, with his forty-five wives, was the father of sixty-five children. John D. Lee, with only eighteen "true wives," fell one short of Kimball's record, and Brigham Young fathered fifty-six children, approximately one for each wife.

Although the issue of the few men of many wives was disappointing in numbers, the rank and file of polygamists made a fair showing. Of 1,651 families, more than four-fifths numbered ten or more children. Half of them had fifteen or more and one-fourth, twenty or more. There were eighty-eight families of thirty or more, nineteen of forty or more, and seven of fifty or more. The average number of children per family was fifteen. And by the third or fourth generation some families had reached rather impressive proportions. When one six-wife elder had been dead fifty-five years, his descendants numbered 1,900.

While polygamy increased the number of children of the men, it did not do the same for the women involved. A count revealed that 3,335 wives of polygamists bore 19,806 children, for an average of 5.9 per woman. An equal number of wives of monogamists, taken from the same general group, bore 26,780 for an average of eight. This suggests the possibility that the overall production of children in Utah may have been less than it would have been without benefit of plurality of wives. The claim that plurality was needed because of a surplus of women is not borne out by statistics.

There is little doubt that the plural wife system went a good way toward making it possible for every woman to marry. According to Mormon teachings a woman could "never obtain a fullness of glory, without being married to a righteous man for time and all eternity." If she never married or was the wife of a Gentile, her chance of attaining a high degree of salvation was indeed slim. And one of the responsibilities of those in official church positions was to try to make sure that no woman went without a husband. When a widow or a maiden lady "gathered" to Utah, it was a community obligation to see to it that she had food and shelter and the privilege of being married to a good man. If she received no offer of marriage, it was not considered inconsistent with feminine modesty for her to "apply" to the man of her choice, but if she set her sights too high she might be disappointed. My grandmother, who did sewing for the family of Brigham Young, was fond of telling how she watched through a partly open doorway while he forcibly ejected a woman who was too persistent in applying to be sealed to him. Her story would always end with the same words: "And I just couldn't help laughing to see brother Brigham get so out of patience with that woman." However, if the lady in search of a husband was not too ambitious, her chances of success were good. It was said of the bishop of one small settlement that he "was a good bishop. He married all the widows in town and took good care of them." And John D. Lee was following accepted precedent when he married old Mrs. Woolsey for her soul's sake.

As for Mr. Kimball's claims concerning the spiritual uplift to be derived from taking a fresh, young wife, what man is going to quarrel with him about that?

IV

The most common reasons given for opposition to the plural wife system were that it was not compatible with the American way of life, that it debased the women who lived under it, and that it caused disharmony and unhappiness in the family. To these charges the Mormons replied that their women enjoyed a higher social position than those of the outside world, and that there was less contention and unhappiness in their families than in those of the Gentiles. There is no statistical information upon which to base a judgment as to who had the better of this argument.

In addition to these general complaints against polygamy, its critics told some fantastic stories about the evils which followed in its wake. It was said that, through some mysterious workings of the laws of heredity, polygamous children were born with such peculiarities as feeblemindedness, abnormal sexual desires, and weak and deformed bodies.

At a meeting of the New Orleans Academy of Sciences in 1861, a remarkable paper was presented by Dr. Samuel A. Cartwright and Prof. C. G. Forshey. It consisted mainly of quotations from a report made by Assistant Surgeon Robert Barthelow of the United States Army on the "Effects and Tendencies of Mormon Polygamy in the Territory of Utah."

Barthelow had observed that the Mormon system of marriage was already producing a people with distinct racial characteristics. He said:

> The yellow, sunken, cadaverous visage; the greenish-colored eye; the thick, protuberant lips; the low forehead; the light, yellowish hair, and the lank, angular person, constitute an appearance so characteristic of the new race, the production of polygamy, as to distinguish them at a glance. The older men and women present all the physical peculiarities of the nationalities to which they belong; but these peculiarities are not propagated and continued in the new race; they are lost in the prevailing type.

Dr. Cartwright observed that the Barthelow report went far "to prove that polygamy not only blights the physical organism, but the moral nature of the white or Adamic woman to so great a degree as to render her incapable of breeding any other than abortive specimens of humanity—a new race that would die out—utterly perish from the earth, if left to sustain itself."

When one or two of the New Orleans scientists questioned the soundness of parts of this paper, the hecklers were silenced by Dr. Cartwright's retort that the facts presented were not so strong as "those which might be brought in proof of the debasing influence of abolitionism on the moral principles and character of that portion of the Northern people who have enacted personal liberty bills to evade a compliance with their constitutional obligations to the Southern States, and have elevated the Poltroon Sumner into a hero, and made a Saint of the miscreant Brown."

Needless to say there is no evidence that polygamy produced any such physical and mental effects upon the progeny of those who practiced it. A study of the infant mortality rate in a large number of Mormon families showed no difference between the polygamous and monogamous households.

It is difficult to arrive at general conclusions concerning this experiment in polygamy, but a few facts about it are evident. Mormondom was not a society in which all men married many wives, but one in which a few men married two or more wives. Although plurality of wives was taught as a tenet of the church, it was not one of the fundamental principles of the Mormon faith, and its abandonment was accomplished with less disturbance than that caused by its introduction. The Saints accepted plurality in theory, but most of them were loath to put it into practice, despite the continual urging of leaders in whose divine authority they had the utmost faith. Once the initial impetus given the venture had subsided it became increasingly unpopular. In 1857 there were nearly fourteen times as many plural marriages for each one thousand Utah Mormons as there were in 1880. Left to itself, undisturbed by pressure from without, the church would inevitably have given up the practice of polygamy, perhaps even sooner than it did under pressure. The experiment was not a satisfactory test of plurality of wives as a social system. Its results were neither spectacular nor conclusive, and they gave little justification for either the high hopes of its promoters or the dire predictions of its critics.

The Political Kingdom as a Source of Conflict

KLAUS HANSEN

Polygamy was, as Ivins has shown, but one of Mormonism's peculiar doctrines. The Mormons saw themselves as heirs to the ancient covenants of Abraham, believing that God had set aside for them a portion of the great West as an everlasting inheritance. They believed that only divinely inspired political leaders could justly govern the society they were destined to establish. They fastened upon the imagery of Daniel, chapter 7, to proclaim in 1844 that the time to establish the Kingdom of God upon the earth had come. In essence the Kingdom of God was anti-pluralistic, combining social, economic, and political power under the leadership of a modern-day prophet who served as mayor, judge, realtor, political boss, and military chief. It was for this reason that many Americans considered the Kingdom singularly anti-American. Klaus Hansen, now at Queens University, Ontario, explores the effect that the political aspects of the Kingdom had in stirring antipathy toward the Mormons from New York to Utah.

The afternoon of October 30, 1838, saw one of the most brutal butcheries of men and children ever to occur in the annals of the state of Missouri. At about four o'clock, relates Joseph Young, one of the eye-witnesses, "a large company of armed men, on horses" advanced toward a mill on Shoal Creek, where about thirty Mormon families had gathered for refuge. Defenseless, the Saints scattered, some into the woods, others into a blacksmith shop. Overtaken by the mob, nineteen men and boys were killed, a dozen wounded. One nine-year-old boy had found refuge under the bellows. Discovered by a mobster, the child was killed by a gun-blast in the head. Boasted the butcher afterwards: "Nits will make lice, and if he had lived he would have become a Mormon."

Klaus Hansen, "The Political Kingdom of God as a Cause for Mormon–Gentile Conflict," *Brigham Young University Studies,* II (Spring–Summer 1960), pp. 241–260. Reprinted by permission of the publisher. Footnotes deleted by permission.

The shots of the Haun's Mill massacre were to keep ringing in the ears of the Saints, reminding them that Satan was fighting with real bullets against the Kingdom of God, a Kingdom that, if it was not of this world, nevertheless marched vigorously and militantly in it. Persecution, then, was to be expected. It had been with the church from the publication of Joseph Smith's first revelation; it was to continue throughout the history of the church in the nineteenth century. Joseph himself was to seal his testimony with his blood. Even the exodus to the Rocky Mountains would not silence the voice of persecution. Not until the Saints had submitted to the government demands for the abolition of plural marriage was the conflict between the church and the world to diminish, finally to end.

To the faithful Saint, the problem of historical causation found a simple and straightforward answer. As already implied, Satan would inevitably have to oppose the work of God; this opposition became in itself one of the touchstones for the divinity of the work; and the blood of the martyrs was transformed into seed for the church.

But in addition to such considerations the historian should search for other objective, historical elements of causation. In the history of Mormon–Gentile relations one of the most significant institutions contributing to the conflict has so far received altogether too little, if any, attention. This institution is the political Kingdom of God.

First of all, then, the development of the political Kingdom of God in Mormon history will have to be outlined. Space limitations will obviously limit the comprehensiveness and scope of this investigation, a task made even more difficult by the fact that large stretches of the course of the political Kingdom of God are still uncharted. Consequently, only a sampling of incidences of conflict at certain crucial periods of church history will be made to suggest general trends.

It should be remembered that in history beliefs are equally as important as facts. Whether or not Joseph Smith actually planned treasonable action against the United States fades into a pale academic question before the bullets of assassins who believed that this was so, irrespective of fact. Likewise, the political Kingdom of God caused persecution more by its distorted image in the eyes of its enemies than by the actual ideals and realities it represented in the eyes of its adherents and defenders.

The strong emphasis on the millennial Kingdom in Mormon thought has led some writers to believe that the idea of a political Kingdom preceding the second coming of Christ was never entertained by the Saints. Mormonism was not to establish a temporal Kingdom, but to wait for Christ. This erroneous notion may have been caused partly by the fact that it is extremely difficult to differentiate between the apocalyptic Kingdom and its predecessor. Since the one was to lead to the other, they were to be almost identical in nature, at least theoretically. The main difference between the two was mostly a matter of chronology. The one would be the kingdom militant, struggling against a hostile world; the other was the kingdom victorious, having subdued all its enemies. The political Kingdom, then, was organized because the Mormons did-not believe that they could wait for Christ to establish his world government without some preparation. The Saints may have believed in miracles; but they were also of a practical mind and thus believed in aiding the Lord as much as they could. Seen in this context, the efforts of the Saints to establish a political Kingdom in preparation for the apocalyptic Kingdom became the application of the belief that, while man can accomplish nothing without the aid of the Lord, God only helps those who help themselves. This idea found expression by John Taylor, who once remarked that "It is not all a matter of faith, but there is some action required; it is a thing that we have to engage in ourselves."

Thus, the Saints had been engaged in temporal matters almost from the day the Church was founded. Experience in government they had gained in Kirtland, Missouri, Nauvoo and, most of all, in Deseret. "The time will come," predicted George Q. Cannon at a missionary conference in 1862,

> when . . . [the elders] will be called to act in a different ambassadorial capacity. The nations are not going to be all destroyed at once, as many have imagined; but they are going to stand and continue to some extent with their governments; and the kingdom of God is not all the time to continue its present theological character alone, but is to become a political power, known and recognized by the powers of the earth; and you, my brethren, may have to be sent forth to represent that power as its accredited agents. . . . Young men now here today may be chosen to go forth and represent God's kingdom. You may be called to appear and represent it at the courts of foreign nations. . . .

What Cannon failed to tell his audience was the fact that the Kingdom of God had already embarked on its political course, almost twenty years earlier.

In the spring of 1844, Reuben Hedlock, president of the British mission, received a letter from Brigham Young and Willard Richards in which the writers informed him that "the Kingdom is organized; and although as yet no bigger than a grain of mustard seed, the little plant is in a flourishing condition, and our prospects brighter than ever." Such news must have seemed strange to a man who had been actively engaged in furthering the Kingdom for some time, unless the term "kingdom" expressed here a more specific meaning than in its usual context which equated it with the church in both its spiritual and temporal manifestations. Young and Richards were, indeed, referring to the political Kingdom of God, whose governing body had been organized on March 11, 1844, as the Council of Fifty by the Prophet Joseph Smith himself. According to one of its members, this council was "the Municipal department of the Kingdom of God set up on the Earth, and from which all Law eminates, for the rule, government & controle of all Nations Kingdoms & tongs and People under the whole Heavens." In order to prepare itself for this ambitious mission, the Council met regularly in Nauvoo to discuss principles of government and political theory under the leadership of Joseph Smith. Before the prophet's death, "a full and complete organization" of the political Kingdom of God had been effected. The basic law of this world government, received through revelation, resembled the Constitution of the United States.

In keeping with a strong Mormon emphasis on the doctrine of individual rights, non-Mormons were to represent the Gentiles in the government of the Kingdom. Whether or not Gentiles actually sat as members of the Council of Fifty is difficult to ascertain, but the possibility points up a significant distinction between the church and the political Kingdom. When, after the death of Joseph Smith, George Miller and Alexander Badlam wanted to "call together the Council of Fifty and organize the Church," apostles George A. Smith and Willard Richards could inform the two petitioners "that the Council of Fifty was not a Church organization." Membership in that group was irrespective of religious beliefs; "the organization of the Church belonged to the Priesthood alone." But if the distinction between the church and the political Kingdom seemed important in one sense, in another it was highly theoretical, for the leading officers of both organizations were identical.

When David Patten became the first apostolic martyr of the church at the battle of Crooked River in Missouri, in October 1838, the doctrine of the political Kingdom of God apparently had not been fully formulated. And yet, even at this time the suspected Mormon ambitions to establish a political Kingdom of God figured prominently in the expulsion of the Saints from Missouri. The testimonies of a number of apostate Mormons before Judge Austin A. King at Richmond, Ray County, in 1838, insisted that Joseph Smith had in mind to establish a temporal Kingdom of God. These testimonies, given by enemies of the church, can hardly be considered accurate and unbiased. Some of them are obvious distortions of Joseph's plans, such as George M. Hinckle's assertion, that

> The general teachings of the presidency were, that the kingdom they were setting up was a *temporal* as well as a spiritual kingdom; that it was the little stone spoken of by Daniel. Until lately, the teachings of the church appeared to be peaceable, and that the kingdom was to be set up peaceably; but lately a different idea has been advanced—that the

time had come when this kingdom was to be set up by forcible means, if necessary.

But in the light of subsequent events the temporal if peaceful plans of Joseph Smith cannot be denied. The fact that Joseph Smith insisted on leadership in both spiritual and temporal matters also caused some internal difficulties in the church. Thus, refusal to acknowledge the authority of the church in temporal matters played an important role in the excommunication of Oliver Cowdery. Answering charges "for virtually denying the faith by declaring that he would not be governed by any ecclesiastical authority or revelations whatever in his temporal affairs," Cowdery declared:

> The very principle of . . . [ecclesiastical authority in temporal affairs] I conceive to be couched in an attempt to set up a kind of petty government, controlled and dictated by ecclestiastical influence, in the midst of this national and state government. You will, no doubt, say this is not correct; but the bare notice of these charges, over which you assume a right to decide is, in my opinion, a direct attempt to make the secular power subservient to church direction—to the correctness of which I cannot in conscience subscribe—I believe that the principle never did fail to produce anarchy and confusion.

But Cowdery's objections were shared by few of the Saints. Neither did the temporal claims of Joseph Smith deter the influx of converts to the city of Nauvoo after the expulsion of the Saints from Missouri, in spite of the fact that civil and ecclesiastical government were practically identical in that city. And to the faithful Saints, who were building the Kingdom by building their city, it may have been difficult to imagine how it could have been otherwise. Thus, they would see no incongruity when their prophet made the celebration of the eleventh anniversary of the organization of the church not only the occasion for the laying of the cornerstone of their new temple, but showed himself head of the Nauvoo Legion in an impressive display of newly acquired temporal power. Carried away by their enthusiasm, the Saints believed that in time this power would be able "to rescue the American Republic from the brink of ruin." Exulted the *Millennial Star:*

> Nauvoo . . . is the nucleus of a glorious dominion of universal liberty, peace and plenty; it is an organization of that government of which there shall be no end—of that kingdom of Messiah which shall roll forth, from conquering and to conquer until it shall be said, that *"the kingdoms of this world are become the kingdoms of our Lord, and of His Christ,"* "AND THE SAINTS OF THE MOST HIGH SHALL POSSESS THE GREATNESS OF THE KINGDOM UNDER THE WHOLE HEAVEN."

The editor of the *Millennial Star* most likely did not know that shortly before this article appeared Joseph Smith had received his revelation concerning world government and the organization of the Council of Fifty. Gentiles, of course, were even less informed about Joseph Smith's plans for the organization of the political Kingdom of God. But after the Council of Fifty had been organized in 1844, its existence may have been kept secret for a while, but not its activities. For it was this Council which organized and supported Joseph's candidacy for the President of the United States as one of several alternatives for the possible establishment of the political Kingdom. Negotiations were also entered in with Sam Houston for the acquisition of a large tract of land in the Texas region as an alternate possibility for the settling of the Saints and the establishment of the Kingdom of God. Furthermore, scouting expeditions were sent west to explore yet another possible location for the future Kingdom.

The secrecy of Council of Fifty deliberations may well have been a protective measure not only against the possibility of misunderstanding by the Gentiles but by the Saints as well. Benjamin F. Johnson, one of the charter members of the Council of Fifty, declared that only after attending some of its meetings did he and his associates begin,

. . . in a degree to understand the meaning of what he [Joseph Smith] had so often publicly said, that should he teach and practice the principles that the Lord had revealed to him, and now requested of him, that those then nearest to him in the stand would become his enemies and the first to seek his life.

But secrecy, to some degree, destroyed its own purpose, for it contributed to false rumors and half truths which gave to the political Kingdom, in the eyes of Gentiles and apostates, the aspect of the sinister and the subversive. The opposition that led directly to the assassination of the prophet was partly caused by rumors "that the Mormons entertained the treasonable design, when they got strong enough, of overthrowing the government, driving out the old population and taking possession of the country, as the children of Israel did in the land of Canaan." The Laws and Foster, in the *Nauvoo Expositor,* objected, among other things, against "any man as king or lawgiver in the church." Wilson Law, after his excommunication, even made an attempt to obtain a warrant against Joseph Smith for treason on the grounds that on one occasion, while listening to the prophet preaching from Daniel 1:44, he heard him declare "That the kingdom referred to was already set up, and that he was the king over it." Governor Ford, in his *History of Illinois,* gives a highly imaginative account of Joseph's temporal aspirations, the source of which must ultimately be sought in the secret deliberations of the Council of Fifty:

It seems, from the best information that could be got from the best men who had seceded from the Mormon Church, that Joe Smith about this time conceived the idea of making himself a temporal prince as well as spiritual leader of his people. He instituted a new and select order of the priesthood, the members of which were to be priests and kings temporally and spiritually. These were to be his nobility, who were to be the upholders of his throne. He caused himself to be crowned the anointed king and priest, far above the rest; and he prescribed the form of an oath of allegiance to himself, which he administered to his principal followers. To uphold his pretensions to royalty, he deduced his descent by an unbroken chain from Joseph the son of Jacob, and that of his wife from some other renowned personage of Old Testament history. The Mormons openly denounced the government of the United States as utterly corrupt, and as being about to pass away, and to be replaced by the government of God, to be administered by his servant Joseph.

Had fact and fiction, curiously intermingled in this document, been separated, and had Governor Ford and the enemies of Mormonism been informed of the truth concerning the Kingdom of God—that it was to be established entirely by peaceful, legal means, and that the Saints believed that worldly governments would dwindle of their own accord, or rather by their wickedness—persecution would most likely have been just as relentless. Theocracy, no matter of what form, was highly obnoxious to most mid-nineteenth-century Americans. The Saints themselves were not unaware of the fact that kingdom-building was a major cause for persecution and to a large degree responsible for the death of Joseph Smith. E. W. Tullidge, writing in the *Millennial Star,* observed:

It is because there has, day after day, and year after year, grown up and fast spread in America a realization, and with it a fear of the empire-founding character of "Mormonism" and the "Mormons," that this Church has such heartrending pages in its history. It is because of the growth of this presentiment and fear that a Joseph, a Hyrum, a Parley, a David Patten, and many others of the chief Elders and Saints have been directly or indirectly Martyred.

Martyrdom, however, contrary to Gentile hopes and expectations, proved no deterrent to Mormon ambitions of building the Kingdom. If anything, the Saints continued their efforts with renewed vigor.

How deeply the idea of the establishment of a theocratic Kingdom of God had been embedded in Mormon thinking was revealed by the succession controversy and its resulting schisms. Alexander Badlam and George Miller, as mentioned previously, wanted to "call together the Council of Fifty and organize the Church." Lyman Wight, who led a colony of Saints to Texas, likewise considered the authority of the Council of Fifty superior to that of the Quorum of the Twelve, and lamented the fact that the reorganization of the church had not taken place under the leadership of the legislature of the Kingdom of God. Splinter groups such as the Hedrickites, Morrisites, Bickertonites, and Brewsterites attempted to establish theocratic governments. Gladden Bishop, who attracted a group of Wisconsin Saints to his cause after the death of the prophet, organized, according to one observer, "what he calls the Kingdom of God, and it was the queerest performance I ever saw." James Strang, one of the most vociferous claimants to the mantle of the prophet, insisted on the establishment not only of a church but a political Kingdom of God and had himself installed as king of a theocratic community on Beaver Island. If Strang may never have been a member of the Council of Fifty himself, his organization, nevertheless, looked like a highly garbled product of that Council. The fact that Strang claimed two former members of Joseph's legislature of the Kingdom as his followers would suggest that any similarities betwen Smith's ideas of the Kingdom and those of his self-styled successor were more than coincidental.

It seems only logical to assume, then, that Brigham Young, whose claim as the rightful heir to the mantle of the prophet was sustained by a special conference of the Church held in Nauvoo on August 8, 1844, would continue the organization of the political Kingdom of God. Under his practical leadership, the Council of Fifty assumed the responsibility of directing both the policies and the administration of the government of Nauvoo. Even more important, the group resumed its earlier activities of looking for a place where the Saints could settle peacefully and establish the Kingdom without Gentile interference. As a result, the Council of Fifty was both to organize and direct the exodus of the Saints to the Rocky Mountains.

It seems not surprising, then, that the Gentiles would capitalize on rumors of the existence of a secret council in the city. In a writ issued for the arrest of prominent citizens of Nauvoo for treasonable designs against the state mention was made, among other things, of a private council of which the accused supposedly were members. And John S. Fullmer, a member of the Council of Fifty, reported while on an errand for the Council that

> . . . the apostates are trying to get up an influence with the President of the United States to prevent the Saints emigrating westward, and that they have written to the President informing him of the resolutions of the General Council [Council of Fifty] [sic] to move westward, and representing that Council guilty of treason, etc.

But as subjective a term as treason leaves wide room for interpretation;

and neither the federal government nor the Council of Fifty saw any impediments that would prevent Mormon men from wearing the uniform of the U.S. Army. If one member of the Council of Fifty, no doubt voicing the sentiments of many of the Saints, nevertheless declared that he "was glad to learn of war against the United States and was in hopes that it might never end until they were entirely destroyed," such a statement must be recognized as an expression of hyperbole caused by the intensity of the persecution. Furthermore, the fine distinction made by Brigham Young betwen loyalty to the Constitution and "the damned rascals who administer the government" was no doubt adopted by most Mormons who saw in this expression a possibility of reconciling American patriotism with kingdom-building. Words that must have inevitably sounded like treason to Gentile ears might well have been uttered, then, by a faithful Mormon who may have considered himself an exemplary patriot. But the enemies of Mormonism, understandably enough, refused to accept what to them may have appeared merely a semantic distinction. And sand and sagebrush proved little more of a barrier than semantics. As a result, controversy followed the Saints to their refuge; only too soon, the halls of Congress would pick up the echoes of conflict from the everlasting mountains and keep them reverberating until not only polygamy, but the political dreams of a Mormon empire, likewise, would be crushed.

But in 1847 and the years immediately following these dreams seemed on the verge of realization. Guided by Brigham Young and the Council of Fifty, the Saints, under heroic sacrifices, began to carve a verdant empire from an arid desert. The reins of government for this empire in embryo were placed in the hands of the Council of Fifty, which controlled the legislature of the state of Deseret and established its ambitious boundaries. Exulted the *Millennial Star:* "The nucleus of the mightiest nation that ever occupied the earth is at length established in the very place where the prophets, wrapt in sacred vision, have long since foreseen it." Brigham Young himself, in a sermon to the Saints, declared that the Kingdom of God was "actually organized and the inhabitants of the earth do not know it." That he was referring to the political Kingdom and not its spiritual counterpart was made clear in the context of the sermon. President Young made this statement in 1855, although the establishment of territorial government in 1851 had, at least nominally, ended theocratic government. This change, however, had diminished the controlling influence of the Council of Fifty but little and was, furthermore, looked upon as merely an expedient until the Saints could obtain statehood for their commonwealth. Statehood, in pre-Civil War days, would have given the Council of Fifty virtually a free hand in regulating the affairs of the Kingdom of God. Frank Cannon's contention that the Mormons attempted to gain admission to the Union in order to escape the Union's authority, as paradoxical as this may sound, has, then, a kernel of truth in it. Thus it was not polygamy alone which was to keep Utah under the rule of carpet-bag federal officials for such a long time.

The opposition which the Kingdom of God was to encounter in its new Zion already began to rise dimly on Utah's political horizon in 1849. If a prophet could have had access to a letter in the territorial papers of the U.S. Senate, referred to the Committee on Territories on December 31, 1849, he would have recognized accusations that were to be reiterated again and again, for over fifty years. This petition of William Smith, brother of the prophet Joseph and former member of the Council of Fifty, and "others, members of the Church of Latter-day Saints, against the admission of the Salt Lake Mormons into the Union as a State," maintained that the petitioners

. . . know most assuredly that Salt Lake Mormonism is diametrically in opposition to the pure principles of virtue, liberty, and equality, and that the rulers of the Salt Lake Church are bitter and inveterate enemies of our government. They entertain treasonable designs against the liberties of American freeborn sons and daughters of freedom. They have elected Brigham Young, (who is the president of their church) to be the Governor of the proposed State of Deseret. Their intention is to unite church and state and whilst the political power of the Roman pontiff is passing away, the American tyrant is endeavoring to establish a new order of political popery in the recesses of the mountains of America. . . .

If the Saints failed to obtain statehood for Deseret in 1850, however, this was not so much due to possible Mormon antagonism in Congress, which at this time was negligible. But the sectional controversy over slavery worked just as effectively to frustrate Mormon ambitions. Territorial government for Utah was one of the results of the compromise of 1850.

The arrival of federal officials in the summer of 1851 gave a preview of things to come. To their perhaps a little naive amazement they found organized government already well established. The celerity with which the Saints had responded to their new status and had called for the election of a territorial legislature and officers gave the newly arrived officials a vague feeling that the Saints were attempting to run things their own way. Whatever the causes for the speedy elections, it seems not unreasonable to suppose that the Council of Fifty may have thought it much easier to exert its influence on the formation of the new legislature without the supervision and interference of possibly unsympathetic Gentile members of the new government. This conjecture may serve as an added explanation for what the federal appointees, on their arrival, considered undue haste in the formation of the new government.

B. D. Harris, territorial secretary, flatly refused to recognize the legislature as a legal body. The secretary's obstinacy, and some unwise and tactless remarks by Judge Brocchus concerning the virtue of the ladies in the territory, touched off a controversy that was to give the Mormons a first taste of the difficulties with federal officials that were to plague them for forty years. If this explosion was ultimately to bring the "twin relic" into national prominence, the immediate cause for the conflict had, nevertheless, primarily been the theocratic nature of the new government. This controversy was to take on larger proportions in the not too distant future. For the time being, however, more serious difficulties were avoided by the rapid departure of the "foreign" officials from the territory.

President Buchanan's ill-starred Utah expedition of 1857–1858 was to a large degree a reaction of the northern Democrats to the Republican "twin relics" platform of 1856. This crusade against polygamy, however, threatened the political Kingdom quite as much, since the two seemed inseparably connected. When the first news of the approaching army reached Salt Lake City, Brigham Young seriously considered secession from the Union. In a speech on August 2, 1857, he declared:

> The time must come when there will be a separation between this kingdom and the kingdoms of this world. Even in every point of view, the time must come when this kingdom must be free and independent of all other kingdoms.
>
> Are you prepared to have the thread cut today? . . . I shall take it as a witness that God desires to cut the thread between us and the world when an army undertakes to make their appearance in this Territory to chastise me or to destroy my life from the earth. . . . We will wait a little while to see; but I shall take a hostile move by our enemies as an evidence that it is time for the thread to be cut.

But the superior strength of Colonel Johnston's troops and Brigham Young's good sense opened a wide interpretation to the term *hostile move*. The mediating efforts of Colonel Kane and the moderation and tact of Governor Cumming further convinced President Young that the Lord apparently did not want the thread cut at this particular time, and the conflict found a peaceful solution.

Young's speech, however, had made it clear that irrespective of historical exigencies the political Kingdom of God was bound to achieve independence. But if the Lord would indicate to the Saints when the propitious moment for cutting the thread with the world had come they must be prepared. They must watch themselves for the time when the political Kingdom of God could send its accredited ambassadors abroad.

The outbreak of the Civil War seemed to portend the speedy consummation of these hopes. Joseph Smith himself had predicted that war, beginning in South Carolina, would envelop the earth and lead to the "full end of all nations." The destruction to be poured out over the United States was to be a punishment for her failure to redress the wrongs committed against the Saints. Such failure, predicted the Prophet Joseph, would result in the utter destruction of the government. "Not so much as a potsherd [would] be left." Remembering these prophecies, the church leaders predicted the inevitability of conflict even before the outbreak of hostilities. Anti-Mormon writers charged the Mormons with desiring a Confederate victory. What the Saints really seem to have hoped for, at least during the beginning of the war, was a mutual destruction of both sides. Such expectations find expression in the diary of Charles Walker who, in 1861, wrote:

> The Virginians are preparing to seize the capital at Washington, and where it will end they know not, but the Saints know and understand it all. . . . Bro. Brigham spoke of the things in the East said he hoped they would both gain the victory said he had as much sympathy for them as the Gods and Angels had for the Devils in Hell.

But whatever the rhetorical expressions of the Mormons and their leaders, no openly hostile actions toward the government occurred. The Saints assumed a waiting attitude; if the Lord saw fit to permit the destruction of the United States they would be ready to take over. Declared Heber C. Kimball: "We shall never secede from the Constitution of the United States. We shall not stop on the way of progress, but we shall make preparations for future events. . . . God will make the people free as fast as we are able to bear it."

In keeping with this idea of preparedness, the Council of Fifty held itself in readiness to take over when other earthly governments would have crumbled. After it had failed to obtain statehood for its revived state of Deseret in 1862, the Council nevertheless continued the state organization in the enigmatic meetings of the so-called ghost legislature of Deseret which convened the day after the close of the session of the territorial legislature during the 1860s. A private message given to this "legislature" by Brigham Young in 1863 reveals its nature and its purpose:

> Many may not be able to tell why we are in this capacity. I do not think that you see this thing as it is. Our organization will be kept up. We may not do much at present in this capacity, yet what we have done or shall do will have its effect. . . . This body of men will give laws to the nations of the earth. We meet here in our second Annual Legislature, and I do not care whether you pass any laws this Session or not, but I do not wish you to lose one inch of ground you have gained in your

organization, but hold fast to it, for this is the Kingdom of God. . . . We are called the State Legislature, but when the time comes, we shall be called the Kingdom of God. Our government is going to pieces, and it will be like water that is spilt upon the ground that cannot be gathered. . . . I do not care whether you sit one day or not. But I do not want you to lose any part of this Government which you have organized. For the time will come when we will give laws to the nations of the earth. Joseph Smith organized this government before, in Nauvoo, and he said if we did our duty, we should prevail over all our enemies. We should get all things ready, and when the time comes, we should let the water on the wheel and start the machine in motion.

But with the victorious emergence of the Union from the Civil War the Council of Fifty would have to find other ways of establishing the Kingdom, and the meetings of the ghost legislature were finally abandoned. There seemed to be no need for keeping the wheel in working order when water apparently was nowhere in sight.

Mormonism itself, nevertheless, seemed viable enough even to its enemies that it apparently would not suddenly fall apart like Oliver Wendell Holmes' celebrated "One Hoss Shay." If vigorous measures seemed indicated to bring it to its doom, the cessation of polygamy alone, which became the avowed primary cause for persecution, would not automatically stop anti-Mormon attacks. The suspected activities of the political Kingdom of God, to some Gentiles, served as quite as important a cause to renew the crusade for the eradication of Mormonism. John Hyde, for instance, a Mormon apostate, declared: "As a religion, Mormonism cannot be meddled with; as a civil polity it may." "From its very inception," maintained another enemy of the church, "Mormonism has . . . been essentially a politico-religious organization, and as such, has clashed with the governmental institutions of every state and territory in which it has acquired habitat."

This clash was to intensify with the increased influx of Gentiles into the territory after the advent of the railroad in 1869. The economic activities of these outsiders threatened the identity of the political Kingdom by drawing it into the economic pattern of the surrounding areas, largely dominated by eastern capital. As a result, the Council of Fifty had to tighten its muscles to protect the Kingdom of God. A program of defensive economic action, stressing self-sufficiency through home manufacture and boycott of Gentile merchants, was, according to the evidence available, decided upon by the Council of Fifty. Its implementation the Council placed in the hands of the School of the Prophets. Under the leadership of the "schools," almost every Mormon community in the territory saw the establishment of a cooperative store.

It is understandable, then, that waning profits would bolster the anti-Mormon sentiments of Gentile merchants and lead to their support of such proposed anti-Mormon legislation as the Cullom Bill of 1870, aimed at wresting political control from the Saints through increased federal controls.

During the 1870s and 1880s, a veritable flood of printer's ink inundated the presses and carried a wave of anti-Mormon sentiment across the country. This sentiment, to be sure, was primarily directed against polygamy and, in retrospect, had somewhat drowned out the voices of those who saw the political Kingdom of God as Mormonism's greatest threat to America. These latter voices, however, were often raised in such a shrill tone that they could be heard even through the din of the anti-polygamy crusade. Beadle, for instance, author of the notorious *Life in Utah,* insisted that it was "the union of Church and State, or rather, the absolute subservience of the State to the Church, the latter merely using the outside organization *to carry into effect decrees already concluded in secret council,* that makes Mormonism our enemy." The following excerpt from one of the numerous anti-Mormon pamphlets of the period further illustrates this position:

Had Deseret been admitted as a state of the Union, the States would been [sic] confronted not only by polygamy, a foul blot upon civilization, but by a state dominated by an autocratic hierarchy, whose cardinal principle it is that the so-called 'Kingdom of God on Earth,' i.e., the Mormon Church-State [sic] is the only legitimate government on earth, and that all other states and nations must eventually acknowledge its sway. The expurgation of this incubus upon the nation would undoubtedly have involved a civil war.

Another pamphlet, entitled *The Mormon Conspiracy to Establish an Independent Empire to be called the Kingdom of God on Earth; the Conspiracy Exposed by the Writings, Sermons and Legislative Acts of the Prophets and Apostles of the Church,* published in Salt Lake City by the Tribune Company, assessed the role of polygamy in the fight against the Kingdom of God:

Congress after Congress has been importuned by the saints for the privilege of coming in [to the Union], but the request has been denied each time, wholly on account of the polygamous practices of Utah's people, which they could not give up. How strange it is, that a matter of comparatively small consequence to the nation as polygamy is, should have served as the sole means of many years to hold in check this diabolical conspiracy for the founding of a theocratic empire in the very heart of the greatest and freest Republic the world has ever known!

However much Mormon ambitions were exaggerated and distorted, these articles, in places, nevertheless come close to the truth. The Saints were certainly not engaged in any evil and insidious conspiracies, but, as demonstrated through the activities of the Council of Fifty, the Kingdom of God was definitely more than merely an ecclesiastical concept.

The death of Brigham Young in 1877 apparently terminated the activities of the Council of Fifty until shortly before the reorganization of the First Presidency of the Church under John Taylor. In the spring of 1880, George Q. Cannon, prominent member of the Council of Fifty and congressional representative of the Territory in Washington, forwarded the records of the Council of Fifty, which he held in custody, to the leaders of the church. On April 10, the reorganization of the Council took place at the Council House in Salt Lake City.

This reorganization takes on special significance in the light of the political circumstances of Utah in 1880 and the following years. In 1879, the U.S. Supreme Court had sustained the conviction of George Reynolds for polygamy. This conviction portended an intensified anti-Mormon onslaught. The available evidence suggests that the Council of Fifty may have become a central committee to direct the defense of the Kingdom. A somewhat cryptic letter by L. John Nuttall, a recent member of the Council, to Bishop William D. Johnson of Kanab, seems to indicate that the Council of Fifty either expanded its organization, or else created subsidiaries to meet with the new emergency. But with the passing of the Edmunds law in 1882, and the Edmunds-Tucker law in 1887, even a Council of Fifty proved powerless to protect polygamy and the political Kingdom of God from destruction. In 1890, the leaders of the church decided to submit to the demands of the government.

With the proclamation of the *Manifesto* not only polygamy ceased to be an issue in Utah politics, but the political Kingdom of God, likewise, gradually lost its controversial nature. A new era in Utah politics obviously had no room for the activities of a Council of Fifty. Thus, with the main causes for persecution removed, Mormonism, in the eyes of the world, became gradually acceptable, finally respectable. A new era had dawned. During this second period of Mormon history the Saints looked upon the restoration of the gospel primarily as a preparation for the Kingdom of Heaven. A carefully worked out plan of salvation, as revealed by Joseph Smith, still required many spiritual and temporal duties of the faithful; but dreams of a political Kingdom of God had faded away into a dim and almost forgotten past.

Statehood for Utah:
A Different Path

HOWARD R. LAMAR

If the Saints, as Hansen has shown, reluctantly surrendered their quest for the political Kingdom of God, they did not yield their pursuit of political self-determination. To the Mormons, the achievement of statehood for Utah would be a means to this end. But for the nation, the Mormons constituted a cultural crisis. How could the American people assimilate a community with institutions so divergent from accepted Protestant standards? Howard R. Lamar gives a cogent explanation of how such a difficult process could be effected within the context of the American political tradition. Significantly, as Lamar observes, the accommodation was accomplished with such finesse that both sides felt they had achieved a victory. The Mormons were able to accept the compromise without surrendering anything essential to their faith. They had come full circle: by leaving behind the political Kingdom of God and polygamy they were left free to continue their original search for a religiously homogeneous community. They still had their prophet, their priesthood, and their sacred books while the nation was now willing to let them continue their pursuit of community largely unmolested.

To suggest that Utah achieved statehood by pursuing a different path from that of other territories is but to repeat the obvious. What other territory began with a government which was run largely by a church operating through an informal but partially invisible Council of Fifty? What other territory during a time of peace has been declared in rebellion against the United States and has been occupied by a federal army? What other continental territory has been the subject of so much special legisla-

Howard R. Lamar, "Statehood for Utah: A Different Path," *Utah Historical Quarterly*, XXXIX (Fall 1971), pp. 308–327. Reprinted by permission of the publisher. This was originally an address given at the 1970 annual meeting of the Utah State Historical Society. Footnotes deleted by permission.

tion, appointive commissions, and exceptional judicial control? What other territory has had to abandon cherished domestic institutions by manifesto, formally declare separation of church and state, and deliberately create national parties in order to get into the union? That Utah's course was unique seems clear. If one views Utah's path to statehood on the occasion of its seventy-fifth anniversary of statehood, however, it tells us as much about American beliefs and values as it does about the distinctive values of members of the Church of Jesus Christ of Latter-day Saints. From the vantage point of 1971 it also begins to look as if the conflict was not so much between American and Mormon values and institutions as it was between a so-called WASP-American view of American values and a Mormon adherence to and espousal of values which, they, too, could argue, were "as American as apple pie."

To explore this argument let us begin with the history of the Mormons as portrayed in American history textbooks. There we are usually told that the Latter-day Saints are a fine example of a burgeoning native American religion born during a period of great millennial, spiritualist, and transcendentalist fervor in the United States. Such comments imply that the Saints started with basic American premises and a home-grown philosophy and tradition. We are told, for example, that the Mormons developed the mysticism which Puritans suppressed in Congregationalism while adopting the often contrary strains of communitarianism, capitalism, millennialism, and manifest destiny so dominant in the age of Jackson. Yet most nineteenth-century accounts see the Mormons as so different that by 1850 they were not only out of the mainstream, they had become, as David Brion Davis has observed in his brilliant article, "Some Themes of Counter-Subversion," the arch symbol of evil subversives to the American public.

It is doubtful that any accusation—apart from questioning the sincerity of their religious beliefs—so angered the Saints as the charge of un-Americanism. In an effort to reconcile or partially explain the assertion that the Mormons had an American religion but were un-American, I wish to argue that building on themes and premises in the American tradition they have taken a different but essentially American path and by so doing helped further define, explore, test, and reveal some fundamental American political beliefs. From the beginning they demonstrated that, like the federal Union with its theory of divided sovereignty, the so-called American tradition was ambivalent, contradictory, and subject to many interpretations. Indeed, one of the difficulties the American historian has with Jacksonian Democracy—the period in which Mormonism began—is that to so many groups democracy meant so many things. To the Brook Farm intellectuals it meant one course of action, to the Shakers another, to Robert Dale Owen another, and to the Whigs, Democrats, States Rights Southerners, and to abolitionists yet other things. America is useful for proving things before untried, the aged James Madison—inventor of divided sovereignty—is supposed to have shouted into Miss Harriet Martineau's ear trumpet. In retrospect it appears that the Mormons likewise tried new ideas, they also drew on both the spiritual and temporal traditions of the United States and in many instances pursued their implications further than anyone else dared or troubled to do. After most groups had abandoned millennialism and communitarianism, the Mormons pursued the idea of a practical gathering of the Kingdom until the end of the nineteenth century. Long after Brook Farm and New Harmony were a memory, and George Rapp's utopian colony had declined, the Mormons experimented with the United Order of Enoch in various Utah communities.

But what has this to do with statehood? A great deal, for defined social and religious goals, experience in practicing them, and persecution to test conviction and provide challenge, had created a true community of Saints before the first Mormons set foot in Utah. Such a community is the basis of a true state. Because they came as a coherent society rather than as individual pioneers who would eventually form a community and then a state, the 1849 Constitution of the State of Deseret was the symbolic expression of an existing condition and not a blueprint for a future commonwealth. The Mormons, as Dale Morgan has said, "simply elaborated their ecclesiastical machinery into a government."

Let us avoid arguments about the real motives which lay behind the 1849 Utah statehood movement and pass on to implications. Whatever the motive, one of the purposes of the proposed State of Deseret was not to bring law and order, but to keep lawlessness and disorder out. In so doing the Mormons took the then respectable doctrines of states rights and popular sovereignty and demonstrated that the doctrines could be used to protect an unpopular religion and its adherents as well as to defend freedom or a domestic institution such as slavery. Just as John C. Calhoun found in states rights a way to protect the minority from the tyranny of the majority, the Mormon statehood proposal was a way to protect a minority religion from the tyranny of a Gentile nation.

Statehood did not come in 1849, nor was the statehood effort of 1856 destined to succeed. By that time the doctrine of polygamy had become general knowledge and had added a vast new dimension to the issues of religious toleration and the protection of unpopular domestic institutions. It is significant that the Republican platform of 1856 not only promised to rid the country of the twin evils of slavery and polygamy, but it beautifully demonstrated what David Brion Davis calls a tendency to see all enemies as one no matter how disparate they may be.

In this case the early association of Mormonism and the slavocracy in the public mind was to endure for nearly half a century. Further the 1856 statehood movement coincided with the Utah rebellion and tested both the theories of states rights and the concept of popular sovereignty by raising the question as to who was supreme in the territories. The irony that it was James Buchanan, leader of the states rights party and future upholder of the Dred Scott decision, who sent an army to Utah has been noted by most historians. His actions simply revealed—four years before the Civil War—the limits of American middle-class tolerance for what it considered an un-American domestic institution whether it was polygamy or an unpopular religion. It illustrated what Calhoun had been arguing all along, that a majority could not be trusted to respect minority rights or dissent without strong guarantees. The Mormon troubles of the 1850s also suggest that in a country as democratic and heterogeneous as the United States was, the Mormons were certain to experience fundamental problems of social, political, and regional alienation from the mainstream even without the presence of such an explosive issue as slavery.

Of particular interest is the way events in Utah tested Stephen A. Douglas's theory of popular sovereignty. Briefly put, Douglas argued that Americans on a frontier are capable of self-government. And certainly actual events seemed to support his thesis: Oregon, California, Texas, Kansas and Nebraska, and the future territory of Dakota had all established their own provisional or squatter governments which had led, or would lead, to regular territorial or state governments between 1836 and 1860. Certainly Utah's State of Deseret deserved to illustrate Douglas's premise as well. After the Kansas–Nebraska issue had erupted into a national crisis, Douglas added a second interpretation by asserting that laws or institutions unpopular with the local citizens would never be upheld locally. Douglas's most famous statement of this argument was at Freeport in 1858 during the Lincoln–Douglas debates when he applied the principle to the problem of slavery in Kansas.

When it came to Utah, however, how far was Douglas willing to follow his own credos? Admittedly Douglas was hostile to the Saints because his Illinois constituency had disliked Mormons ever since the days of Nauvoo. When he heard that Utah was defending polygamy he urged in 1857 that the territory be divided between other territories or revert to the sole and exclusive jurisdiction of the United States. In either case non-Mormon courts could try Utah people for their crimes. Repeating most of the charges which anti-Mormon federal officials had filed in Washington since 1854, Douglas maintained that nine-tenths of the Mormons were aliens and were dominated by an all-powerful Brigham Young who wanted statehood for evil purposes. Therefore he urged repeal of the Organic Act for, said he, "you can never rely on the local tribunals and juries to punish crimes permitted by Mormons in that territory." Utah, unlike Kansas, was not to be allowed to practice home rule or popular sovereignty. Abraham Lincoln was quick to note that in backing down on self-government for Utah, Douglas had demonstrated what was "plain from the beginning, that the doctrine was a mere deceitful pretense for the benefit of slavery." Douglas's arguments bore some resemblence to those used by the Radical Republicans ten years later: namely that the South, having taken itself out of the Union by certain un-American acts, could be treated as conquered territory. The arrested logic of the anti-Mormons was also borne out by a Republican congressman, Austin Morrill, who said in 1857 that the Mormons were hostile to the republican form of government, favored slavery, polygamy, and violence, but worst of all, they were Democrats!

The theorizing was not all on the congressional side. When a Utah memorial asking for admission finally reached Washington in 1858 after the Mormon War had subsided, it is interesting to see Brigham Young arguing that the Ordinance of 1787 was directly contrary to the genius of the Articles of Confederation—an American constitution of which he approved. It was not without careful forethought that the memorial asked that Utah be given admission "as a free and sovereign State in the great *confederacy* of our republic."

Some historians have not seen the efforts of 1849 or 1856 as serious attempts to achieve statehood, or as being different, since the constitution presented to Congress on each occasion was virtually the same. But while the 1858 constitution still asked for the creation of the State of Deseret, the memorial of that year stressed that Utah had a republican form of government and was "another link in the chain of states" between the East and the West and could serve as a path to the Orient. Seeing the state as a "star shedding a mild radiance from the tops of the mountains midway between the borders of eastern and western civilization," the memorial represented both a step away from a policy of total isolation and a step toward some role as a geopolitical middleman. A legislative memorial of that same year exclaimed: "Withdraw your troops, give us our constitutional rights, and we are at home." Patriotic Mormon public rhetoric certainly did not reflect private Mormon feelings of anti-Americanism but it reflected an awareness of the situation they were in.

In carrying out the abortive statehood efforts of 1861–1862, Young, Delegate William H. Hopper, and George Q. Cannon used arguments familiar in most territorial statehood movements: a desire for full rights in the Union, a wish to be governed by local residents, and the ploy that statehood would save the federal government money. Young posed a bargain: the Mormons would be loyal and stay in the Union in return for statehood and home rule. But in this case the argument was particularly unpursuasive for the Mormons were handicapped more than they knew by the tyranny of the analogy between Utah and the South, the church hierarchy and slavocracy, polygamy and slavery, and the 1857 rebellion and southern secession.

If the curious juxtaposition of southerners and Mormons affected the public's views of Utah before the Civil War, the war itself was to have a profound effect on both federal and Mormon policies for the territory. On the congressional side, for example, the war established prededents of authority for the federal government, which before 1861 would have been considered unthinkable. Pursuing a theory of Congressional supremacy, Radical Republican congressmen were to use control of courts, disfranchisement, practice of discretionary appointive powers, and economic attrition both in the reconstruction of the South and in accomplishing what Richard Poll has called the "Political Reconstruction of Utah." Not only are the parallels between Utah policy and southern policy remarkable, the authors of the two policies overlapped like an interlocking directorate.

In April 1866, a Civil Rights Act sponsored by Congressman James M. Ashley of Ohio was passed by Congress giving federal district courts jurisdiction over all civil rights matters. The Freedman's Bureau Act and the First Reconstruction Act also circumvented southern state and local courts. Three months after the Civil Rights Act was passed, Ashley's friend and fellow radical, Senator Benjamin F. Wade, introduced a bill to circumvent Utah's courts. During the next three years other bills affecting Utah courts were introduced by Senators Aaron H. Cragin (in 1867) and by Ashley (in 1869) in which the theme of federal control was reiterated. Then in 1869 Senator Shelby M. Cullom introduced a bill to disfranchise polygamous Mormons just as leading southerners had been disfranchised in the Second and Third Reconstruction Acts. Utah citizens would have done well to listen to Senator Newton Edmunds of Vermont who said in February 1873 that "the Supreme Court has decided that no one of the provisions of the Constitution has any application as it respects what we may do in the territories." Such thinking led to the enactment of the Poland Act of 1874, which established further federal control over courts and juries in Utah.

Two years before Congress passed the Poland Act, Utah once again tried to gain statehood by holding a constitutional convention and by ratifying the proposed state constitution which it produced. While the memorial which accompanied the 1872 document used the standard argument for statehood—that the territorial system was an "inherently oppressive and antirepublican" colonial system run by nonresidents—the Mormons began to pursue a policy at this time which for want of a better term one may call a policy of superior virtue. The policy was simply to demonstrate beyond any doubt that the Mormons were not only good Americans but super-Americans in their habits, virtues, and patriotic loyalty. In 1872 this policy was manifested first by Mormon willingness to let non-Mormons represent them in Congress. Tom Fitch, the silver-tongued orator-politician from Nevada and Arizona who had been invited to Utah to help the statehood cause, was to be a United States senator; and Frank Fuller, the territorial secretary, was to be a congressman. Further, Brigham H. Roberts suggests that at this time the Saints were willing to let Congress present conditions for entry and have them submitted to a vote of approval by the people of Utah.

The Mormons also argued that they were overburdened with court cases, and if that seemed a plea for escape from prosecution as polygamists, it was also a plea for a restoration of their civil rights. The Saints would, in fact, soon take a stand that they were crusaders for civil rights. Still another argument using the virtue theme was that because of Mormon industry and energy the territory was now economically developed both in agriculture and mining. Unlike virtually all other territories Utah's warrants were worth ninety-eight cents on the dollar. It was not only fiscally sound to a remarkable degree, it was noncolonial in its economy and had as yet escaped the clutches of the national railroad monopolies. The argument that Utah was exceptionally virtuous in areas of endeavor where other territories were usually wracked by scandals was a solid one.

Equally significant was the constitutional clause providing for female suffrage, which the legislature had enacted by territorial statute two years before. However cynical one may be about the basic motives behind the decision to give women the vote in Utah at this time, it is clear that once again Utah carried to its ultimate point a long delayed promise of equality by realizing a goal of suffragettes everywhere while demonstrating the unusually ambivalent meaning equality and civil rights had for most Americans. As both Thomas Alexander and T. A. Larson have shown in recent articles, Congressman George W. Julian, a Radical Republican, had urged in 1868 that Congress give Mormon women the vote. Again the southern analogy is applicable. Julian saw plural wives as slaves of a sort and felt the vote would liberate them just as the vote was supposed to give the ex-slave equality. Upon reflection, however, both Julian and Congress decided that voting Mormon wives would simply echo their husbands. By 1878 Governor George B. Emery was urging the abolition of female suffrage in Utah.

If the proposed 1872 constitution for Utah represents the beginning of a politics of superior virtue and patriotism for the next two decades, it was paralleled by increasing control of Utah by the federal government.

With the passage of the Poland Act in 1874 the theme of court control became established policy. Governor Eli Murray—obviously reflecting the thought of certain senators—set the second theme when he wrote in his 1880 annual report: "Time will not prove the remedy. It is revelation (so-called) against statute law." Murray was rebutting those who said the transcontinental railroad would Americanize Utah. The governor proposed a return to a discarded form of territorial rule which had been used in the Old Northwest, Louisiana, and Michigan: a federally appointed council or commission to govern Utah. Council government had been justified in these territories by the fact that they had a non-American population which was presumably unready for self-rule.

Murray's suggestion eventually found elaborate expression in the Edmunds Act of 1882 which created the five-man Utah Commission. The role of that controversial body in the history of Utah is not the subject of this paper, but it is useful to note that the Commission was, among other things, a compound of the governing council of the Old Northwest and ideas taken from the Second and Third Reconstruction Acts. The compounding was symbolized by one of the few light moments in the debate over this important act. The Edmunds bill was opposed by southern Democrats and especially by Senator Joseph G. Brown of Georgia who used every opportunity to question Edmunds. On this occasion Senator Brown referred to the brass plates of the Book of Mormon. Edmunds replied that they were gold. Brown insisted over and over that they were brass. Finally the annoyed Edmunds said: "We will compound it and call it silver, which is a popular thing." [laughter]

Perhaps the greatest irony about the first Edmunds Act was that the bill would not have passed without the pressure exerted on members of Congress by Protestant churches and the national religious press. The coalition of churches and government to achieve separation of church and state in Utah again demonstrates what a limited and ambivalent meaning "separation" had for most Americans. At the very moment this crusade was taking place the government turned Indian agencies over to sectarian religious bodies to run. Under this portion of the "Peace Policy" the Episcopal Church in Dakota Territory became so strong it emerged as a major patronage force in local politics. At the same time the Catholic Church was so powerful in New Mexico it determined elections. Throughout the North, Protestant churches were involved in legislative struggles to curb Catholic educational and social policies. These ironies reached an absurd climax when it is remembered that Gentile missionaries brought religious schools to Utah to save education from Mormon "church" influence.

It was in the shadow of the recently passed Edmunds Act of 1882 that the fifth major effort to gain statehood took place in Utah. While all of the seventy-two delegates to the 1882 convention were Mormons several women were present, and elaborate committees drew up a long constitution which contained many clauses on education. This time the theme of superior virtue was stronger than ever. Listen to the words of the legislative memorial which justified the calling of the convention: " 'It is the right and duty of the people of Utah . . . to plead for and demand a republican form of government, so that they and their posterity may enjoy the blessings and liberties, to secure which the founders of this great nation lived, labored, and struggled and died.' "

The close—if new—identification with the American past was made even greater three years later when John T. Caine, speaking at a Mormon protest meeting against the injustice of the Edmunds Act, explained that in Utah in 1849 it was not a government of church and state, but a "government of the Church without the State" and exhibited "in modified form the influence which the pilgrim fathers exercised in the settlement of the New England states, and from whom we receive much of our civilization and the fundamental principles of our republican institutions." That same year Governor Eli Murray reported to the Secretary of the Interior that "a good Mormon cannot be a good citizen." Yet the evidence begins to suggest that by 1882 the beleaguered Saints had begun to identify themselves with what they saw as a true and ideal American republic, a republic whose freedom was in danger from the excesses of Gentiles in Congress. It was a very different republic, however, from the states rights confederacy which Brigham Young had espoused in 1858.

At the same time important changes were occurring in Washington. It is probable that the election of Grover Cleveland as President of the United States in 1884 was as significant a development for the history of Utah as the theories of congressional reconstruction had been after the Civil War. For the first time since Andrew Johnson's Administration a Democrat sat in the White House—a Democrat with strong southern backing. Even before Cleveland was elected, a proposal to extend and expand the Edmunds Act aroused some southerners nearly as much as it did the Saints, for they saw it as a threat to civil rights generally and specifically as more an attack on freedom of religion than on the domestic institution of polygamy. Senator Brown of Georgia urged Edmunds to forget the bill and instead to lead 50,000 New Englanders to Utah to convert rather than crucify. Then said Brown, "the whole state will adopt the more refined, delicate, voluptuous and attractive practices of the people of New England."

Cleveland and the Democratic party exhibited signs of sympathy for very practical reasons. If territories could be made Democratic in their party politics, they might become states and add Democratic senators to

Congress. The political efforts the Democrats engaged in to make solidly Republican Dakota, New Mexico, and Wyoming Democratic overnight ranged from serious intelligent maneuvers to absurd and laughable sleights of hand, but they engendered a statehood fever so widespread that by 1887 the Dakotas, Wyoming, Montana, Washington, New Mexico, and even Arizona were full of great expectations about admission. Here at last was a situation in which Utah might find a way to bypass the anti-Mormon Republicans in Congress—and the hated Liberal Party in Utah—and gain statehood by declaring for the Democrats.

Such hopes had dramatic results. Not only did embryo Republican and Democratic parties spring up in Utah, but Delegate John T. Caine was identified as a Democrat in Congress, and appears to have been encouraged by the Administration to try for statehood. Rumors of debates within the Mormon church as to the best way to achieve statehood implied that the church itself might split along party lines.

Given all these hopes it is wrong to suggest that the 1887 constitutional convention in Utah was but another response to new anti-Mormon federal legislation which in March 1887 took the form of the famous Edmunds–Tucker Act. Moreover, the policy of superior virtue reached a climax in this convention. Not only were the delegates all nonpolygamists, but only nonpolygamists voted at the time of ratification. Further, women did not vote on the document in order to avoid any accusation that the ratification vote might be rigged. The constitution itself declared polygamy a misdemeanor and guaranteed that the clause containing this declaration could not be changed without specific repeal by Congress. In effect the clause was made unrepealable.

This policy of superconformity was also reflected in the statehood memorial to Congress in 1887. "Congress has not imposed unusual requirements upon a new state, but the people have placed these restrictions upon themselves in order to meet prevailing objections and secure political harmony with the existing states." Then the memorial went on to say: "Virtually the whole population are desirous of becoming fully identified as a State with the institutions of this great republic and of taking part in national affairs as loyal and peaceful citizens." With the exception of the Liberals who boycotted the ratification election, the voting population of Utah declared strongly for statehood.

Despite all these extraordinary efforts the statehood movement of 1887 was unsuccessful. The failure was a bipartisan one in a way. Not only did the majority of the Utah Commission and the territorial governor still oppose statehood, a nonsouthern reform group of Democratic congressmen were unhappy about the burgeoning Mormon–Democratic alliance. The split in ranks came when Senator Samuel J. Randall, whom Delegate

Caine had failed to consult about Utah's admission, announced his opposition. Other Democrats began to back away from the issue and once again Utah failed to achieve statehood.

Meanwhile Senator Edmunds, supported by religious pressure groups, managed to pass the harshest of the anti-Mormon laws, the Edmunds–Tucker Act of 1887, which marked the high tide of Reconstruction legislation against Utah, for it allowed seizure of church property and dissolved the Nauvoo Legion, the Perpetual Emigrating Fund Company, and the church itself as a property-holding institution. The act also extended court control and instituted a test oath.

As had been the case earlier, southerners opposed the new Edmunds–Tucker bill. Their arguments about an invasion of rights and freedom of religion were familiar ones. As Senator Brown had done previously, Congressman Risden T. Bennett of North Carolina used humor to attack the 1887 bill. "This bill," he said, "should be entitled a bill to put the Mormon church in liquidation. We are going to appoint a receiver for the assets of the Lord." The test oath, he declared, was one of "the sharp weapons which young oppressives first learn to wield."

While the evidence presented here represents only a sampling, it looks as if the passage of the first Edmunds Act marked the point at which disinterested parties began to see the Mormons as basically good citizens who were being deprived of their civil rights. When such distinguished lawyers as George Ticknor Curtis agreed to defend Mormon Church officials during the 1880s the good citizen case became stronger. It also seems significant that the pro-Mormon pamphleteers began to defend their cause with exceptional decorum and propriety during the decade.

A new variation of the virtue theme apeared in the annual report of Cleveland's appointee, Governor Caleb West. There is, he said, a "bridging of the chasm that has separated the Mormon and non-Mormon people." The former were now helping in school matters, trade associations, Fourth of July celebrations, and were electing liberalized municipal governments. West himself felt that he might be able to declare for statehood once he could be sure there would be a lasting separation of church and state.

Another kind of psychological barrier fell in 1889 and 1890 when, after a decade of statehood movements, six western states were admitted to the Union. A desire to round out the Union of states had begun which was not to end until New Mexico and Arizona were admitted in 1912. But that trend, while important for Utah, was far less significant than the psychological impact of the famous and dramatic Manifesto of 1890 which seemed to settle the questions of polygamous marriages and of a church-dominated political party once and for all. Both the Saints and the Gentiles of Utah would undoubtedly agree that the Woodruff Manifesto of 1890 seemed a reversal, a turning point, and a surrender on the part of the church. In the perspective of time the Manifesto appears to be less of a reversal than the true climax of the policy of superior virtue and hyperconformity in public life, which brought the Gentiles around to a more tolerant view.

It would be misleading to say that after 1890 all was a bed of roses in Utah. Many federal officials remained skeptical; the Liberal party and its anti-Mormon friends in Congress died hard; the Utah Commission continued to be split between pursuing severe and lenient policies. Harrison's gubernatorial appointee, Arthur Thomas, remained deeply suspicious of the Saints. Within the church itself there were bitter fights between the older and younger generation of leaders, and over secular and religious policies. But there had been a remarkable shift. Governor Thomas himself reported as early as 1889 that not only had a marvelous change taken place, but he implied that the change had been effected by the Mormons themselves. By 1890 he was reporting that the happy, stabilized mining conditions in Utah were due to Mormon resistance to uncontrolled mining development in the territory.

By 1891 the doubting Thomas had even come to accept as sincere the Mormon commitment to a two-party system. "I believe," he wrote, "the mass of the people have gone into the party movement in perfect sincerity and that it is their present determination not to retrace their steps." Ironically, the first legislature elected on clearly national party lines behaved so badly, Thomas was disgusted with it. Progress in the thinking of Congress was also evident. In 1892 Congressman William Springer of the House Committee on Territories saw that polygamy was no longer the question; it was whether Congress would exclude Utah simply because a majority of her population belonged to one church. If that proved to be the case Springer felt that Congress, not Utah, would be guilty of faulty thinking.

From 1892 until statehood was achieved the policy of superior virtue and patriotic conformity continued to pay off. Harrison and Cleveland granted acts of amnesty to former polygamists; a return of church property followed; and Utah entered the final stages of the statehood movement. Governor West, who had succeeded Thomas, paid an unconscious tribute to such a policy when he wrote in 1893:

> I know of no people who, in their preparation for statehood, have been
> confronted with as delicate and grave questions and as radical differences,
> requiring the cultivation and exercise of the highest public qualities. Yet
> the responsibility has been met with patience and forbearance, and our

people, after years of earnest effort, have peacefully solved their difficulties and satisfactorily settled their differences.

It seems especially ironic that the church, by means of exercising its traditional power over the Saints and by pursuing a conscious policy, managed to create the image of the disciplined, virtuous Mormon-American whom the Gentile now admired and respected.

By 1894 Utah's path to statehood seemed a broad road unobstructed except for lingering Gentile suspicions and the usual partisan problems. The Enabling Act of July 1894 was followed in September by Cleveland's allowing ex-polygamists to vote. In effect, the national Administration was now vying for Utah's vote. The constitutional convention, meeting from March 4 to May 8, 1895, wrote an acceptable constitution and on January 4, 1896, President Cleveland signed the act admitting Utah as a state.

When news of admission arrived in Utah, Salt Lake City gave itself up to expressions of joy and celebration. The ceremonies attending the inauguration of the state government on Monday, January 6, were such a mixture of Gentile and Mormon, local and federal, military and civilian that one could call it a cultural, social, and political proportional representation ritual. Governor West was not present at the ceremonies, but he was so profoundly moved by the account of that day he congratulated both the Cleveland and the Harrison Administrations on the success of the federal government's wise, "firm and beneficent policy" which had resulted in statehood. One could also argue, however, that the policy was successful because the Mormons had decided it would be, for they, too, had worked out a policy which allowed them to adjust their beliefs and reverse their unfavorable public image as American subversives without disastrous results. What Saint need be bothered by a separation of church and state when such statements as one made by Brigham Roberts, on the occasion of admission, represented the new Mormon rationale. "It is the mission of the church to make men," Roberts wrote, "leaving the men to make the state—the community."

It is amusing and instructive to see what newspapers around the nation felt about statehood for Utah. The *New York Times,* suspicious and uncertain, simply remarked that the public had better watch out for the constitutional implication of Utah's coming into the Union as less than an equal state because of Congress's unusual right to pass on polygamy. The *Washington Post* admitted jealousy. Utah had finally escaped government by the infamous Commission, it noted, but poor Washington was still being ruled by an autocratic congressional commission. Such parochial responses were even more pronounced in the *New Orleans Times Picayune* and the *San Francisco Chronicle.* The former acted as if a very distant region of

Mongolia had joined the Union, and in a search for relevance, noted that Albert Sidney Johnston, a southerner, had been in Utah during the 1857 rebellion. The *Chronicle,* on the other hand, welcomed Utah into the Union and wished her well, but for a selfish reason:

> In one respect Utah is an enormously valuable accession to the family of States. She is sound as a dollar on the financial question. The Citizen of Utah, no matter what his political affiliation may be, is not to be persuaded that silver is not a true, genuine, historical and necessary money metal, or that the prosperity of the American people is not to be promoted by a return to free coinage.

The *Chicago Tribune* put the admission story on the front page and gave it full coverage by printing a short history of Utah and a special message by Governor Wells. Elsewhere Utah statehood was pushed aside by news about Venezuelan guerrilla activity, English problems in South Africa, and the appointment of a new poet laureate.

Three final observations about the different course of Utah's statehood struggle and the genuine Americanism of the state by 1890 seem pertinent. First, a reading of documents and speeches from 1849 to 1896 suggests that while Utahns were exceptionally proud of their pioneering heritage, the local subculture was not necessarily western and certainly not "cowboy" western. Utah became American by following paths different from those posed by Frederick Jackson Turner while coming to accept as gospel some of Turner's precepts about America. Second, Utah's achievement of statehood was due in part to deliberate change of the unpopular stereotype of the Mormon of the 1850s to that of the solid, energetic, conservative American citizen of the 1890s. Third, while church revision of the Mormon image may have begun cynically or to escape persecution, by 1880 the Saints had convinced themselves of their own true Americanism.

The genuine Americanism was dramatically demonstrated at the famous 1897 jubilee held in honor of Utah's fiftieth anniversary of settlement. There the pioneer theme was strong as floats depicting the handcart expeditions, the pony express, overland coaches, Jim Bridger's cabin, the first house, and the first saw pit in Utah came down the main street of Salt Lake City. For those pioneers present who had come to Utah fifty years before, there were gold badges but they had been made by Tiffany's in New York.

The celebrations featured a "wild east" show at which the celebrated Sie Hassan Ben Ali and his band of Bedouin Arabs did acrobatic and gymnastic feats. Bannock and Shoshoni warriors from Fort Hall danced war and ghost dances. A daring balloon ascension and parachute jump by Professor Wayne Abbott and the Leadville Drum Corps doing their sensational silent drill were featured highlights of the jubilee. But there were also fireworks at Saltair, baseball, concerts, baseball, operatic solos, baseball, and 1,000 children singing "How Like a Voice from Heaven" by Donizetti, as well as the "Pilgrim's Chorus" by Verdi. Billed as a "Pageant of Progress," it was also a sincere expression of middle-class American values and habits.

The image of the Mormon as super-American has waxed rather than waned in the years since 1896. A recent article in the popular French magazine L'Express suggesting that the young Mormon missionary abroad is perhaps the best representative of the true American "silent majority," indicates how consistent the devotion to middle-class values has been.

What larger meaning, if any, does the history of the statehood struggle suggest? Certainly it is clear that in trying to establish cultural and institutional pluralism in the United States in the nineteenth century, the Mormons came up against deep-set conformist beliefs, in defense of which anti-Mormon Americans proved to be willing to suspend civil rights, use force, and violate traditional Constitutional limitations on the power of the government. Today, once again we see various groups urging variations of cultural pluralism whether it be in behalf of Hispanos, Black Americans, women's liberation forces, or genuine social and political radicalism. Both they and the forces which oppose them, whether government or private, might study the long history of the difficulties Utah experienced before achieving religious toleration and cultural survival through home rule within the Union. In looking back over the history of Utah from the vantage point of seventy-five years of statehood, one can even say that the difficulties ended because both sides thought they had won. It was an outcome which neither group had predicted. Back in the 1860s Brigham Young is reported to have said to Delegate Hooper as he was boarding the stage for Washington: "Remember Brother Hooper, anything for Statehood. Promise anything for Statehood." In the light of history, that was a prophetic, positive, and even patriotic remark.

PART III

THE MORMON COMMUNITY: TWENTIETH-CENTURY CHALLENGES

Achievement of statehood for Utah in 1896 symbolized for the Mormons the end of one era and the beginning of another. The age of initiating settlements was over, and so too was that of confrontation with a hostile federal government. But rapid economic and social change brought new challenges.

By 1900 the state's economy was not developing rapidly enough to support continued large migration into Utah. Joseph F. Smith, President of the church, recognized this and emphatically told European converts in 1910, "At present we do not advise you to emigrate." There followed what one historian has termed a Mormon diaspora—the Saints increasingly had to look outside Utah for business and educational opportunities. But as Mormons left to make their homes in many parts of the United States, they had to reinterpret their concept of community: Where the community had been a region, now it became the local "ward," or congregation. Only in this limited society could the modern Latter-day Saint find the kind of intimate relationships he had enjoyed in agrarian Utah.

The twentieth century provided a different kind of challenge than that of mastering a frontier, bringing a need to maintain within the ward the same relevance to everyday life that had characterized the kingdom in an earlier age. The church responded with the expansion of several auxiliary programs which absorbed its members' spare time. These programs, which paralleled those of the institutional church in many Protestant denominations, included a broadening of the functions of the Women's Relief Society, the establishment of Sunday School classes for adults, an expansion of teenage programs to include Boy Scouts, dance festivals, instruction in speech and drama, as well as a full range of athletic activities symbolized by the incorporation of a gymnasium in most wards.

Meanwhile, major economic adjustments were also necessary for the church. As Leonard Arrington has shown in *Great Basin Kingdom,* the pattern of economic development in Utah was reoriented to resemble more closely that of the rest of the nation. Although the church had never prohibited private enterprise, the shift now was away from the cooperative enterprises of the nineteenth century and toward greater integration with the market-oriented businesses and industrial economy of modern America. Total economic isolation, of course, had never prevailed in Zion, but now even the ideal was no longer advocated. A new identification with the American big-business community may have contributed to the political and economic conservatism that characterized many high ranking church leaders. Among some churchmen William Graham Sumner's ideology, which Richard Hofstadter termed "Social Darwinism," became synonymous with church doctrine. The assimilation of conservative business values was at once an example of accommodation and an effort to preserve the integrity of the traditional faith. Thus J. Reuben Clark, Jr., a member of the First Presidency, reconciled economic individualism with the early Law of Consecration by emphasizing its capitalistic rather than its communal aspects.

Beginning in the early 1900s an increasing number of non-Mormons who were opposed to church domination of secondary education became influential in Utah political life. They were joined in their demand for state-supported public high schools by many church members, who not only preferred a more professional educational system but also objected to financing both church and state secondary schools. The movement for public high schools became so powerful that in 1920 the church turned over most of its academies to the state, and initiated in their place a seminary system which provided daily religious education to supplement secular learning.

Adjustments were also made at the level of higher education. Recognizing the need for Mormons to obtain advanced training in all fields, the church gave increased support to Brigham Young Academy, which advanced to the level of a university in 1903 and since then has expanded to an enrollment of over 25,000 full-time students, mostly Mormon, who are instructed in every aspect of secular knowledge. This investment was justified by the church not only on the basis of the need for secular training but also with the hope of tempering secularism with traditional religious values. At Brigham Young University the College of Religion, with indoctrination its primary goal, became central to the education process; all undergraduates were required to take religion courses every semester. For Mormon students attending other institutions of higher learning, the church provided adjacent institutes of religion which offered religious instruction and social activity and opportunities for regular church activities in student-oriented wards. Thus the accommodation to secularism in education was tempered with innovative institutional responses designed to maintain conservative values.

The increasing complexity of the modern world also made necessary the development of a new professionalism in other areas. Large numbers of professional and technical people who performed basically nonreligious functions were increasingly hired by the church on a full-time basis. These included business managers, attorneys, editors and publishers, building engineers, architects, communications specialists, computer programmers, and social workers. Church leadership, however, remained in the hands of laymen who resisted any effort to introduce a professional clergy. As a result, Mormon thought and church polity remained relatively responsive to the predilections of the common rather than those of professional theologians.

The institutional changes wrought in Mormondom corresponded with much of what was happening in the rest of the United States. But during the early part of the twentieth century Americans had experienced what historian Henry May calls "the decline of American innocence"[1]—the end of the long held faith that due to its isolation America had escaped the strictures of the Old World and had launched a new and more natural social order. By the 1920s many American writers began to view European culture with its tolerance and sophistication as more "natural" than their own, which seemed too tradition bound. During that decade and again in the 1960s the young revolted against confining archaic forms and standards. Yet in Mormondom the nineteenth-century idealism, the commitment to traditional moral standards, as well as the overriding sense of uniqueness, remained dominant. To the Mormons innocence was not a naive set of social values but eternal truth. Perhaps more rigorously than any other large group in the nation, the Mormons sought to maintain traditional ways. By the 1970s Mormondom had become in its ideals a microcosm of what America was, not what it was becoming. What emerged as part of the radical counterculture in the 1830s was in the 1970s strongly conservative.

[1] Henry F. May, *The End of American Innocence* (New York: Knopf, 1959).

Sources of Strain in
Mormon History Reconsidered

THOMAS F. O'DEA

In 1957 Thomas F. O'Dea, a sociologist, published *The Mormons,* a sympathetic but detached analysis of the dilemmas faced by the Mormon community in the modern world. In his trenchant chapter on "Sources of Strain and Conflict," he depicted several fundamental dilemmas confronting the church, including the disharmony between rationality and charisma, the contradiction between authoritarianism and the ideals of democracy and individualism, the dichotomy between patriarchal family organization and the ideal of female equality, and the conflict between political conservatism and social idealism. O'Dea believed that for most of the Mormons these sources of stress were not discomforting because they found satisfaction in the activities of the church. But for the intellectuals, there seemed an ambiguity which was often disillusioning, although many still remained committed to the Mormon community. Regardless of difficulties the church seemed to O'Dea to retain great vitality and flexibility which augured well for the future.

How would the same observer view Mormonism in the early 1970s when a new set of problems face both the church and the nation? At the invitation of the editors, Professor O'Dea wrote a new article early in 1971, especially for inclusion in this volume. Here he reconsiders some of the observations made in his earlier work and places the strains he perceived in Mormonism against a contemporary American background. Since the 1950s the problem of race relations has had some effect in creating an unfavorable public image of the Mormon community. O'Dea focuses on this issue as potentially diagnostic in an effort to determine how well the Mormon people are meeting the contemporary problems that confront their society. While the question of the relationship of black people to the church comprises the bulk of this article, O'Dea is

Thomas F. O'Dea, "Sources of Strain in Mormon History Reconsidered." This article has been especially prepared for inclusion in this volume.

really raising a more fundamental question: is the Mormon community preparing its members and converts to do whatever it is that man ought to be doing in this new, complex society? While placing the black issue in this broad context, O'Dea suggests that it has come to symbolize the threat of modern America to all that the Mormons hold dear—perhaps even the perpetuation of their unique community. At its crux the question is "What kind of society shall Zion be?" Such questions are always traumatic ones, whether they are asked by Mormons or by a broader community of Americans. How the church, as well as the nation, responds will, O'Dea suggests, go far toward providing an answer.

A decade and a half has elapsed since we examined in *The Mormons* various strains in Mormon life;[1] yet many of them remain real and visible within the church. The decade of the sixties continued to bring Mormonism into increasing contact with the larger non-Mormon world, with its challenge to religion and its eroding effects upon all provincialisms and traditionalisms. Moreover, internal developments in Utah and the intermountain West, still the Mormon homeland despite the vastly increased importance of the Mormon diaspora, brought fundamental change into the heart of Mormondom itself. The continued urbanization of the Wasatch Front meant that Utah was no longer primarily an agricultural community, and that the economic base upon which the Mormon way of life had traditionally rested was being completely transformed. Secularization and its consequences in public and private life were increasingly visible. Urbanization brought all the challenges of modernity in its wake. Salt Lake City continued to take on a metropolitan character with modern business practices, the latest consumer tastes, and the affluence of middle-class groups as visible an aspect of its life as the new freeways that run through the city to connect the valley with the world. All contemporary social problems were to be found in the heart of Mormondom, from juvenile delinquency to the high toll of highway deaths and from the use of drugs to the counterculture. One even heard rumors of "communes" in the canyons made up of "hippies" of Mormon background seeking to "modernize" and relive the spirit of the United Order, the socialistic Mormon communities of the nineteenth century. At the same time there existed Fundamentalist groups still practicing plural marriage and excommunicated from the church itself. There was, of course, student unrest, although even at the end of the decade the state university and college campuses in Utah were still orderly, their atmosphere still civil, and the general emphasis upon the importance of learning still quite dominant. At Brigham Young University, strict authoritarian regulation kept such phenomena as student unrest

[1] Thomas F. O'Dea, *The Mormons* (Chicago: University of Chicago Press, 1957). See especially pp. 222–263.

and the usual dramatization of student dissent in dress and hair style at bay. What unrest and discontent might lurk beneath the surface was not easily gauged, but a recent student poll showed that 38 percent of the student body did not conform to conservative dress standards set by the university.[2]

In the face of this continuingly changing situation, the Mormon church structure appeared not to have changed at all and there was little visible updating of policy. Earlier trends continued, as dramatically symbolized in the accession of President Joseph Fielding Smith, another nonagenarian like his predecessor. There was clearly visible the tendency for conservative religious people to ally themselves with conservative politics. This even assumed an extreme form when the John Birch Society found palpable sympathy, at times in high places, in the church. Yet Utah continued to vote more or less like the country as a whole. As it shared in the Roosevelt landslide of 1936, so it shared in the Johnson landslide of 1964. Moreover, in the 1970 election the liberal Democratic incumbent in the U.S. Senate was returned to office by a substantial margin, despite the somewhat strained efforts of the Republican Administration in Washington to unseat him. Most interesting was the fact that in 1970 the Wallacite American Independence Party ran candidates in Utah and did poorly, receiving around 1 percent of the total votes cast. It could be said that the older tendency for church leadership to be conservative and for the electorate to exhibit a considerable degree of political independence continued to be characteristic of the 1960s as it was of previous decades.

How did the Mormon church face this difficult decade of the 1960s, which brought change of a marked character to the nation as a whole? What ideas and what programs did it generate to enable it to grapple with increasing secularization? What contribution did it make to the understanding and facing by the American people of the new problems made visible by prolonged war and the managing of a highly developed industrial society? Did the older elements of agrarian thinking in much official policy-making give way to contemporary attitudes more appropriate to the new conditions? There is not available sufficient evidence to treat these questions adequately, but even the partial response possible at this time falls short of providing positive answers.

THE 1960S: A NEW SITUATION FOR CHURCH AND NATION

The decade of the 1960s brought many Americans a new and disturbing awareness that we as a people were undergoing a profound transformation,

[2] *The Daily Herald* (Provo, Utah), April 22, 1971.

one in which the destiny of the nation was fatefully involved, and whose basic character was far from clear. Every society is in a certain sense an acted out implicit answer to the question "What ought man to be doing here on earth being the kind of being that he is?" Every society enacts its answer under the press of concrete historical circumstances, and its answer —that is to say, its institutions, its goals, and its fundamental values—bear the marked influence of the conditioning exigencies. Americans have for two centuries settled the continent and built a vast advanced technologically based society; they have assimilated millions of immigrants into that society to produce considerable consensus; and they have created the world's most affluent community. In the process there was evident a seamier side, which involved violence, exploitation, deprivation, and banality. But to most Americans it seemed that their country was moving toward the fulfillment of their dream of a humane, prosperous, and demo- cratic society. It would take generations, but it would be done. Even the Great Depression of the 1930s did not succeed in overthrowing that idea in the mind of Americans, though it did indeed threaten it. But the decade of the 1960s appears to have brought into existence something new. There was doubt about the efficacy of technology, the authenticity of democracy, and the meaningfulness of the basic tasks that constituted the "world's work" for most Americans. The idea suggested itself to many that perhaps the acted out answer to the question of what man ought to be doing that had characterized American society up to the present was now becoming obsolete. The self-evidentness of our conventional values and the premises upon which our taken-for-granted sense of direction rested were being called into question. The youth especially harbored serious doubts, but they were far from alone in this.

For nearly a century and a half the Mormon church, as the nation as a whole, acted out its own answer to the basic question of what man *ought* to be doing. It was an answer that at first involved building a separated Mormon community embodying peculiarly Mormon values and a Mormon sense of direction, a Mormon notion of the goal of history. Later, defeated in conflict with the general American community and the federal govern- ment, it had to reconcile itself to that general community, but it continued to assert its own particular values in that general context. At all times its goals involved proselytization and the building up of the Mormon church itself.

Has the Mormon church too come to a place in its history where the concrete form in which it has acted out its answer to that fundamental question must now be reconsidered? Because the church now gives its answer not in the institutional form of a separated Mormon community, but within the context of the general American society, it would appear that the crisis of the larger society must in significant ways be its crisis too. Does indeed the Mormon church have significant tasks of its own in terms of which it acts out a meaningful answer to the constitutive question today? To ask how the church faced the 1960s is to ask to what extent such important issues have surfaced in the consciousness of church members and especially in the consciousness of the church leadership.

Mormonism's answer may be stated by saying that man was placed on the earth by God, after a period of preexistence, that he might continue to work out his own development, a progression that would in after-lives bring him to God-like status. The Mormon church and the immensely impressive settlement of the intermountain West long provided the institutional context and the active meaningful content of that developmental process. It has been suggested again and again by the church's critics, some even within its ranks, that the tasks that made Mormonism meaningful had been accomplished and that consequently Mormonism was becoming obsolete. In 1957, the present writer summarized the ideas of these critics as follows:

> The religious outlook of Mormonism, they say, met the needs of men in the first half of the last century, embodying for them meaningful and challenging ideals that inspired their undoubted heroism. These ideals and the action they infused combined with the circumstances of westward movement to evolve the greatly proliferated Mormon organization, which settled the intermountain West. The church and its institutions became a perfected expression of a pioneering cooperative community, a mighty instrument for taming the desert. . . . Now, say these critics, Mormondom has defeated its foes, but it has been frozen in the posture of combat and cannot relax and meet the new situation that victory brings into existence. It stands today, advocating and acting out the highly organized behavior that was both the product and the tool for dominating older pioneer situations. In short, it is their contention that the Mormon church is obsolete, that it has been the strategic weapon for conquering the wilderness, but that the measure of its success is at the same time the index of its obsolescence. The church, these critics claim, is an elaborate pioneering mechanism, a vast sociological apparatus nicely modeled for tasks now finished, leaving it functionless.[3]

At that time the writer felt strongly that those who held to the idea of Mormon obsolescence underestimated seriously the religious vitality of Mormonism. While he conceded that the church "was not so well adapted or prepared to meet new problems as it was at times in the past," he argued that it still provided "a meaningful context to great numbers of its adherents" and that its history of past flexibility, despite a palpable increase

---

[3] O'Dea, pp. 258–259.

in rigidity of structure and of attitude, and "its viability under the most diverse conditions," did not "augur badly for its future." He felt that those who saw the Mormon future as simply "a stereotyped lack of creativity and a routine running down" were wrong. "There is still too much vitality—the characteristic Mormon vitality—remaining for such a prognosis to be likely."[4]

How do such prognostications appear a decade and a half later? The changes that have come upon the country in this time have rendered every challenge more urgent and every inadequacy more fateful. Has the Mormon church met the newer, more intensified crisis conditions with any degree of adequacy? These are difficult questions, and any assessment will inevitably reveal some degree of individual bias for they involve profound existential implications. Yet to understand Mormonism and the sources of strain characteristic of the contemporary Mormon experience it becomes necessary that some assessment be attempted. The answers to these questions must be sought in performance. What did the Mormon church do during the 1960s and how does its performance measure up against the yardstick of the great problems that the spiritual crisis of that decade revealed?

First, it must be recognized that the Mormon church in 1971 still provided, as we said it provided in 1957, "a meaningful context for great numbers of its adherents." Moreover, it continued to achieve striking successes in the missionary field, especially in Great Britain and South America. These phenomena are signs of vitality and evidence of continuing viability. These are most important observations and they confirm the positive prognostications we made at the earlier time. Yet concerning these positive data certain critical questions arise. How satisfactory when weighed in the scales of the existential predicament of modern Americans and of men generally in the modern Western world is the meaningful context that the Mormon church still provides its adherents? In our prior statement we suggested some real problems in this respect. The modern state and modern secular institutions, we said, had taken over most of the nonreligious activities formerly carried out by the churches—welfare measures, education, recreation, and the like. We noted that this was a continuing trend and that it was especially important for Mormonism because it was these "typically this-worldly spheres of activity that Mormonism has emphasized," and that in the period ahead these spheres would be "precisely those areas of human action where more inclusive, more secular, and less peripheral organizations can make a more attractive appeal to the consciences and idealisms of men." Against that background it was noted:

[4] *Ibid.*, pp. 263, 262.

Moreover, it would seem a grave mistake for a religious movement to concentrate its attention on this-worldly activities, since it is precisely this-worldliness and activism that modern man appears to be finding inadequate. For organized religion to offer competition in spheres of life in which non-religious organizations do better—spheres themselves inadequate to the facing of deeper human problems—is to be found wanting. The basic need of Mormonism may well become a search for a more contemplative understanding of the problem of God and man.[5]

The meaning of life has become more consciously problematic for many during the last decade and a half. As a consequence we find experimentation with bizarre cults and syncretic religious movements. As a student of the counterculture observed, "At the level of youth we begin to resemble nothing so much as the cultic hothouse of the Hellenistic Period, where every manner of mystery and fakery, ritual and rite, mingles with marvellous indiscrimination."[6] In addition we find adult disillusionment, nihilism, and even despair. Again, particularly among the youth, we find new versions of older political ideologies appealing to many as offering some shreds of meaning and some sense of direction. Has the Mormon church spoken relevantly to these problems? Has it attempted to devise new programs to point the way to meaningful action that are in any way commensurate with the magnitude of the problems themselves? Or has it continued by and large its older, highly active and highly organized programs along conventional lines, programs that the critics of Mormonism a decade and a half ago saw as stereotyped routinization and fast becoming "activity for activity's sake"?

With respect to the remarkable success of Mormon missionary efforts, questions also arise. Conversion, as a sociological phenomenon, is not a matter of the spirit alone, nor is it simply involved with religious belief. In the nineteenth century the Mormon religious message combined with the attraction of the call to build Zion in the mountaintops to attract many converts. Once in the church these people found themselves involved in a task that assumed meaning for them in both a religious and a secular sense, and that, moreover, represented a genuine objective contribution to the development of America. What of today's converts? Do they join because of the call of a vocation that will give them subjective satisfaction and at the same time involve them in activities of authentic objective significance? Are they being involved in a movement destined to provide some degree of guidance for modern men caught in the various versions of the modern

---

[5] *Ibid.*, pp. 261–262.
[6] Theodore Roszak, *The Making of a Counter Culture, Reflections on the Technocratic Society and Its Youthful Opposition* (Garden City, N.Y.: Doubleday, Anchor Books, 1969), p. 141.

predicament? One becomes a convert to a church, to a religious movement, or even to a political movement because it appears to offer revitalization through new values, a genuinely worthwhile set of goals, and an authentic community. In the crisis conditions of our time, any community or doctrine that appears to offer something in this respect is bound to find adherents. We have noted that among the youth even the most bizarre find a following—at least for a time. But the question is whether there is really a viable objective basis for that subjective feeling, a basis grounded in both the subjective finding of a viable path to a more abundant life in the spiritual sense and a set of activities in the world of real significance as was the task of settling the intermountain West in the last century. Such a basis means that conversion really becomes an inner turning, out of which a creative transformation of the person comes about, one that eventually will have a vitalizing effect on the community about him. It clearly involves some activities in the world that will contribute to the search of modern man for relevant and authentic vocation and not simply the continuing acting out of older patterns fast becoming obsolete. It is possible for people to join religious or political groups because they find in them communal and ideological support for a defensive posture that enables them to survive amidst conditions of anomie, because they find in them surrogates and substitutes for deeper values, genuine community, and authentic vocation. Their conversions become the taking on of a shared defensive posture. Such a posture soon proves to be a halfway house and not a pathway to the solution of the homelessness and social anomie characteristic of our times.

Does the Mormon church offer its converts a pathway to significant living amid the great transition of our age or does it offer them a defensive halfway house in which they can escape the confrontation that modernity presents to them? Does it offer them a context for growth and maturation in the face of the enormous challenges of the times or does it give them an anachronistic community, segregated in spirit, that makes life easier but avoids precisely those challenges that the modern religious man must face if he is to find ethical and religious authenticity?[7] In short are the Mormon converts converted because they find in the Mormon church a deeper understanding of the divine–human encounter and consequently a more authentic religious life that enables them to live reasonably and ethically with the upsetting crisis of our day? Or are they converted because they find in the Mormon church a reinforcement of older values and attitudes that had been undermined and threatened by the conditions of

---

[7] I have discussed some aspects of this problem under the rubric of religion and maturity in Thomas F. O'Dea, *The Sociology of Religion* (Englewood Cliffs, N.J.: Prentice-Hall, 1966), pp. 101 ff.

our times? We cannot answer these questions; it is doubtful at this juncture if anyone can answer them. To find even tentative answers would require a large-scale study and subtle instruments of observation and interviewing, more subtle perhaps than exist at present. Yet such questions must be posed because we are dealing with the viability of a religious movement and the adequacies of its responses. Such questions delineate the universe of discourse within which a true appraisal of Mormonism in our day would have to be made.

It is obvious that because we cannot answer these questions we cannot make the kind of assessment that a profound appraisal of Mormonism would require. Perhaps, however, having posed such questions as a background to suggest the scope and profundity of the problem, we might have recourse to procedures that could offer us a partial view a partial suggestive answer to the problems involved in an assessment of the situation of contemporary Mormonism. There is one area of attitudes and activities in which Mormonism has been profoundly involved—not of its own choosing—and it is an area that has become diagnostic for the understanding of significant aspects of the present crisis in America. Perhaps the adequacy of the Mormon response in that area might indicate something about the adequacy of the Mormon position as a whole.

RACE: A DIAGNOSTIC ISSUE?

In the decade of the 1960s, two issues in the United States came to express and focus the American problem as it came to the surface of American consciousness. These issues acted as catalysts to precipitate in the awareness of many the inadequacy of our present acted out response to the constitutive question of what man ought to be doing. The first was the issue of race. The black man had been shamefully treated by Americans for three centuries. When the decade began he was, on the whole, the most ill-housed, ill-clothed, ill-fed, and poorly educated member of society. He was not part of the affluent society and he was typically deprived of civil rights, de jure in the South, de facto in the rest of the country. More and more, particularly in the minds of young people, the problem of the black population came to be the visible sign of the inadequacies of our achievements, the inauthenticity of our goals, and the unethical character of the way we lived our lives. The second issue to take on such catalytic significance was the war in Southeast Asia. We had entered that war without a formal declaration and we found ourselves vastly overextended with respect to men and resources. The question of *why* had to arise, and when it arose it brought with it a questioning of fundamental policy. Is this how a successful, technologically based, presumably democratic society allocates its resources? Is this the way we act out the meaning of man in America and of America in the world in the third quarter of the twentieth century? As the war continued, its costs in lives and treasure had an impact upon the national consciousness that brought an almost unprecedented bitterness of contention into American life.

At first the race problem seemed a leftover problem—the shamefully overlooked problem of Reconstruction. But as time went on and we saw how embedded were certain attitudes, and how far-reaching would be the reforms necessary to change matters, we saw that this question was also most diagnostic concerning our basic unstated beliefs and values—our real goals and our practiced morality. Race like war raised the basic question of how we should allocate our energies and our resources. Many in America began to feel that we should have to rewrite the script of the drama of our national life and change the plot thoroughly. Yet no one except the rigid and naive ideologies of the extreme right and left pretend to know how it can be rewritten. That does not mean, of course, that some reallocations are not fairly evident, and these appear to have a good measure of popular support.

The fundamental constitutive question of what ought men to be doing on earth, being the kind of beings that they are, became for many in this country the question of what ought America to be doing with its enormous productive potential, human and material, to lead men in this century in their quest for a meaningful and humane way of life. Against this background race tended to become a key symbol and a diagnostic issue. Attitudes toward racial justice came to indicate how seriously one took one's morals. Moreover, they indicated how deeply one grasped the new situation and its challenge which demands that Americans restructure their lives and reform their social order. Those who saw it only as a threat and wished to avoid it, or to keep it constrained within the conventional limits, showed themselves as poorly prepared to face ethically the great changes that will have to be made in the decades to come if America and the Western world are to make the great transition with some measure of success— indeed possibly if they are to survive, for the moral issue of race tests the willingness of men to give up old securities and old conventions in the search for genuine justice. Thus race became a diagnostic issue indicating how profoundly one saw the demands of human vocation in our day. For religious groups it was a particularly significant diagnostic element. Biblical religion claimed to point out to men in a most profound manner what human vocation really was. It claimed to provide the sense of direction and the ethical norms for genuine vocation; it claimed to bring man into an authentic relationship with God and to show him his true destiny, his real calling. How did the Mormon church meet the problem of race within its own ranks?

When the decade of the 1960s brought the issue of race to the fore in the Mormon church as it did in the country as a whole, Mormon history had already endowed the issue with a particularly Mormon significance. Here too Mormonism was typically American and peculiarly itself. It is a tragic fact that while the Mormons developed markedly favorable attitudes toward the American Indians, while they developed quite favorable attitudes toward the Jews—indeed they went far in overcoming the elements of traditional Christian attitudes that gave rise to anti-Semitism and toward creating a "new relationship to the old Bible people and its religious world"[8]—they developed a highly derogatory conception of the black man. Joseph Smith had made two kinds of statements during his career that could have affected Mormon attitudes with respect to blacks. It appears that the prophet took over many of the standard ideas and prejudices of his time and country on this question, and his earlier statements reflect such attitudes. In 1843, he seemed to change toward a more liberal attitude and when he was running for President of the United States in 1844, just before his death, he made statements that could have become the basis for a genuine Mormon abolitionism. It is the earlier attitudes that became accepted as scripture and revelation, while the latter became looked upon as merely the secular utterances of the prophet–founder acting in a merely political capacity.

The Mormon scripture chiefly involved in this matter is the Book of Abraham. Here Pharaoh is presented as a descendant of Ham and therefore "a partaker of the blood of the Canaanites by birth." Consequently he is seen as "cursed . . . as pertaining to the priesthood." Another Mormon scripture, the Book of Moses, declared that "a blackness came upon all the children of Canaan, that they were despised among all people." In 1836, a black, Elijah Abel, was given the priesthood, and some of his descendants may have been also—even as late as 1935[9]—but on the whole the church's policy became antiblack with respect to priestly participation. Since the priesthood is the institutional context within which all "worthy" Mormon males really participate in the church, blacks are in effect unworthy and cannot become full church members. Said a *New York Times* reporter in a study of this problem in 1966:

---

[8] Rudolf Glanz, *Jew and Mormon, Historic Group Relations and Religious Outlook* (New York: Published with the help of the Lucius N. Littauer Foundation, 1963), pp. 331–332.

[9] Wallace Turner, *The Mormon Establishment* (Boston: Houghton Mifflin, 1966), pp. 242 ff. It seems also quite possible that the church has "been ordaining priests who are part Negro" in Brazil. See *ibid.*, p. 263.

The most serious problem facing the LDS church today is the Negro question. The church has successfully become everyman's church— except it cannot be the African Negro's church. . . . The Negro is barred from the priesthood purely on racial grounds.[10]

It has been said that the Book of Abraham "in effect crystallized Joseph's hitherto vacillating position on the Negro problem."[11] At any rate attitudes originally inherited from the general cultural milieu of early nineteenth-century America took on theologized form within early Mormonism and affected its evolving position. Such tendencies were strengthened by the difficulties of the Missouri experience. Here the Mormons made what has been called their own "Mormon Missouri Compromise"[12] in an attempt to clear themselves in the eyes of the Missourians, many of whom seemed to regard them as Yankee abolitionists. Thus unfortunately was created the basis of future church policy.

The events of the 1960s brought the issue to a head, and the Mormon church was widely criticized throughout the nation for its racial policy. Within the church more liberal members and leaders tried to bring about some kind of change. But as the decade closed no changes had been made nor did any seem to be in sight. Even the conversion of a group of Nigerians did not lead to change. The Nigerians established their own church independent of the Utah church, although there had been contact between them and Utah in the process. Moreover, some of the Nigerians did join the Utah church and some of their young people have attended the Brigham Young University. Yet no real change occurred. The issue of the black man and the priesthood became an important intrachurch matter.

There are many positions taken within the Mormon world on these matters. The ultraconservatives look at the problem for Negroes as just one of those things that are inflicted unhappily on other people who should accept their fate humbly—and quietly. The conservatives believe that the Lord has told them that the Africans are not to be taken into the priesthood, and that's that. The ultraliberals take the position that this interpretation of the scriptures is absolute nonsense. The scholars attempt to reason a way out of it. The vast center of the church just accepts it without question. The apostates, who hate the church anyway, take the position that it's all to the good, that maybe the Saints will wreck themselves, and the rising aspirations of the American Negro will help shove them onto the rocks.[13]

[10] *Ibid.,* p. 218.

[11] Fawn M. Brodie, *No Man Knows My History: The Life of Joseph Smith the Mormon Prophet* (New York: Knopf, 1960), p. 173.

[12] David L. Brewer, "The Mormons," *The Religious Situation: 1968,* Donald R. Cutler, ed. (Boston: Beacon Press, 1968), p. 521.

[13] Turner, pp. 218–219.

The position of the church generally appears to be that only a new revelation from God can alter the present impasse.

In 1970 a book written by a church member, who died before its publication, examined the evidence and concluded that "The Negro policy and its attendant teachings all developed on an informal basis in response to historical circumstances rather than through revelation." Stephen C. Taggart, the author, stated explicitly that "The weight of evidence suggests that God did not place a curse upon the Negro—his white children did," and that "The evidence also suggests that the time for correcting the situation is long past due."[14]

Moreover, the salience of these issues in public awareness has caused the Book of Abraham, supposedly translated by Joseph Smith from Egyptian papyri, to be given new attention. A few years ago fragments of the originals were found in New York's Metropolitan Museum. One consequence of this discovery was reported somewhat cautiously in the *New York Times* on May 3, 1970: "Examination of these originals has heightened the confidence of some Egyptologists that the Book of Abraham is not a translation." And the same year a group of intellectuals in the Reorganized Church of Jesus Christ of Latter-day Saints issued a pilot issue of a journal called *Courage: A Journal of History, Thought and Action.* The Reorganized Church is made up of people whose ancestors did not go West with Brigham Young but who were part of the original Mormon movement. They often refer to themselves as "Josephites" and to the Utah church as "Brighamites." The Reorganized Church rejects many of the innovations made in the church at Nauvoo and they have never accepted the Book of Moses and the Book of Abraham. In that issue of *Courage,* Richard P. Howard, official church historian, called the Book of Abraham "simply the product of Joseph Smith Jr's imagination," and declared that "Whatever the intent of Joseph Smith in expounding this view of the Negro . . . it is clear that the ancient papyri from Egypt contain no such information."

An important long-time student of Mormonism declared in a public lecture given in Salt Lake City on October 3, 1970:

> The Church today, as everyone knows, is faced with mounting pressure for a repudiation of its practices concerning blacks. What makes a solution so agonizing is the unfortunately controversial nature of the Book of Abraham. Here is a dramatic example of the scientific past smashing into the Mormon past. The truly devout find it impossible to accept the word of the Egyptologists, whose translations of the newly discovered papyri from which the Book of Abraham "translation" was

14 Stephen G. Taggart, *Mormonism's Negro Policy: Social and Historical Origins* (Salt Lake City: University of Utah Press, 1970).

made differ totally from that of Joseph Smith. To give the blacks the priesthood without a new revelation or a new manifesto means an implicit repudiation of countless quiet decisions by Mormon leaders in the past. But to continue to deny the Negro full privileges of membership in the Mormon church is to do so on the basis of a book that is the least securely established among Mormon holy works. To an increasing number of Latter-day Saints this stand appears unjust and alien to the ideals of the Declaration of Independence.[15]

The issue has obviously put the Mormon community at odds with itself and the discovery of the original papyri has obviously exacerbated the difficulties in the short run, although in the long run it may indeed contribute to a solution.[16] It has also put the Mormon church at odds with the general thrust of opinion in the country. One should note, however, that if the Wallacite American Independence Party expected to garner a blacklash vote as a consequence of this situation in the 1970 elections, it was severely disappointed.

What we see here is a new challenge giving new expression to many of the older sources of strain that we identified a decade and a half ago, and focusing them upon this significantly diagnostic issue of racial justice. The church comes to this issue with its values crystallized in concrete, historically conditioned forms as a result of the last century and a half of the Mormon experience. In all human communities, religious or other, the process of institutionalization involves not only the concretization of the implications of the values concerned, but also a certain degree of foreshortening of them. They become understood in certain contexts and thereby limited and constrained in their implications.[17] In the nineteenth-century Mormon experience the idea that God had reopened converse between heaven and earth, and had prepared the way for the spread of the new gospel by the development in America of democratic political institutions, both pillars of the Mormon belief, came to be seen as not standing in contradiction with such a palpable denying of religious universalism and democratic principles as was involved in accepting the general American attitudes toward blacks.

Two contexts of past experience affected the way in which the Mormon church came to define the problem of race. The first was the Missouri experience which gave a racist cast to Mormon thinking. The second was the

[15] Fawn M. Brodie, *Can We Manipulate the Past?* (Salt Lake City: Center for the Study of the American West, First Annual Lecture, 1970), p. 13.

[16] One should consult in this respect the translations of the original papyri by several Egyptologists and the comments on them by members of the Utah church and the Reorganized church in the summer and autumn issues of *Dialogue*, 1968.

[17] Cf. Thomas F. O'Dea, *Sociology and the Study of Religion, Theory, Research, Interpretation* (New York: Basic Books, Inc., 1970), pp. 240 ff.

experience of accommodation that followed the defeat of the church in its struggle to defend plural marriage against the federal government and general public opinion in the 1880s. At that time, under severe government pressure and indeed even persecution, the church gave up plural marriage and following that renunciation adopted a policy of general accommodation to the values and way of life of the general American community. From then on it tended to emphasize its patriotism and how it was like the others while at the same time continuing to emphasize its peculiarity in less dramatic and less consequential ways that had been the case in the nineteenth century, when its cooperative ethic and its marriage mores gave it a marked nonconformist character. During those years, when America neglected its responsibilities to the emancipated slaves and their descendants, the bias that Missouri had built into Mormonism was congruent with that of the nation as a whole, and fitted in well with the policy of accommodation. But as we have seen the decade of the 1960s gave new life to the issue of racial justice, and it tended to become a touchstone with respect to both biblical ethics and American democratic values. This was not without its effect on members of the Mormon church. Previous to this time a small number of church members had always advocated a change of the policy that barred blacks from participation, but the issue remained a minor one. A decade and a half ago when we analyzed the major sources of strain it did not possess sufficient prominence to warrant consideration. In 1971, however, this situation was completely changed. Many members of the Mormon church found themselves endeavoring with great difficulty and against great odds to work the church out of its historic cul de sac.

In summary, then, it must be said that "the modern Negro problem symbolizes for Mormons a dangerous and powerful worldly influence," threatening the basic Mormon values and the concrete community togetherness as they have evolved through Missouri and the accommodation of the last four generations, by threatening to bring into the church the most obvious "outsiders," the most "different" kind of people. Although the Mormons may be able eventually to work their way to comprehend that such an introduction does not threaten the real basic values of the church, they will do so only by being able to separate that basic meaning from the concrete, compact, symbolic meanings that time and experience have made of it. Consequently, the black issue has "come to stand for the whole breaking through of the outside world into the holy community."[18]

This is as much as to say that it has come to signify the threat of modernity and has therefore reactivated the old sources of strain and

[18] Brewer, p. 529.

focused them upon itself as a major issue. Hence in the face of it many display the old defensive responses. At the same time, the issue of racial justice remains for those church members aware of the larger ethical context and the need to meet honestly the authentic challenge of modernity, and aware that the church cannot go on forever meeting problems in this realm in a defensive and provincial manner, an issue diagnostic of the church's most profound problem. That problem can be stated in a number of ways; here we shall attempt but one brief and insufficient formulation: How to renew the original democratic and ethical spirit of Mormonism, free its religious message from the institutional and conventional restraints built up in the experience of the last century and a half, and thereby provide the basis for a more contemporary and more vital understanding of Mormon values. The race issue has become symbolic of the entire complex of problems involved in that challenge and the defensive attitude against the idea of change with respect to it stands surrogate for "standpatism" generally in the face of the larger challenge. The church's adequacy to handle the problems of its encounter with modernity will eventually be judged by the adequacy of its response to the problem of racial justice.

Beneath the layers of the problem that we have tried to indicate lies another that renders it exceedingly recalcitrant to easy solution. Indeed this deeper layer of implicit significance is one that is extremely difficult to make explicit and understandable in all its ramified emotional implications. The priesthood is not only the basis upon which all Mormon males participate fully in the church, it is also closely tied to the whole complex of Mormon values concerned with family, temple marriage, and offspring. The priest is also a husband, and wives share in the blessings of the Mormon gospel—and are believed to share in its promises for another life— through their relationship to their husbands. Thus when Mormons think of the priesthood, they also have in mind the family. One scholar of contemporary Mormonism has written:

> Another reason for resistance is the fear of intermarriage, already deeply embedded in American culture and thought by some social scientists to be the central meaning in most opposition to racial equality. In Mormondom this dread both reinforces and is reinforced by the priesthood concept of worthiness and the doctrine of the curse. Mormons are likely to feel that admitting Negroes to the temple would encourage intermarriage.[19]

Here too Mormonism reveals itself to be both typically American and peculiarly itself.

[19] *Ibid.*, p. 524.

Many church members no doubt feel about this issue like Mrs. George W. Romney, who said in 1967, "At this time in history, the Negro does not hold the priesthood in our church. I personally am sorry for this, but I have no authority to do anything about it."[20] Her husband, at one time a candidate for the Presidential nomination in the Republican Party, and now a member of President Nixon's cabinet, has always taken a progressive position in his political life with respect to civil rights for black people. This can be seen in his record as Governor of Michigan and his record as Secretary of Housing. But he has not strayed from the orthodox position on intrachurch matters, at least not in public. It is widely rumored that Mr. Romney has tried hard in a private manner to bring some rethinking and change in this situation. A professor at the University of Arizona, himself a church member, is reported to have said when the Romney candidacy made the Mormon stand on race a national issue: "George Romney has precipitated a crisis in the Mormon Church that may rank with the plague of the locusts."[21] Yet the church remains where it was at the time. In 1964, President David O. McKay, then ninety-one years of age, and speaking from a wheelchair, was asked at a press conference when the time would come that blacks would be given access to the Mormon priesthood. He replied, "Not while you and I are here."[22]

What evaluation can be made of the response of the Mormon church to this new diagnostic challenge, which it still faced undecided and undeciding as it entered the decade of the 1970s? The response of church authorities appears not to be meeting the challenge with any degree of adequacy. Both as Americans sharing the general problems of their country and as Christians facing what is perhaps the consequence of the gravest sin in their country's history, their performance seems highly deficient. The picture is redeemed only by the fact that the present situation is not a final one, and the inadequacy of the church's official response must be seen together with the real anguished dissatisfaction of those who work and wish for change.

One must also remind oneself that change comes slowly in matters of deep concern. When deep concerns come to symbolize a larger set of implicit issues as this one has come to symbolize the larger threat of the modern world to the older concrete forms of Mormon values, then additional obstacles to change are created. To say this is not to excuse, but it is to attempt to understand a community confronting a great challenge and responding to it highly inadequately. The issue of race comes to challenge

20 National Observer, Monday, April 10, 1967.
21 T. George Harris, Romney's Way (Englewood Cliffs, N.J.: Prentice-Hall, 1967), p. 207.
22 National Observer, Monday, April 10, 1967.

the Mormon church in the context of already existing problems—that is, of the sources of strain we delineated some fifteen years ago. It comes as part of the challenge of modern secular thought, for although it involves the gravest problems of Christian ethics, it is also to be seen as an element of modern secular liberalism by which Mormonism is challenged on the score of its concrete religious position and its old-fashioned socioeconomic ideas. As such it carries disturbing—deeply disturbing—connotations for conservative churchmen. Indeed the issue has picked up a complex of meanings for all groups. The conservative sees it as a strategic issue on which the church must hold the line; otherwise it will open the way to the intrusion of a host of damaging secular influences and disrupt the Mormon community. For apostates and enemies, it has become the great club with which to traduce the church and all its values. Caught up in this complex are other sources of strain, all of them bothersome enough in themselves. Obviously involved is the conflicting issue of a literal understanding of scripture and taking it on the authority of the church as against a more liberal and critical perspective. Here too is to be seen the older conflict between acceptance of authority and unquestioning obedience to it as against an emphasis upon democracy and individualism. Most significantly intertwined with the racial issue is the long-standing conflict of political conservatism versus social idealism, both based upon important elements in the Mormon tradition. We must add to this the strain deriving from the anxiety concerning the possible consequences of an abrupt change of position. Would that shake confidence in the general authorities? Or in the peculiar Mormon scriptures? The situation here is somewhat analogous to the abandonment of plural marriage which came in response to outside pressure. This change was accepted by the membership generally, but it did lead to the establishment of the Fundamentalist sect whose members still practice plural marriage in Utah and the intermountain West today. At the same time the issue brings the church into a new kind of conflict between belief and environment. Today the Mormon church stands before enlightened American opinion at worst as guilty of unchristian behavior, or at best as being tied up in obsolete provincial American and Mormon racist attitudes and unable to shed them.

How this issue involves such a complex of strains and stands surrogate for a host of unvoiced defenses and anxieties was illustrated by the warning in the summer of 1970 by W. Cleon Skousen. Mr. Skousen, a right-wing Mormon and a public figure in Salt Lake City, declared that "the Communist Party has apparently decided to take over the leadership" of the growing agitation against the church.[23] He circulated reprints of an

---

[23] W. Cleon Skousen, "Communist Press Calls for Attack on LDS Church," mimeographed circular distributed in the summer of 1970, n.d., n.p.

article originally published in the October 18, 1969 issue of *World Maga-zine,* which is an insert distributed with the communist papers *Daily World* and *People's World.* The article states that blacks are mistreated in Utah because of the Mormon numerical superiority in the state's population. It also gives a list of some of the church's financial interests as well as pic-tures of politically prominent Republicans who are church members whom it captions as "Nixon's Mormons." In distributing the article Skousen attached to it his own analysis stating that it was "a signal for the com-munist 'transmission belt' to go to work" in an attack on the church orga-nization.

The seizure of the communist issue in order to make it a scapegoat for all those causes that bring about social change of a disturbing kind is a frequently observed phenomenon in American life. It derives from deep anxieties that are the consequence of threatening changes. It has the psy-chological function of enabling those suffering from such strains to "identify" some surrogate causes and to take symbolic action against them. It is not a way that leads to open confrontation and successful handling of real problems. Such scapegoating may provide for those involved a simpli-fied and manageable definition of the situation under whose disturbing stress they react, but it helps little in arriving at a realistic understanding of the deeper issues involved. Should the Mormon church take such a stand (and the indications are that it will *not*), it would undoubtedly condemn itself to precisely that obsolescence of which its critics have accused it.

How does the Mormon church's overall treatment of the diagnostic racial issue throw light upon the larger question of the adequacy of the church's general response to the challenges of the time? We have sug-gested that the great constitutive question of what ought man to be doing on this earth being the kind of being that he is has become no longer a theoretical one for Americans, but that in our day it lurks beneath and often surfaces within every major contemporary issue facing the nation. Because religious bodies have long aimed to offer definitive answers to this ques-tion, the great issue for them today becomes the adequacy of their accepted answers. It is widely being faced in theological and religious circles that a radical reformulation is necessary—one that would recast the interpreta-tion of Christian vocation to render it relevant to the times. It is for all religious bodies a time of molting of old forms and the development of new ones. The Mormon church in its defensive and stand pat position reveals itself as responding inadequately to a most diagnostic issue. Such a response does not augur well for the answer to the other questions we have raised: does the meaningful answer offered by the church to its members today measure up against the yardstick of the predicament of modern men and modern society? Does the church offer its converts the basis and grounds for genuine religious conversion that will have personal and social consequences commensurate with the needs of men caught in the modern crisis of vocation? However, it must in justice be conceded that we deal here with suggestive indications and by no means with direct evidence concerning those questions themselves.

Moreover, we must emphasize again that the racial issue, either as an issue on its own right or as an issue diagnostic of a larger complex of problems as we have indicated, has not been given its final solution within the Mormon church. There are numbers of people in the church disturbed by it. As Lowell L. Bennion, former Director of the LDS Institute of Religion in Salt Lake City and now a dean at the University of Utah, observed, there is a considerable "diversity of feeling and opinion" concerning the matter and "even general authorities are not of one mind on this problem and struggle over it as does the body of the Church."

> Institutional factors stand in the way of change. Authority is vested in the prophet–president of the Church. He alone is authoritative in matters of doctrinal interpretation and Church policy. Mormons are loyal to their prophet, believing him to be spokesman for God. In their basic moral conviction, many would like to see the Negro have all the gifts and privileges of life which they themselves enjoy. But many Mormons do not agitate for this change because their tradition is to believe in prophetic leadership. To question this is to question the vitality of their faith. Most Mormons would adjust quickly, many happily, to a prophetic announcement that the time has come for all men to enjoy the gifts of God on the same impartial basis.[24]

Will the Mormon church have a renewal of spirit and of vigor that will enable it to work its way out of the difficult situation in which it now finds itself? Will the new converts change the character of the church in a way to make change more or less likely? Will new leadership arise out of the inner anguish that many suffer over this issue? Will the surfacing of this issue of blacks and the priesthood enable the church to get a better explicit grasp on the total complex of problems and the sources of strain involved in them which this issue has come to symbolize? Or will it make the church more defensive and less capable of working through the difficult complex position to which history has brought it? We have not offered here sufficient evidence to answer such questions; we have, however, provided enough background to indicate how serious such questions are concerning the destiny of the Mormon church today. As regards the answer to such questions, the outside observer can only wait and see.

[24] Lowell Bennion, "Commentary" on David L. Brewer, "The Mormons," in Donald R. Cutler, ed., *The Religious Situation: 1968* (Boston: Beacon Press, 1968), p. 551.

Writing in 1957, I stated, "It is a tremendous presumption to attempt to judge the future of a movement like Mormonism." And despite the inadequacies of the present, which this article points out, that future remains unjudged. It cannot be denied that the Mormon church displays genuine vitality in its missionary work. The appearance and apparent prospering of *Dialogue,* an independent quarterly journal of Mormon thought, now in its sixth year, testifies to a continuation of that intellectual and ethical seriousness that this writer found among young Mormons a decade and a half ago. In the Mormon academic community many are generally heartened by the recent appointment of Dallin H. Oaks, a young, energetic professor of law from the University of Chicago and a former law clerk for Chief Justice Earl Warren, as president of Brigham Young University.

The Mormon church like the nation as a whole faces a vast challenge and the need for a great transformation. Like the nation as a whole it faces that demanding situation with much confusion and inner turmoil. Yet intelligence, vitality, and ethical concern are still important components of the Mormon makeup as they are indeed of that of the country as a whole. They are integrally related to that meaningful context that Mormonism still provides great numbers of its adherents. Fifteen years ago we found that the flexibility of Mormonism in the past and its viability under the most adverse conditions did not augur badly for its future. The situation for both the church and the nation is a much more difficult one today. Yet the profound turmoil over the problem of race, which the Mormon church experienced throughout the 1960s and still experiences in the new decade, may indeed prove to be the painful propaedeutic of the kind of transformation that would renew and reinvigorate the spirit of the original open and innovating Mormonism.

Crisis in Identity:
Mormon Responses in the
Nineteenth and Twentieth Centuries

LEONARD J. ARRINGTON

If O'Dea has delineated an area of life where the Mormons have not been able to adjust effectively to the contemporary world, nonetheless there seem to be many areas where they have maintained vitality as well as commitment. Fifty years ago Ephraim Ericksen warned that with the conquering of the Utah frontier Mormons faced the necessity of finding new goals and new programs if the church were to retain its vigor and relevance. Leonard Arrington details how the Mormons have dealt successfully with several "identity crises" in the past, and how today programs of great variety continue to absorb the time and talent of its membership, thus providing a kind of relevance still meaningful to the Latter-day Saints.

During its 141-year existence the Church of Jesus Christ of Latter-day Saints has been confronted with at least four critical crises which have constituted threats to its identity and perhaps to its survival. The first occurred between 1830 and 1838 and had to do with the formulation of a general program for the "restoration" of the "true church" and the commitment of the Saints to gathering in the West to make ready for the coming millennium. The second crisis was one of leadership between the time of Joseph Smith's death in 1844 and the assuming of the role of prophet by Brigham Young in 1848. A third crisis involved the struggle to preserve the independent kingdom between 1868 and 1882, when the imminent completion of the transcontinental railroad forced an agonizing

Leonard J. Arrington, "Crisis in Identity: Mormon Responses in the Nineteenth and Twentieth Centuries." This article has been especially prepared for inclusion in this volume.

reappraisal of economic and political policies. A fourth crisis developed during the church's conflict with the federal government between 1890 and 1911. It was precipitated by the decision of the U.S. Supreme Court to uphold the Edmunds–Tucker Act, which disincorporated the church, and continued until the disorganization of the Anti-Mormon American Party in 1911.

Each of these identity crises has affected the relationship of the Mormon community with contemporary American culture, but in each case the church through minimal adjustment and pragmatic compromise successfully handled the crisis. In many cases it was accomplished by launching a program or series of programs oriented toward minimizing the effects of the threat and at the same time retaining the loyalty and commitment of its people. Today the church finds itself confronted with a fifth crisis of sizable proportions: the confrontation with modern scepticism and hedonism and the counterculture of youth. Again it has responded with what it hopes are appropriate programs.

The first period of testing, then, was in the early 1830s, when the church's basic beliefs and practices were formulated. Mormonism emerged from this period with its own set of scriptures, a prophet, an ecclesiastical organization, an extensive missionary system, and a program of assisting converts to "gather out of Babylon" to live, work, and worship together in distinctive communities. This program had particular relevance to church members in the early nineteenth century, who were convinced that American democratic society was on the verge of disintegration.[1]

The second crisis followed the brutal assassination of Joseph Smith in June 1844. Convinced that Mormonism was hardly more than a personality cult, the murderers predicted the imminent demise of the church. Many claimants to the prophet's mantle emerged, including Sidney Rigdon, James J. Strang, Lyman Wight, and William Smith, the prophet's sole surviving brother, who modestly announced that he would serve as interim prophet until his martyred brother's oldest son assumed his rightful position as head of the church. Brigham Young, meanwhile, advanced the proposition that the prophet should have no successor, but that the Twelve Apostles with himself at their head should build up the kingdom in Joseph's name. Young, by not overplaying his role, and by encouraging the Saints to remain in Nauvoo and rally to the program of completing the temple, won the loyalty of most of the Saints and was eventually "sustained" as prophet, seer, and revelator as well as president of the church in 1848. After following Young to the Great Basin, the Mormons renewed

---

[1] See Marvin S. Hill, "The Role of Christian Primitivism in the Origin and Development of the Early Mormon Kingdom 1830–1844." Unpublished Ph.D. dissertation, University of Chicago, 1968, pp. 64–71.

their effort to build a latter-day Kingdom of God and within twenty years they had founded five hundred self-sufficing communities in Utah and other western territories, dispatched hundreds of missionaries to places as far away as Hong Kong, Santiago, and Constantinople, and established the ecclesiastical, political, and economic basis for a culturally distinctive community.

The third crisis occurred with the approach of the transcontinental railroad in the late 1860s—a development that threatened to convert the closed Mormon society into an open one. The railroad made it possible profitably to extract the rich store of minerals in the region and to import heavy machinery and equipment, as well as an abundance of consumer goods, from the East. A small group of Latter-day Saint businessmen and intellectuals under the leadership of William S. Godbe proposed the immediate accommodation of the Mormon economy to the greater economy of the nation. They hoped this would lead to cultural and political accommodation as well. Brigham Young and his closest advisers, however, regarded these proposals as a betrayal of the Mormon dream of separateness, and Godbe and his friends were excommunicated for apostasy. Church officials then launched a massive program to preserve the political, cultural, and economic integrity of the Latter-day Saint community by insuring that the mining and trading economy of the incoming Gentiles would constitute no more than an enclave within the self-sufficient, theocratic commonwealth of the latter-day Zion. The Mormon protective program included the establishment of town councils called Schools of the Prophets, community cooperatives called United Orders, and exclusively Mormon promotional and regulative associations called Zion's Boards of Trade. Cooperative railroads were constructed and operated, as were textile mills, clothing factories, tanneries, iron works, furniture factories, and wholesaling and retailing establishments.

The Mormons were viewed as models by many social reformers in America and England, one of whom exulted that the despised Mormons had "created a soul under the rib of death."[2] But to the majority of Americans this distinctive and exclusivist society was intolerable. To Protestant leaders in particular it was unthinkable that the United States would permit the continuance of a theocratically directed closed society within its borders. Especially reprehensible to these persons was the Mormon practice of plural marriage. Nor were non-Mormon enterprisers in the region prepared to tolerate the restrictiveness implicit in the Mormon system of economic cooperation.

Thus, the fourth Mormon crisis began in the 1880s during the anti-

[2] Bronterre O'Brien, as cited in *Tullidge's Quarterly Magazine,* II (January 1883), p. 400.

polygamy crusade which followed the passage of the Edmunds Act (1882), establishing heavy penalties against polygamists. Thousands of Mormon leaders were placed in the penitentiary, the voting franchise was taken away from loyal Mormons, and much of the government of the territory was vested in a commission of five men appointed by the President of the United States. With the passage of the Edmunds–Tucker Act of 1887, the funds and assets of the Mormon Church, except houses of worship and burial grounds, were confiscated and placed in the hands of a government receiver. When the Supreme Court, by a 5 to 4 decision, upheld the constitutionality of the Edmunds–Tucker Act, Mormon President Wilford Woodruff made a grave decision to comply with the national mandate in marriage practices, politics, economics, and education. He first issued instructions in 1890 that no more plural marriages were to be performed. At the same time the church political party (Peoples Party) was dissolved, and the Saints were divided up among the Republican and Democratic parties. Many church-founded business enterprises were sold or farmed out to private interests. Finally, steps were taken to institute a public school system for Utah. These accommodations were sufficient to induce Congress to approve an enabling act granting statehood to Utah. After almost fifty years of incessant application, Utah became a state in 1896.[3]

Conformance to national norms in marriage practices was fraught with difficulties for the Latter-day Saints. At the time of the Woodruff Manifesto in 1890, several thousand plural families were in existence. Some national leaders insisted, in stern Puritan tones, that every married male must immediately sever his connections with his plural wives. A few Latter-day Saints took this step and the children were reared from that point by one (but not both) of the parents. These separations were difficult to maintain. Recognizing this, most national leaders tolerated the continuation of those plural marriage relationships contracted before the Manifesto, and so the institution was prolonged until well along in the twentieth century.

At the same time, a few Mormon authorities regarded plural marriage as a divinely ordained practice which could not be outlawed by national legislation, and they continued to perform plural marriages in Canada, Mexico, and on the high seas. The number of such post-Manifesto marriages was not large, but there were enough of them to constitute an embarrassment to the church. Two members of the Council of Twelve Apostles who had performed such marriages were disfellowshipped in 1904 and a strong statement was issued by the church presidency that the performance of plural marriages must cease. A few Latter-day Saints have covertly at-

[3] Gustive O. Larson, The "Americanization" of Utah for Statehood (San Marino, Calif., 1971).

tempted to keep the practice alive, but in every instance in which these have been discovered, the participants have been promptly excommunicated.

The abolition of plural marriage called forth a renewed emphasis on theology supporting the sacredness of the marriage covenant. The eternality of family relationships and the overwhelming importance of the family in the church and society has become the single most important theme of Mormon sermons in this century. Part of this response consists of the construction of several new temples and earnest efforts to encourage all couples to have their marriage solemnized "for time and all eternity" in these especially sacred structures.

Mormon leaders were also reluctant to abandon the drive to establish their own political Kingdom of God. Some federal officials and congressmen of the 1890s insisted that the Mormons must not only share the principal political offices with non-Mormons—a concession that Mormons were quite willing to make—but also that Mormon ecclesiastical officials must not be candidates for these offices. Mormon leaders, determined to save as much of the kingdom as possible, declined making such a commitment. In 1899, Brigham H. Roberts, a member of the First Council of Seventy of the Church, was nominated for Congress by the Democratic Party and won the ensuing election. Roberts was not only a high ecclesiastic, but also had two wives, both of whom he had married before 1890. There was an immediate protest against seating Elder Roberts, a campaign was waged by several national women's groups, and eventually a petition bearing more than seven million signatures was presented to Congress. By a vote of 268 to 50 Congress refused to seat Roberts, and the office was declared vacant.[4]

A second test of national attitudes toward Mormon leadership occurred four years later when Reed Smoot was nominated by the Republicans and subsequently elected to the U.S. Senate. Smoot was a member of the Council of Twelve Apostles, but strictly monogamous. There followed a three-year congressional investigation of the Mormon church and its leaders. After almost four thousand pages of testimony, a senatorial committee recommended the expulsion of Senator Smoot. Only with the active support of Theodore Roosevelt and other prominent Republicans were Smoot's supporters able to override the committee's recommendation and permit Smoot to retain his seat—a seat he held for the next thirty years.[5]

---

[4] R. Davis Bitton, "The B. H. Roberts Case of 1898–1900," *Utah Historical Quarterly,* XXV (January 1957), pp. 27–46.

[5] Milton R. Merrill, "Reed Smoot, Apostle in Politics." Ph.D. dissertation, Columbia University, 1950.

The Smoot controversy stirred passions, both nationally and locally. The national muckraking press issued dozens of anti-Mormon books which in hatred and vituperation matched anything previously published against the Roman Catholics and Jews. Articles and cartoons in leading newspapers and magazines of the time were equally acrid. A new theme of some of these articles was the charge of an unholy alliance between the Mormon Church and the trusts. The church, it was alleged, had linked up with big business to exploit the American people.[6] In Salt Lake City, an anti-Mormon political party, the American Party, was organized; talented writers were employed by the *Salt Lake Tribune;* and a mayor and other city officials were elected on anti-Mormon platforms.

By the time of World War I, however, the bitterness had subsided. Non-Mormon businessmen, tired of the insults directed against their Mormon associates, discontinued their support of the American Party. The anti-Mormon campaign was called off, and positive attempts were made during the years that followed to dissolve the bitterness between Mormons and non-Mormons.[7] The *Salt Lake Tribune,* still owned by a Roman Catholic family as it had been earlier in the century, now played a leading role in promoting an era of good feeling which has continued to the present.[8] One evidence of this good feeling is that despite the continuing predominance of the Mormons in Utah (about 70 percent over the years of the twentieth century) three non-Mormons have been elected governor: Simon Bamberger (1916–1920), George H. Dern (1924–1932), and J. Bracken Lee (1952–1960). Every election has produced charges that the Mormon church was attempting to influence the outcome, but most of these seem traceable to particular interested parties who seek to use the church, or motivate the electorate, for their own purposes. The president of the church publicly advocated a vote for Taft in 1912 (Taft did receive a plurality in Utah), a vote for Hoover in 1932 (Utah voted over-

[6] See Alfred Henry Lewis, "The Great Mormon Conspiracy," *Collier's Weekly,* March 26, 1904, pp. 11 ff.; Richard Barry, "The Political Menace of the Mormon Church," *Pearson's* (September 1910), pp. 319–330; Barry, "The Mormon Method in Business," *Pearson's* (October 1910), pp. 571–578; Alfred Henry Lewis, "The Viper on the Hearth," "The Trail of the Viper," "The Viper's Trail of Gold," *Cosmopolitan,* LI (March, April, May 1911).

[7] The first undeviatingly favorable national publicity received by the Mormons came during World War I, when they furnished 200,000 bushels of wheat to provide food for America and its allies, and demonstrated their support of the war effort by heavy enlistments, extensive support of the Red Cross, and oversubscribing Liberty Bond drives.

[8] Today the *Tribune* and the *Deseret News,* which is the official newspaper of the LDS Church, share the same printing, circulation, and advertising facilities in Salt Lake City. O. N. Malmquist, *The First 100 Years: A History of the Salt Lake Tribune, 1871–1971* (Salt Lake City, 1971).

whelmingly for Roosevelt), and a vote for Landon in 1936 (Utah again voted overwhelmingly for Roosevelt), but other than these instances the church's influence has been directed toward issues and policies rather than toward personalities and parties. Church control of the political life of the region, designed to assist in the realization of the Kingdom of God in the nineteenth century, has dissolved in this century to the point that the church is just one of the many interest groups (business corporations, labor unions, the medical profession, teachers) which politicians must recognize as they wage their campaigns and vote on issues.[9] Thus, in seeking a new image after the fateful decision of the Supreme Court upholding the Edmunds–Tucker Act, the church reluctantly moved from the tight theocracy that had characterized its political institutions in early Utah to the near separation of church and state that has characterized Mormon political relationships during the past thirty or forty years.

A similar, though less reluctant, adjustment was made in the fields of economics and business. In 1882, the year the Edmunds Act was passed, Mormon leaders officially announced that the boycott of Gentile stores was over. The Saints, in good conscience, were free to launch out into new enterprises on their own, and the ecclesiastically sponsored cooperatives would no longer occupy a favored position. This initiated a "boom" in the creation of new stores, shops, and factories, particularly in Ogden and Salt Lake City. It also removed the stamp of disapproval from the efforts of Mormon entrepreneurs to join with non-Mormon businessmen in and out of the region. An economic diaspora began as gangs of Mormon workmen left their homes to work under subcontracts with railroad companies in the Pacific Northwest and Canada; Mormon cowboys began to ride the range in Idaho, Wyoming, Colorado, Arizona, and Nevada; hundreds of Mormon settlers moved on their own initiative to Oregon where they farmed and worked in lumber mills after completion of the Oregon Short Line Railroad. At the same time, hundreds of non-Mormons from the East and Midwest moved into the Mormon commonwealth to engage in mining, trading, banking, manufacturing, transportation, and other services. Mormons occasionally elected non-Mormons to the boards of their key businesses, and non-Mormons returned the favor. When the Mormon church sold its controlling interests in the beet sugar, salt, hydroelectric power, railroad, and other interests to eastern capitalists after the turn of the century, the economic interests of Mormons and non-Mormons became so

---

[9] Many Mormon candidates who have waged campaigns against non-Mormons in the twentieth century will testify to their failure to attract Mormon votes from the opposite political party. Mormon voters seldom vote for Mormons unless they agree with them on parties and issues. A recent thoughtful and forthright article is J. D. Williams, "The Separation of Church and State in Mormon Theory and Practice," *Dialogue: A Journal of Mormon Thought,* I (Summer 1966), pp. 30–54.

inextricable that the mutual suspicions and name-calling that were a part of the anti-Mormon clamor from 1904 to 1911 failed to halt the gradual coalescence.

At the same time, however, the church still attempted to maintain its own religiously derived values. As public education gradually replaced the nineteenth-century church schools, Religion Classes were instituted, beginning in 1890, in order to insure proper weekday religious training for Mormon children in both the elementary and secondary schools. These were established for all age groups and were conducted by qualified persons, usually women, after school was dismissed. At the same time, Theological Classes were given by university-trained people to students at the church-oriented colleges. In the early 1920s Religion Classes were dropped for students in the grade schools on the assumption that their needs were adequately met by other church programs. At the secondary levels the Religion Classes were converted into full-time seminaries which functioned on a released-time basis in buildings adjacent to high-school campuses. In 1926 the church began to establish Institutes of Religion at all college and university campuses where there were substantial numbers of LDS students.

With the renunciation of plural marriage, with a largely accomplished separation of church and state and church and business, and with its children now trained in public rather than church school systems, Mormonism had made the minimal accommodation required of it by the American people at the end of the nineteenth century. That Mormon leaders continued seeking to implement traditional community values, however, is indicated by the inauguration of the Church Welfare Plan in the 1930s. The Great Depression had a particularly severe impact on the Great Basin and Rocky Mountain regions. The Welfare Plan provided a means of helping the "worthy poor" by establishing agricultural and factory enterprises which would provide work for the unemployed and produce goods for their families. A chain of 150 bishop's storehouses was established to receive the goods produced by these projects and to make food available to the poor. The surplus foodstuffs and other products raised in one area were transported to deficit areas, which in turn produced other surplus crops for exchange. By the 1950s the Church Welfare Plan owned and operated some 700 separate enterprises throughout the nation, including peanut farms and peanut butter factories in Texas, cotton farms and grapefruit orchards and canneries in Arizona, orange groves and canneries in southern California, apple orchards in Washington, pineapple and sugar plantations in Hawaii, shaving cream and toothpaste factories in Chicago, dairies and cheese plants in northern Utah, salmon canneries in Oregon, a gelatin factory in Kansas City, vitamin pill and shoe polish factories in New

Jersey, and cattle ranches in Wyoming. About 100,000 Latter-day Saints were given an estimated seven million dollars in cash and welfare products each year. A related program saw the establishment of the Deseret Industries, which utilized unskilled and handicapped labor to reprocess discarded goods and distribute them through Deseret Industries stores in the more heavily populated areas. The cooperative effort of the 1930s differed from that of the 1870s, however, in that the Mormons generally no longer sold these commodities on the open market, nor competed as they had in the past with the products of non-Mormon manufacturers.

But what of the recent crisis? In the face of a growing sense of irrelevance of organized religion among adults and the youth of today, how have the Mormons reacted in the last decade? The stepped-up secularization of American life;[10] the "God is dead" movement; the youth revolt; the widespread circulation of works previously regarded as obscene; the banning of required prayers and Bible readings from the nation's public schools; the easing of requirements for divorce, abortion, and the use of contraceptives; the drug culture; and the growing violence of protest demonstrations—all of these inevitably have been unsettling to Mormonism, a religion that prides itself on its high standards of personal and group morality.

The principal source of strain in modern Mormonism seems to be sociological in nature: namely, the problems of adjusting its programs and living patterns as the Mormons become more and more urban and cosmopolitan rather than rural and localized in orientation. Over half now live outside the Mountain West and probably as many as 70 to 80 percent live in an atmosphere that the U.S. Census Bureau would classify as "urban." The overwhelming majority of these represent tiny minorities in the vast metropolitan centers of the North and South America, Europe, and Asia. How has the church attempted to maintain its vitality as well as its traditional values among the young people reared in these settings?

There can be little doubt that Mormonism has managed to retain the loyalty and active participation of the overwhelming majority of its increasingly scattered membership—and this in the face of declining commitment among many religious groups. The population of the Mormon church rose from 1.6 million in 1960 to approximately 3 million in 1970 —a gain of about 8 percent per year. In 1960 there was but one Mormon stake (diocese) outside the United States and Canada. Today there are more than fifty stakes organized in foreign lands. The decade of the 1960s began with 290 stakes and 2,600 wards and branches (congregations);

---

[10] See the thoughtful essay by James L. Clayton, "The Challenge of Secularism," *Dialogue: A Journal of Mormon Thought*, III (Autumn 1968), pp. 63–76.

it ended with 500 stakes and 5,000 wards and branches. There were 5,500 full-time volunteer missionaries when the decade started and more than 12,000 in 1970. During the 1960s the church erected and paid for 2,158 chapels, of which 1,558 were in the United States and Canada, 214 in Europe, 204 in Mexico and Latin America, 133 in the South Pacific, and 28 in Asia. Moreover, the average attendance of all members at the Sunday worship service rose from 35 percent in 1960 to 42 percent in 1970.

A review of the most important areas of Mormon activity as of 1971 suggests the nature of the church's programs and illustrates the total commitment required of active members. A typical week begins on Sunday with males attending early morning "Priesthood meeting." Six groups of priesthood holders, which include nearly all male members over the age of twelve, meet separately to discuss their weekly assignments and to participate in religious instruction. Later in the morning all church members attend Sunday School, and on Sunday evening a Sacrament meeting (worship service) features the Lord's Supper and a doctrinal sermon by one or two appointed members of the congregation. Each Tuesday morning the women of the local church meet for an hour and a half for study courses in cultural arts, social relations, theology, and homemaking. These Relief Societies, as they are called, also have "work days" on which various arts and crafts are pursued. On Tuesday evenings, the young people from twelve to twenty-five attend meetings of the Mutual Improvement Associations, where they receive training in the cultural and performing arts, socialize, and discuss some aspect of the gospel relevant to their lives. Each Wednesday after school, children from the ages of three to twelve attend Primary, where they are taught religious music, history, and doctrine, interspersed with recreation and training in manners and morals. In addition, on Monday evening, each family is expected to hold a "Family Home Evening," at which family members discuss how to improve themselves religiously and otherwise, try to solve family problems, and "have fun together."

A vital aspect of Mormonism's continuing sense of identity is its emphasis on missionary work. Approximately 14,000 young men (and some women), usually between the ages of nineteen and twenty-five, annually volunteer for two years of service as missionaries. Some 100 missions are located throughout the world, communist countries and many new African nations excepted. Entirely at their own expense, or with the support of friends and relatives, these missionaries assist in teaching, converting, and baptizing some 80,000 persons per year. Several hundred of these missionaries are from foreign lands, many of them financed by members in the United States. In addition to these proselyting missionaries, the church has recently begun to call missionaries from various professional fields, who help to build meetinghouses, teach, and render medical aid in underdeveloped countries.

Responding to the increasing needs for education in the modern world, the church has made heavy investments in education. It has constructed and supports not only Brigham Young University, but also the following institutions: Ricks College, Rexburg, Idaho; Church College, Laie, Hawaii; Church College, Temple View, New Zealand; LDS Business College, Salt Lake City; high schools in Tonga, Western Samoa, American Samoa, and Mexico; and elementary schools in Tonga, Western Samoa, Tahiti, Mexico, Chile, and Bolivia.[11] Some 60,000 young Mormons are enrolled in full-time instruction in these schools. In addition, about 200 released time or early morning seminaries in all states of the Union and in seven foreign countries serve more than 140,000 junior-high and high-school students; and Institutes of Religion adjacent to the campuses of about 250 universities in the United States and five foreign countries, serve approximately 40,000 college-age LDS students. All told, some 211,000 students are enrolled in church schools.[12]

The Latter-day Saints have paid particular attention to the American Indian as the current national concern with the status of minority groups has served to rededicate them to what they have always implicitly regarded as a major responsibility. The church maintains a number of grade schools, nine Indian seminaries at which some 15,000 students are enrolled, and a comprehensive program for more than 500 Indian students at Brigham Young University. Because of the lack of adequate schooling in many Indian villages, the church conducts an Indian Placement program, whereby some 5,000 Indian students are received in the homes of Mormon families and supported by the host family while they attend local schools. The church also has about 30 full-time missionaries who reside on reservations and assist Indian groups with their agricultural problems in the same manner that county farm and home agents have done in rural counties.

Genealogical and historical activities absorb much of the time of many Mormons, and contribute much to the continuing sense of Mormon com-

[11] The most extensive system outside the United States is in Mexico where there are 7,615 students in LDS schools. Because of Mexican law, the schools are incorporated under the name of Sociedad Educativa y Cultural, S.C. Since 1960 the church has opened 31 primary schools, 1 secondary school (with others planned), and a center in Mexico City for teaching teachers.

[12] Students away from home have the advantage of belonging to student wards, branches, and stakes, which are specifically geared to their needs and interests. There are perhaps 300 such wards in the church. The churchwide LDS Students Association assists college-age students to achieve academically, spiritually, and socially.

munity. In cooperative arrangements with local governments, parishes, churches, and other agencies, the church has microfilmed more than one trillion pages of historical records and placed a copy of 800,000 rolls of these films in a huge bombproof storage vault carved into the granite mountains southeast of Salt Lake City. The church supports a busy genealogical society, as well as a network of local genealogical libraries in areas where there are large numbers of Mormons. It has also constructed information centers and restored historical structures and sites in many parts of the nation. Nauvoo Restoration, Inc., a creature of the church, is in the process of restoring Nauvoo, Illinois, with an objective similar to that of Colonial Williamsburg.

In an effort to provide its young people with ample sports and recreational activity that will still identify them with the Mormon community, the church sponsors competitive leagues for different age groups in basketball, softball, volleyball, golf, and tennis. There are also local and regional festivals of speech, music, theater, art, and dancing. Approximately 660,000 young people participated in these activities in 1970, representing about 55 percent of the youth in the church.

The church has also moved to assist in the amelioration of poverty and want. The most significant new feature of the Church Welfare Plan is the dispensing of emergency assistance in areas affected by natural and war-born calamity. At the close of World War II, 140 railroad cars of food, clothing, bedding, and other items were shipped to devastated Europe. In 1953, when a flood occurred in Holland, quilts and blankets were sent. In 1954 canned fruits, vegetables, and flour were dispatched to Greece, following an earthquake. In 1960, when Chile suffered an earthquake, food, bedding, and medicine were flown to relieve the suffering. In February 1962 floods in northern Utah, southern Idaho, and parts of Nevada caused untold damage, and dozens of huge trailer trucks were dispatched with emergency aid. In recent years the Plan has given large-scale and immediate aid after earthquakes, hurricanes, and floods in Peru, Turkey, and Japan, as well as in the United States, Canada, and Mexico. This is a service of the church and its members to nonmembers and thus represents a Christian work which looks outward toward the problems of humanity.

A Church Social Services Department was established in 1969 to help leaders of local congregations solve the social-emotional problems of their members. The department maintains twenty local offices in ten different states, which provide psychiatric and psychological help, youth guidance, and vocational and marriage counseling; assist in rehabilitating the handicapped; supervise the Indian Placement Program; and maintain an adoption service for the children of unwed mothers. There is also a program to help those in prisons. Drug abuse, alcoholism, divorce, and crime come within the department's purview as its facilities expand throughout the continent and overseas. It is billed as "a program to put the Good Samaritan story to work in the lives of thousands."[13]

In addition to these welfare and social services, the church maintains fifteen hospitals in various locations in Utah, Idaho, and Wyoming. Particularly noteworthy is the Primary Children's Hospital in Salt Lake City, which has received much national recognition. Its patients have included children from the Americas and from the South Pacific as well. It not only provides care for nonpaying welfare cases, but recently has become Utah's major pediatric center as other Salt Lake City hospitals have found it financially impossible to continue such services. Under the direction of the Church Commissioner of Health Services, arrangements have been made whereby the church is able to provide medical services in many parts of the world for members who are unable to pay for their own medical care. The latest development is an experiment with paraprofessionals (persons without a medical degree but trained in some specialty) to work among its members in Latin America and the South Sea Islands, where physicians may not be available.

Identity and communication within Mormonism is assisted through a vast publication program. A daily newspaper, the *Deseret News,* with a Saturday supplement called the *Church News,* goes to approximately 100,000 families. It also publishes separate monthly magazines for adults, youth, and children, with a combined circulation of about 350,000. All church auxiliaries publish manuals and lesson plans and the church-owned Deseret Book Store as well as several privately owned houses publish many books of interest to the LDS community. To meet the needs of its increasing membership in foreign lands, the church has greatly expanded a program of translation and distribution. Church lesson manuals, instruction materials, and records are now published in 21 languages. There are translation and distribution centers in Salt Lake City, Mexico City, Sao Paulo, Frankfurt, Copenhagen, Liege, Hong Kong, Seoul, Tokyo, and Auckland. A unified church magazine is published in 17 languages.

All of these programs are basically financed by a system of voluntary tithes, in which individuals contribute one-tenth of their net income to the church on a continuing basis, as well as special fund-raising projects for the poor, the expenses of local congregations, missionary upkeep, and new buildings. There has been no decline in either the amount of such revenues or the proportion of persons who make such voluntary offerings. None who hold ecclesiastical offices receives a salary. The expenses of administering the church—travel, the maintenance of offices, and the like—are paid

[13] Stephen W. Gibson, "Their Job—To Solve Problems," *Church News,* October 16, 1971, p. 5.

out of revenues from church investments, so that tithing funds can be used exclusively to finance its programs.

This brief review of church programs suggests two major trends involved in Mormonism's accommodation to the modern world: a growing professionalism in handling church programs and a stepped-up internationalization. The first trend is suggested by the reliance upon professionals in the Church Building Department, Unified Social Services, Health Services, and in the computerization of much of the record keeping. The internationalism is reflected in the organization of stakes in such unlikely places as Amsterdam, Johannesburg, and Buenos Aires, the necessity of making simultaneous translations in nine languages of the sermons presented in the church's April and October general conferences, and in the establishment of church educational programs in many nations. At the August 1971 general conference held in England (the first to be held outside the United States), President Joseph Fielding Smith stated:

> We are members of a world church. . . . The day is long since past when informed people think of us as a strange group in the tops of the Rocky Mountains in America. . . . We are coming of age as a church and as a people. We have attained the stature and strength that are enabling us to fulfill the commission given us by the Lord through the Prophet Joseph Smith that we should carry the glad tidings of the restoration to every nation and to all people. . . . Thus the church is not an American church except in America. In Canada it is a Canadian church; in Australia it is an Australian church; and in Great Britain it is a British church. It is a world church; the gospel is for all men.[14]

But despite its evident growth and success in recent years, the church is not without problems, both internally and externally. One of these relates to a continuing, though healthy, tension between what might be called conservatives and liberals within the church. In an imaginative use of Mormon symbolism Richard Poll has suggested that these might be referred to as the "Iron Rod Saints" and "Liahona Saints."[15] Both terms come from the Book of Mormon: The Iron Rod was the word of God; persons who held on to the rod could follow the straight and narrow path to the fruitful tree of life. The Liahona was the compass that the emigrés

[14] "To the Saints in Great Britain," *The Ensign* (Salt Lake City), September 1971, pp. 204–207.

[15] Richard D. Poll, "What the Church Means to People Like Me," *Dialogue: A Journal of Mormon Thought,* II (Winter 1967), pp. 107–117. In another context, Father Eugene Kennedy of the Roman Catholic Church suggests the terms "extrinsic" religionists, who rely on rules, rituals, and dogmas, and seek authoritative answers to all their questions, and "intrinsic" religionists, who constantly raise questions, are willing to undergo a life of risk, and emphasize the humanness in man and society. See *Newsweek,* October 4, 1971, p. 88.

from Israel used to point the way—but it did not fully mark the path and the clarity of its directions varied with the circumstances of the user. As suggested by the symbolism, the Iron Rod Saint finds the answers to all his questions, both large and small, in scripture, the works of prophetic authority, and the Holy Spirit. Revelation, both past and present, is the iron rod that will lead one to exaltation in the Kingdom. The Liahona Saint, however, is skeptical of the answers Iron Rod Saints think they have found in their sources. No human instrument, the Liahona Saint feels, is capable of transmitting the word of God so clearly and comprehensively that it can be universally understood and easily appropriated. Both of these groups, Dr. Poll insists, are "good" Latter-day Saints—deeply committed, living the standards, and active in their wards and stakes.

That both Iron Rod and Liahona Saints have been converted to Mormonism and have remained loyal and active is further evidence of its vitality and vigor. Like fundamentalists in other faiths, conservative elements among the Mormons emphasize strong reliance on the wording of scripture, the authoritative structure of church government, the desirability of a theocratic social system, and the strength of the pioneer tradition. Liberal elements emphasize the boldness and innovative character of the Restoration, faith in the essential goodness of man and his possibilities of eternal progression, and the church's commitment to education and the resulting emphasis on rationality. The checks and balances inherent in the two traditions and types of membership give Mormonism both stability and progressivism.

Observers are perplexed by the comparative absence of generational conflict, student militancy, and youthful protest among the Mormons. The usual interpretation is that Mormon students are "not with it"; they are apathetic and not facing up to the realities of modern life. But there is a possible alternative explanation based on Mormon cultural patterns and inherent in the program-oriented church life described above. In contrast with the permissiveness of many post-World War II American families, the Mormon family has typically provided a definite standard against which Mormon youth could vindicate themselves and react to establish their own identities. Mormon parents are supported in setting firm standards by the ward or local congregation. Young people in the process of achieving self-definition are also encouraged and assisted by teachers and religious advisers. Indeed, although it is organized along geographical rather than functional lines,[16] the ward is essentially an extended family. Members of the ward teach and counsel children of various age groups,

---

[16] Functional wards, which cross other ward boundaries, include Spanish-speaking wards, wards for the deaf, and wards for married and for single university students.

take them on trips, help them obtain employment, provide emergency financial help, visit them when they are ill, counsel them on courtships and marriages, and in general fulfill the channelizing role once performed by the village neighborhood. Central in the life of the Mormon youth is the ward bishop, a lay member who usually serves for a period of five years as "father of the ward." He appoints persons to fill the 150 or so positions in the ward (many of which are held by teenagers), conducts or presides at all meetings, arranges frequent interviews with young people, and sees that widows, the aged, and the unemployed are adequately cared for. The familistic nature of the ward, including wards specifically organized for students at universities, may help explain the relative freedom from rebellion and tension in the Mormon educational environment.

A related problem, often remarked by non-Mormon activists, is that Latter-day Saints are so busy attending meetings and doing the things asked of them by the church that they do not have time for community services. The First Presidency of the Church have been aware of this tendency and have published the following statement:

> The growing worldwide responsibilities of the Church make it inadvisable for the Church to seek to respond to all the various and complex issues involved in the mounting problems of the many cities and communities in which members live. But this complexity does not absolve members as individuals from filling their responsibilities as citizens in their own communities.
>
> We urge our members to do their civic duty and to assume their responsibilities as individual citizens in seeking solutions to the problems which beset our cities and communities.
>
> With our wide ranging mission, so far as mankind is concerned, Church members cannot ignore the many practical problems that require solution if our families are to live in an environment conducive to spirituality.
>
> Where solutions to these practical problems require cooperative action with those not of our faith, members should not be reticent in doing their part in joining and leading in those efforts where they can make an individual contribution to those causes which are consistent with the standards of the Church.
>
> Individual Church members cannot, of course, represent or commit the Church, but should, nevertheless, be "anxiously engaged" in good causes, using the principles of the Gospel of Jesus Christ as their constant guide.[17]

Has Mormonism, then, been able to meet the needs of its people in the contemporary world but at the same time retain its most basic values? While it may be argued that its complex organization, multiple programs,

[17] Published in the *California Intermountain News,* September 19, 1968.

and paternalistic atmosphere tend to shield its youth from modern realities, it may also be true that these very things help combat the social deterioration often wrought by current forces. In a sense the church seeks to demonstrate through its policies and programs that the cultural imperialism that wrote "finis" to its Great Basin Kingdom could not completely stamp out the nucleus of the kingdom in the hearts of its three million members. Indeed, for the committed Latter-day Saint, the church continues to bear testimony of the direct intervention of a loving God in the affairs of men. Whether a program-oriented approach to the ideological and social conflicts of today can continue to receive the full commitment of the Mormon people, and especially the young, remains to be seen. As of the moment there is impressive external evidence that it is doing so.

Selected Bibliography

There are several articles on Mormon bibliography that students might consult. These include Marvin S. Hill, "The Historiography of Mormonism," *Church History,* XXVII (December 1959), pp. 418–426; Leonard J. Arrington, "Scholarly Studies of Mormonism in the Twentieth Century," *Dialogue: A Journal of Mormon Thought* I (Spring 1966), pp. 15–32; Thomas G. Alexander and James B. Allen, "The Mormons in the Mountain West, A Selective Bibliography," *Arizona and the West,* IX (Winter 1967), pp. 365–384; James B. Allen and Leonard J. Arrington, "Mormon Origins in New York: An Introductory Analysis," *Brigham Young University Studies* IX (Spring 1969), pp. 241–274; and Ralph W. Hansen, "Among the Mormons," a survey of current literature, which appears in each issue of *Dialogue: A Journal of Mormon Thought.* For serious scholars a comprehensive bibliography is currently being prepared for publication at Brigham Young University by Chad Flake, special collections librarian. An interesting essay that views the writing of Mormon history in a broad context is Rodman W. Paul, "The Mormons as a Theme in Western Historical Writing," *Journal of American History,* LIV (December 1967), pp. 511–523.

General histories of Mormonism are few, and usually biased toward or against the church. Two examples are Brigham H. Roberts, *Comprehensive History of the Church of Jesus Christ of Latter-day Saints* (6 vols.; Salt Lake City, 1930), which is a standard general history but lacks the breadth of view needed to place Mormonism in its national setting, and William A. Linn, *The Story of the Mormons* (New York, 1902), which sees Mormonism as a great threat to American institutions. Thomas F. O'Dea's *The Mormons* (Chicago, 1957) is an excellent brief history with fine sociological analysis. *Among the Mormons,* edited by William A. Mulder and A. Russell Mortensen (New York, 1958), through a careful selection of original sources, captures much of the drama and a good deal of the meaning of Mormon history. A work that considers Mormon ideals thoughtfully in the context of Western philosophy is Sterling McMurrin, *The Theological Foundations of the Mormon Religion* (Salt Lake City, 1965).

Additional perspectives on Mormonism as a part of American culture are contained in scholarly articles. William Mulder's "Mormonism in

American History," *Utah Historical Quarterly,* XXVII (January 1959), pp. 59–77, finds many parallels between the American and Mormon experience, but deals mostly with the nineteenth century. Thomas F. O'Dea's "Mormonism and the American Experience of Time," *Western Humanities Review,* VIII (Summer 1954), pp. 181–190, treats the sense of new beginnings in Mormon thought, while Mulder's "Image of Zion, Mormonism as an American Influence in Scandinavia," *Mississippi Valley Historical Review,* XLIII (June 1956), pp. 18–38, analyzes the cultural impact of Mormon missionaries as evangels of American ways from 1850 to 1900.

The works by Alice Felt Tyler and Whitney Cross discussed in the introduction to this volume provide indispensable background for the social context in which Mormonism emerged. Others that say little or nothing about the Mormons but provide important insights into the cultural milieu are John Humphrey Noyes, *History of American Socialisms* (New York, 1961), Ralph Henry Gabriel, *The Course of American Democratic Thought* (New Haven, 1940), and John William Ward, *Andrew Jackson, Symbol for an Age* (New York, 1955). Ernest Lee Tuveson, *Redeemer Nation* (Chicago, 1968), a study of American apocalyptic expectations, includes a large section on the Mormons.

Some of the general surveys of American culture give the Mormons more than passing mention. Stow Persons, *American Minds* (New York, 1958), argues that the Protestant dream of a millennial kingdom was the dominant motif in Mormon thought. Daniel Boorstin, *Americans: The National Experience* (New York, 1967), includes the Mormons among "the transients," and Charles L. Barker, *American Convictions: Cycles of Public Thought 1600–1850* (Philadelphia, 1970), sees the Mormons as postmillennial perfectionists who, like others, experimented with some basic American institutions.

On the early Mormons an important documentary source is Joseph Smith, *History of the Church of Jesus Christ of Latter-day Saints* (6 vols.; Salt Lake City, 1930). The best, though not wholly satisfactory biography of Smith, is Fawn Brodie, *No Man Knows My History* (New York, 1945), which handles the milieu perceptively, while Klaus Hansen's *Quest for Empire* (East Lansing, 1967) treats with insight some of the early ideals which shaped the Kingdom of God.

In addition to the articles by Davis and De Pillis which appear in this book, others are important for understanding Mormon origins. Mario De Pillis has reopened the question of roots in "Social Sources of Mormonism," *Church History,* XXXVII (1968), pp. 50–79, challenging Cross's thesis that Mormonism emerged from a culturally mature region. De Pillis sees the roots as rural, essentially southern and western. Marvin S. Hill, on the other hand, takes issue with a western approach in "The Shaping of the Mormon Mind in New England and New York," *Brigham Young University Studies,* IX (Spring 1969), pp. 351–372.

Other works that treat important individuals or topics associated with the initial movement are George Arbaugh, *Revelation in Mormonism* (Chicago, 1932), which ignores the institutional aspects of Mormon revelation; James H. Kennedy, *Early Days of Mormonism* (New York, 1888), dealing with the Ohio period; and Robert Bruce Flanders, *Nauvoo: Kingdom on the Mississippi* (Urbana, 1965). There is no comprehensive study of the Mormon exodus, but colonization of the Great Basin is handled effectively in Milton R. Hunter, *Brigham Young, the Colonizer* (Salt Lake City, 1940).

On economic and social experimentation in Utah, Hamilton Gardner's "Cooperation Among the Mormons," *Quarterly Journal of Economics,* III (May 1917), pp. 461–499, is suggestive, while more substantial is Leonard J. Arrington's *Great Basin Kingdom* (Cambridge, 1958). Social aspects of Utah history are considered in Nels Anderson, *Deseret Saints: The Mormon Frontier in Utah* (Chicago, 1942) and Lowry Nelson, *The Mormon Village: A Pattern and Technique of Land Settlement* (Salt Lake City, 1952).

Recently there have been many competent studies of the politics of the Mormon kingdom. The student might begin with Norman F. Furniss, *The Mormon Conflict, 1850–1859* (New Haven, 1960), and follow this with Richard D. Poll, "The Political Reconstruction of Utah Territory, 1866–1890," *Pacific Historical Review,* XXVII (May 1958), pp. 111–126, and Gustive O. Larson, *The Americanization of Utah for Statehood* (San Marino, 1971). Internal strife between Mormons and non-Mormons is considered in Joseph Dwyer, *The Gentile Comes to Utah* (Washington, D.C., 1941). For a definition of Mormon political intentions Klaus Hansen's *Quest for Empire* is important, as are J. Keith Melville, "Brigham Young's Ideal Society, the Kingdom of God," *Brigham Young University Studies,* V (Autumn 1962), pp. 3–18, and James R. Clark, "The Kingdom of God, the Council of Fifty, and the State of Deseret," *Utah Historical Quarterly,* XXVI (April 1958), pp. 131–150. Students should not ignore Ephraim Ericksen's incisive estimate of Mormon communal values in *Psychological and Ethical Aspects of Mormon Group Life* (Chicago, 1922). A study that deals with some unfortunate aspects of Mormon psychology is Juanita Brooks, *Mountain Meadows Massacre* (Norman, Okl., 1962).

There are very few adequate biographies of Mormon leaders in Utah. A hasty and superficial attempt to assess Brigham Young was made by Stanley Hirshon in *Lion of the Lord* (New York, 1970). Such pillars of the Mormon establishment as Heber C. Kimball, Orson Hyde, John Taylor, and many more have not been given scholarly study. Harold Schindler has written an interesting study of a secondary figure, *Porter Rockwell, Man of God Son of Thunder* (Salt Lake City, 1966), and Juanita Brooks has written vividly regarding *John Doyle Lee* (Glendale, Calif., 1961).

Although there is a plethora of popular periodical material on Mormonism in the twentieth century, relatively little of a scholarly nature has been published. The books by Whalen, Mullen, and Turner, cited in the introduction, are generally interesting but superficial. Very sketchy is James B. Allen and Richard O. Cowan, *Mormonism in the Twentieth Century* (Provo, U., 1967). In *Sociology and the Study of Religion* (New York, 1970), Thomas F. O'Dea reprints four of his most important articles that deal with the nature of the Mormon community during both the nineteenth and twentieth centuries.

Mormon reaction to race problems is objectively but not exhaustively treated in Stephen G. Taggart's *Mormonism's Negro Policy: Social and Historical Origins* (Salt Lake City, 1970). John J. Stewart, *Mormonism and the Negro* (Orem, U., 1960), shows a pro-Mormon bias. The student should also consult Utah Academy of Sciences, Arts, and Letters, *The Negro in Utah* (Salt Lake City, 1954); Armand L. Mauss, "Mormonism and Secular Attitudes Toward Negroes," *Pacific Sociological Review,* IX (Fall 1966), pp. 91–99, and "Mormonism and the Negro: Faith, Folklore and Civil Rights," *Dialogue: A Journal of Mormon Thought,* II (Winter 1967), pp. 17–29; David L. Brewer, "Religious Resistance to Changing Beliefs About Race," *Pacific Sociological Review,* XIII (Summer 1970), pp. 163–170.

Other miscellaneous but important considerations of the modern Mormon community include Leonard J. Arrington and Wayne K. Hinton, "Origin of the Mormon Welfare Plan," *Brigham Young University Studies,* V (Winter 1964), pp. 67–85; Jan Shipps, "Utah Comes of Age Politically: A Study of the State's Politics in the Early Years of the Twentieth Century," *Utah Historical Quarterly,* XXXV (Spring 1967), pp. 91–111; Frank H. Jonas, "Utah: Crossroads of the West," in Frank H. Jonas, ed., *Western Politics* (Salt Lake City, 1961); Edward L. Schapsmeier, "Eisenhower and Ezra Taft Benson," *Agricultural History,* XLIV (October 1970), pp. 364–378, which discusses the controversial Mormon apostle's role as Secretary of Agriculture.

Especially lacking are scholarly studies of Mormon activities in the twentieth century outside the United States. Some of the problems Mormons faced south of the Rio Grande are described in B. Carmon Hardy, "Cultural 'Encystment' as a Cause of the Mormon Exodus from Mexico in 1912," *Pacific Historical Review,* XXXIV (November 1965), pp. 439–454, and Karl E. Young, *Ordeal in Mexico* (Provo, U. 1968). Mormon expansion into other parts of the world is recorded in annals like Gilbert W. Sharffs, *Mormonism in Germany* (Salt Lake City, 1970). For the beginning of a more analytical approach see Wesley W. Craig, Jr., "The Church in Latin America: Progress and Challenge," *Dialogue: A Journal of Mormon Thought,* V (Autumn 1970), pp. 66–74.

The best source for scholarly writing within the church is *Dialogue: A Journal of Mormon Thought,* which was inaugurated by a group of Mormon intellectuals in 1966 as an independent journal devoted to exploring all aspects of Mormon culture. Some of the more important articles pertaining to modern times include J. D. Williams, "The Separation of Church and State in Mormon Theory and Practice," I (Summer 1966), pp. 30–54; Dean E. Mann, "Mormon Attitudes Toward the Political Roles of Church Leaders," II (Summer 1967), pp. 32–48, which focuses on Mormon involvement in the recent right-to-work issue; J. Kenneth Davies, "The Accommodation of Mormonism and Politico-Economic Reality," III (Spring 1968), pp. 42–54; a "Roundtable" on "The Church and Collective Bargaining in American Society," III (Summer 1968), pp. 106–133; Knud S. Larsen and Bary Schwendeman, "The Vietnam War Through the Eyes of a Mormon Subculture," III (Autumn 1968), pp. 152–168; O. Kendall White, Jr., "The Transformation of Mormon Theology," V (Summer 1970), pp. 9–24. In addition, *Dialogue* has published two special issues that consider Mormonism's cultural problems: "The Mormon Family in the Modern World." II (Autumn 1967), pp. 41–108; and "Mormons in the Secular City," III (Autumn 1968), pp. 39–108. Particularly relevant in the latter are William H. Robinson, "Mormons in the Urban Community," and James M. Clayton, "The Challenge of Secularism."

72 73 74 7 6 5 4 3 2 1